DATE DUE

JUN 1 0 2011		
JUL 1 2 2011		
AUG 1 1 2011		
OCT 1 9 2011		
NOV 1 7		

The WEEPING GOLDSMITH

Discoveries in the Secret Land of Myanmar

W. JOHN KRESS

FOREWORD BY WADE DAVIS

ABBEVILLE PRESS
New York   London

This book is dedicated to all the scientists and explorers of the world who are striving to understand the natural world and our place in it. And in admiration and respect for the commitment of the Myanmar foresters in their efforts to conserve the biodiversity and natural environments of their country.

FRONT COVER: The misty summit of Mount Popa, the "Mountain of Flowers" at over 4,000 feet (1,219 meters) elevation.

BACK COVER: The Weeping Goldsmith, called *Globba magnifica* by botanists.

PAGES 2–3: The full moon rising over the plains of Bagan at the end of the first day of the festival of Kathina.

PAGE 8: The ancient city of Bagan, situated along the Irrawaddy River. Established in 849 AD, the city was the site of the First Burmese Empire.

EDITOR: Susan Costello
PRODUCTION MANAGER: Louise Kurtz
PRODUCTION EDITOR: Austin Allen
COPYEDITOR: Miranda Ottewell
DESIGNER: Patricia Fabricant

First published in the United States of America in 2009 by Abbeville Press, 137 Varick Street, New York, NY 10013.

First edition
10 9 8 7 6 5 4 3 2 1

Library of Congress Cataloging-in-Publication Data

Kress, W. John.
 The weeping goldsmith : discoveries in the secret land of Myanmar / W. John Kress. — 1st ed.
  p. cm.
 Includes bibliographical references.
 ISBN 978-0-7892-1032-6 (alk. paper)
  1. Natural history—Burma. 2. Plants—Burma. 3. Burma—Description and travel. I. Title.

 QH193.B93K74 2009
 508.591—dc22

                    2008055031

For bulk and premium sales and for text adoption procedures, write to Customer Service Manager, Abbeville Press, 137 Varick Street, New York, NY 10013, or call 1-800-ARTBOOK.

Visit Abbeville Press online at www.abbeville.com.

Photo Credits

All photographs are copyright © John Kress except for the following:

P. 10, top left; pp. 38, 80; p. 42, left; p. 114, above; p. 124, opposite; pp. 151, 152, 163, 178: Photo by James Henry Green, c. 1920s, courtesy of The James Green Centre for World Art.

P. 10, top and above: photographer unknown, c. 1980s.

P. 60, left; pp. 160, 168, 169: Photo by F. Kingdon-Ward, c. 1940s, courtesy of the Royal Geographical Society.

P. 61, opposite top: Photo c. 1940s, courtesy of the Royal Geographical Society.

P. 171, above right; pp. 185–86, 219: Printed with permission from the Botany Department, The Natural History Museum, London.

Contents

Foreword

BY WADE DAVIS

It is difficult to describe to those who have not experienced it the overwhelming yet subtle grandeur of a pristine tropical rain forest. From the edge of trails creepers lash at the base of trees, and herbaceous heliconias and calatheas give way to broad-leafed aroids that climb into the shadows. Overhead, lianas drape from immense trees binding the canopy of the forest into a single interwoven fabric of life. In the air is a fluid heaviness, a weight of centuries, of years without seasons, of life without rebirth. Making sense out of these infinite sensations, giving form to the raw fecundity of the forest, bringing focus to the immense challenges of scientific inquiry in a place of such wonder, is the notable achievement of field botanists, such as my good friend John Kress, author of this wonderful new book, *The Weeping Goldsmith*, an account of botanical exploration that will, I believe, rank among the great memoirs of natural history.

John and I first met as students at Harvard, where we both studied under the direction of the legendary plant explorer, Richard Evans Schultes. Schultes devoted his entire academic life to the Northwest Amazon of Colombia. Following in Schultes' footsteps, John Kress in the early years of his career became an authority on the Andes and the Amazon in his own right, a superb field botanist and a master of two charismatic and complex families of plants: the gingers and heliconias, and the more modest and utilitarian of monocots, the plantains and bananas. No one, I suspect, in the world knows more about these singular plants, and this alone is a remarkable achievement.

But as a plant explorer firmly in the tradition not only of Schultes but also of his other hero, Francis Kingdon-Ward, John inevitably turned his attention to Asia. Of all the lands Kingdon-Ward came to know, Burma was the place that most captured his heart. When John Kress decided to travel to Myanmar, he knew that he would be walking in the shadow of greatness. At the height of his professional career, John elected to become a botanical neophyte in a completely new and wondrous floristic realm. This in itself was a courageous intellectual deed.

To work today as a western scientist in Myanmar, as this book reveals with great wit, compassion and sensitivity, is not without its challenges. The complications of logistics and access as well as the miscellaneous perils are intense.

No doubt adding to the challenge, I suspect, were the voices lingering at home among certain academic circles suggesting that any research activities in a place as politically repressive as Myanmar were suspect and run the risk of implicitly legitimizing the regime. Such concerns, I believe, while understandable, in a sense miss the point. Both Schultes and Kingdon-Ward traveled through lands convulsed in violence. These conflicts and atrocities, terrible as they were, are today largely forgotten, filed away among the countless sordid memories of the most violent century in human history. This is not to absolve scientists of social responsibility, but it is to suggest that solitary students of plants have a mission that in many ways transcends history and time.

The hundreds of living plants, the seeds and cuttings brought back from the wild by Schultes and Kingdon-Ward brighten to this day the gardens of the world. Their purpose is to reveal to the world the transcendent wonder of the Earth, as made manifest in the dazzling diversity of the botanical realm. Schultes knew a world still familiar to our fathers when the tropical rain forests of the world stood immense and inviolable. Sadly that era is long gone. The consequences of the destruction of tropical rain forests, whether in Southeast Asia, South America, Equatorial Africa, or Australia are being felt around the world.

Perhaps most tragically, the destruction of the tropical rain forest is resulting in the massive loss of biological diversity. Although extinction is a global problem, these rain forests are particularly susceptible because many species tend to occur in low densities with restricted ranges. The elimination of life, of course, is nothing new in the history of the Earth. What has changed in a disturbing way in the last fifty years is the rate of disappearance. E. O. Wilson believes that within the last twenty-five years of the 20th century, one million species may have been lost.

Unfortunately, as John Kress reminds us, just at the time when the plight of the forests is calling out for armies of young naturalists to enter the field, the culture of science has shifted and fewer young scientists are being trained as taxonomists. Without a cadre of dedicated plant explorers the fundamental quest to systematize creation will never be realized. To destroy these forests, before even making an effort to name or know the plants and animals that dwell within them is a gesture of such callous disregard that it will shame our children and grandchildren. It is my hope that this book will fire the hearts of a new generation of field botanists, who will be inspired to carry on the work of all the great plant explorers in whose footsteps they will walk.

Prologue

Some authors and historians have called the country of Burma, now known as Myanmar, *"terra incognita."* Some have labeled it "isolated," "inaccessible," "remote," "solitary," "forbidden," "hidden," and "out-of-the-way." Some describe it as "secret." All of these epithets are correct, yet the political, social, and economic reasons for the current state of affairs are varied and complex. There is little doubt that the contemporary military government controlling Myanmar is repressive, and is the immediate cause of the isolation of this potentially wealthy Southeast Asian country. But the present book is not about political and social repression in Myanmar.

This book is about the natural landscapes and people of Myanmar as interpreted through the eyes of a modern-day scientist and plant explorer. Over the course of nine years I explored many areas in this enigmatic country as I surveyed the teak forests, bamboo thickets, timber plantations, rivers, and mangroves to document the plant diversity of this vast unknown land. Myanmar is one of the great biodiversity hot spots in Asia, but because of its social isolation and reputation for political repression, it has been off-limits and avoided by many biologists, conservationists, and environmentalists.

I first went to Myanmar in 1996 with few preconceived notions about the country. I knew that political and economic turmoil in Myanmar during much of the twentieth century had prevented many biologists from thoroughly exploring the country.

For that reason I suspected that the mountains, valleys, and coastal areas harbored many exciting plant species to be discovered and described. Furthermore, many of the plants had not been studied since Western botanists first observed them over a century ago. And I knew that after close scientific observation many of these species would prove to be new to science. British and Burmese foresters and plant hunters in the nineteenth and early twentieth centuries, such as George Forrest, J. H. Lace, H. G. Hundley, U Chit Ko Ko, and Frank Kingdon-Ward, had collected and recorded many exotic species in the mountainous regions of Myanmar. They had left accounts of their observations in the books they wrote and the botanical specimens they collected, which were deposited in natural history museums around the world. Now it was my turn.

I had previously traveled extensively in the tropical regions of Central America and South America. From the dry forests of the Yucatan to the rain forests of Costa Rica and Panama as well as throughout the Andean mountain range and the Amazon Basin, I collected plants and conducted field studies in an effort to understand the ecological processes that controlled the functioning of the forests. My scientific work had also taken me to Madagascar and New Guinea as well as parts of Indonesia, Malaysia, southern China, and the islands of the South Pacific in search of new plant species. In each place I encountered multiple habitats and experienced many different cultures.

TOP LEFT: Shwedagon Pagoda in the city of Rangoon as it appeared in the 1920s. Photograph by James Henry Green.

TOP: H. G. Hundley, Burmese botanist and coauthor with U Chit Ko Ko (ABOVE) of an early version of the checklist of plants known from Burma.

OPPOSITE: Shwedagon Pagoda, the largest and most sacred of Buddhist shrines in Myanmar, as it appears today.

I did not anticipate that in my exploration of the natural environments of Myanmar I would become engaged in a culture and social landscape so different from anything I had experienced in all of my travels to the tropical areas of the world. Myanmar would be one of the most fascinating lands I would ever visit and one of the most extraordinary opportunities of my life. Despite the difficulty of my first visit to Rangoon, I was enchanted with the country and the people, and knew that I would be back many times.

The present book is about how I came to appreciate the people and culture of Myanmar as a result of my quest to understand the plants in the natural habitats and human-dominated environments of the country. I went to Myanmar to help conserve biodiversity. I ended up experiencing a culture with a system of values completely different from what I expected after reading the daily accounts about the country in Western newspapers. I am a historian of nature, a Darwinian evolutionist who studies how life evolved on our planet. In order to understand the diversity of life present today, one must also uncover and document the past histories and lineages of living organisms that exist in the present. However, during the time I spent in Myanmar while conducting my studies on biodiversity I learned as much about the history of the land and its people as I did about the thousands of species of plants that I recorded from its forests.

The chapters that follow are built around the experiences I had during many visits over a nine-year period exploring Myanmar; I trace the encounters, incidents, and insights I had in this "secret" land. The sequence of the chapters roughly follows the natural cycle between the monsoon season and the dry season. In some instances, I have presented events slightly out of the order in which they actually occurred in order to clarify a particular theme or to simplify a situation. As some who read this book may know, the military junta that came to power in 1962 decided to change the name of the country from Burma, as used by the British, to the Union of Myanmar, or Myanmar. The junta also altered many of the city and place names. It is not uncommon to find both pre- and post-junta names included on maps of the country, and many local Burmese, sometimes depending on their age, cite one or the other as the proper usage. For these reasons, I have decided to use both the old and the new place names interchangeably, selecting the name that seemed to be most appropriate for the situation. I hope this will not cause any undue confusion for readers, although the confusion would mirror the situation that already exists in the country.

The modern world is changing fast, but Myanmar seems to have been held back in an ancient past. Perhaps tomorrow will bring the possibility of new developments to this land—a new government, a new economy, a new openness—which do not now exist. Yet perhaps some places on Earth, like Myanmar, will always live in another time.

OPPOSITE: Topographic map of Myanmar, indicating places and localities, including important cities, rivers, and wildlife sanctuaries, visited by the author.

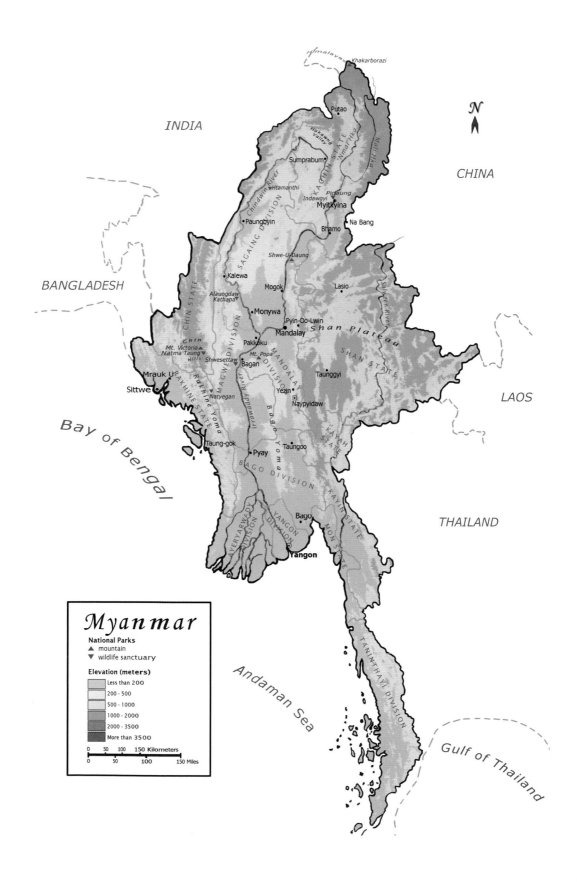

INDIA

CHINA

Khakarborazi

Himalayas

Putao

Hukawng Valley

Sumprabum

Chindwin River

KACHIN STATE

Nmai Hka

Htamanthi

Pidaung

Indawgyi

Myitkyina

Na Bang

BANGLADESH

Paungbyin

Bhamo

SAGAING DIVISION

Shwe-U-Daung

Kalewa

Mogok

Lasio

CHIN STATE

Monywa

Pyin-Oo-Lwin

Shan Plateau

Salween River

Alaungdaw Kathapa

Mandalay

Pakkoku

Mt. Popa

SHAN STATE

Mt. Victoria

Natma Taung

Chin Hills

Shwesettaw

Bagan

MANDALAY DIVISION

Taunggyi

Mrauk U

Yezin

Naypyidaw

Sittwe

MAGWE DIVISION

Irrawaddy River

Natyegan

RAKHINE STATE

KAYAH STATE

Rakhine Yoma

Bay of Bengal

Taung-gok

Bago Yoma

Pyay

Taungoo

LAOS

THAILAND

Bago

BAGO DIVISION

KAYIN STATE

AYEYARWADY DIVISION

YANGON DIVISION

Yangon

MON STATE

Andaman Sea

TANINTHAYI DIVISION

Gulf of Thailand

Myanmar

National Parks
▲ mountain
▼ wildlife sanctuary

Elevation (meters)
Less than 200
200 - 500
500 - 1000
1000 - 2000
2000 - 3500
More than 3500

0   50   100   150 Kilometers
0   50   100   150 Miles

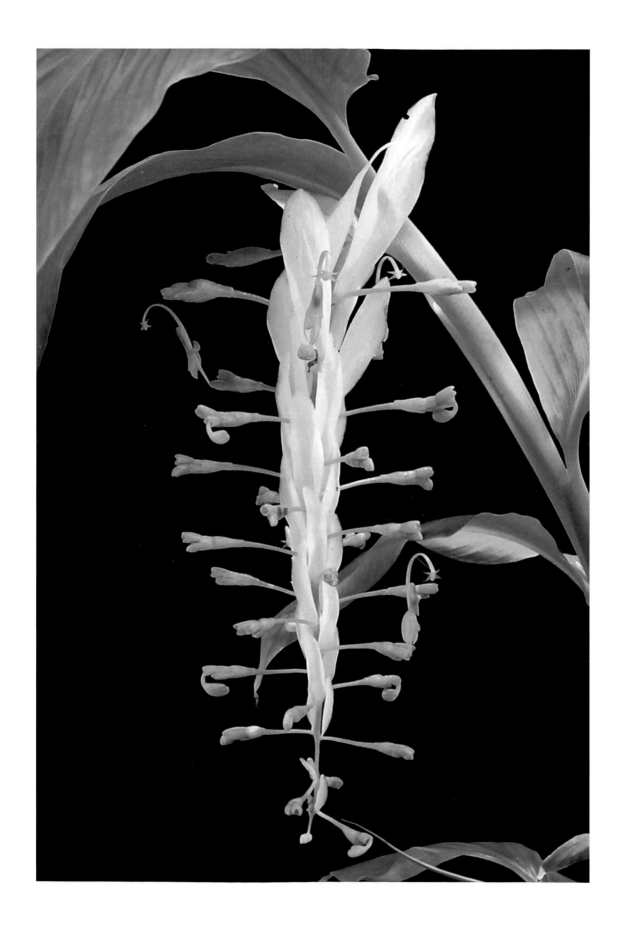

CHAPTER I # *The Weeping Goldsmith*

"And I found that in my recollections, so vague and uncertain, the Shwe Dagon rose superb as on that first morning it had risen, glistening with its gold, like a sudden hope in the dark night of the soul of which the mystics write, glistening against the fog and smoke of the thriving city."

W. Somerset Maugham, *The Gentleman in the Parlour*, 1930

The flower called by the Burmese "The Weeping Goldsmith," and by botanists *Globba magnifica*.

The goldsmith was weeping. No matter how hard he tried, with all his skills, his tools, his experience, and his love, he could not re-create nor imitate the intricate structure of this delicate white and yellow-gold flower. He and his fellow craftsmen had worked tirelessly to capture in gold the intimacy and simplicity of the individual parts of the flower. It looked possible. He just couldn't do it. Perhaps the sacredness of this flower was what prevented him from fully understanding its nature in order to reproduce it. Many had tried, but no one had succeeded. The plant itself could easily be grown in the garden of the monastery, but the goldsmith could not work his precious metal into its gentle form. And so the natural flower itself must be gathered from the fields to serve as a special offering to the Buddha in the village pagodas and household shrines.

Such is the legend behind a real flower that is commonly found in Myanmar. The first time I saw *padeign gno*, which literally means "weeping goldsmith" in Burmese, the flowers were in a giant pile in a basket. This basket was perfectly balanced on the head of a lovely, slim Burmese woman who wore a long pink *longyi* as she headed for the local market in Bago. Bago is about fifteen miles (25 km) from Rangoon, the former capital city of Burma—or Myanmar, as it is now called by the military regime currently in control of the government. The renaming of places in modern-day Myanmar is extensive. In fact, in ancient Burma, Bago used to be called Pegu. Rangoon is now referred to as Yangon.

And the famous Irrawaddy River has become the Ayeryarwady. As a newcomer myself to this mystifying country I soon realized that the goldsmith was not the only one having trouble understanding the secrets of this forbidden land.

Padeign gno is the Burmese name for a species of plant in the ginger family, in a genus known to botanists by the Latin name *Globba*. I should have known the species name for this flower. After all, for a professional botanist specializing in gingers and with access to the latest laboratory methods and DNA tests for determining the identification of any plant species, ordinary plants found in everyday markets should pose no problem. I had prepared for my work in Myanmar by studying botanical specimens in museums and compiling lists of species already reported from the country. Yet here I was in the flower bazaar of one of the most populated areas of Myanmar, and I, like the goldsmith, was mystified. *Padeign gno* is a striking flower, its bright green leaves and long stems topped with a drooping cluster of white bracts enclosing the golden yellow flowers, each on a thin pale green stalk. I knew it should be classified in the genus *Globba,* but I didn't know in which species. Here I was, my first time in Myanmar, and I could not properly identify a common flower sold in the market. I was humbled, but I also felt myself being drawn into this country by these simple flowers in the marketplace. I knew they represented only a tiny fraction of the plant life waiting to be discovered in this puzzling land.

In addition to its golden flowers, Burma is often called the Golden Land because of the thousands of gilded pagodas and shrines that have been built there over thousands of years to honor the Buddha. There is almost no place you can go in the country without encountering a shrine to the Buddha. As you sail along the Irrawaddy River, not half a mile will pass without your sighting at least one brilliant white and gold pagoda perched on the crest of a hill or rise. Far from any city, deep in the middle of a pristine teak forest, it is also not uncommon to encounter a small, always elegant Buddhist statue placed on a special boulder or neatly carved into a rock face. About 90 percent of the population of Myanmar practices Theravada Buddhism, which permeates every aspect of the daily social life, behavior, and professional interactions of the Burmese. In fact, beautiful *padeign gno* serves as a frequent offering at Buddhist shrines, both large and small. The basketful of flowers I first saw was on its way to be respectfully placed at the feet of the giant reclining Shwethalyaung Buddha in Bago.

A woman in a flower market in the city of Bago with "The Weeping Goldsmith."

CHAPTER 1

ABOVE: The gilded Shwedagon Pagoda during the monsoon season in Yangon.

RIGHT: Images of the Buddha and his disciples along the courtyard of Shwedagon Pagoda.

LEFT: A small Buddhist shrine in a local restaurant in Taunggyi, with containers of "The Weeping Goldsmith" as an offering of respect.

OPPOSITE, TOP: Ginger "root" being sold in the market in Yangon.

OPPOSITE, BOTTOM: Gingers growing in the country.

Why was I, a botanist and plant expert, in Burma? Was it by chance, by luck, or even by fate? My passion for tropical plants had taken me to tropical places in many countries around the world in search of species that were poorly known, new to science, or in need of conservation. I started my career first as a researcher at a small tropical botanical garden in Florida and then as a scientist and curator at the Smithsonian's National Museum of Natural History in Washington, D.C. I worked nearly twenty years in the tropical lands of Central and South America before my growing interest in the classification of gingers and their relatives demanded that I begin some exploration of the tropical areas of Southeast Asia. In Thailand, Laos, Vietnam, Cambodia, southern China, and Myanmar, gingers are abundant, especially in the monsoonal regions, which have distinct dry and wet seasons. Some gingers are important medicinals used as local curatives; others provide distinctive and essential flavors in daily cooking rituals; and still others have entered the international cut-flower trade because of their horticultural beauty.

My interests were primarily scientific. I am one of the dwindling cadre of scientists called taxonomists who devote their careers to the discovery, description, and classification of plants. Many species, particularly in the tropical zones of the earth, are yet to be found and given a scientific name. One of my jobs as a taxonomist is to travel to remote areas to document the remaining unknown plant diversity. Yet providing a botanical name for a specimen is not my only goal. Each plant species fits into a community of other plants and animals in a unique way. Understanding how a species interacts and evolves with other species is a scientific challenge that requires the patience of observation, the

CHAPTER I

ingenuity to devise critical experiments, and the skill to interpret the data and results. Science is puzzle-solving, and each species I found in Myanmar provided one piece of a very large evolutionary puzzle that I was trying to decipher. For me the gingers were a key ingredient. But first I had to know their names.

My work on gingers and other related plants had focused my geographic sights on Southeast Asia. In 1996 I learned that a field trip to Myanmar was being planned by a group of conservationists at the research center of the Smithsonian's National Zoo under the leadership of Dr. Chris Wemmer. Chris and his colleagues at the zoo were studying populations of wild elephants and endangered deer in the teak forests of central and upper Burma. I had heard that he needed a botanist as part of his team to help record and describe the vegetation in the habitats where the elephants and deer were found. During my earlier work on gingers I had thoroughly checked our botany library at the museum and could not find a recent book about the plants of Myanmar. I knew that if I could accompany Chris and join this group of scientists heading to Myanmar, I would have an unbelievable opportunity to get a glimpse of a country and a land that had been only poorly explored for plants. When he invited me to go with him to Myanmar, I quickly accepted the invitation. At the time I knew nothing about *padeign gno*, nothing about goldsmiths, and very little about Myanmar, but all of that would soon change.

CHAPTER 2 # *Waiting in Rangoon*

"My Burmese friends offered to take me and I put my Western pride in my pocket. It was midnight. Arriving at the temple we went up a long stairway on each side of which were booths; but the people who lived in them to sell the devout what they might require had finished their work and some were sitting about, half naked, chatting in undertones, smoking or eating a final meal, while many in all attitudes and abandonment were asleep, some on low native beds and some on the bare stones. Here and there, left over from the day before, were masses of dying flowers, lotus and jasmine and marigold; they scented the air heavy with a perfume in which was already an acrid decay. At last we reached the great terrace. All about shrines and pagodas were jumbled pell-mell with the confusion with which trees grow in the jungle. They had been built without design and symmetry, but in the darkness, their gold and marble faintly gleaming, they had a fantastic richness. And then, emerging from among them like a great ship surrounded by lighters, rose dim, severe, and splendid, the Shwe Dagon."

W. Somerset Maugham, *The Gentleman in the Parlour*, 1930

The monsoon had started, and it was raining hard when my plane landed in Yangon. I had been traveling for over thirty hours straight, from Washington, D.C., to London, to Bangkok, and now to Myanmar. As I stepped off the final flight from Bangkok to Yangon, the rain poured down; before I reached immigration and customs everything I had brought with me was completely soaked. Myanmar was clearly not prepared for more than a few international guests at that time, and the small, disheveled, and disorganized airport was a distinct challenge for a jet-lagged botanist. It was dark and wet. The smell of tropical mildew, tobacco and herbs, various cooking odors, and diesel fuel penetrated the moist night air. A chorus of *Ya ba de, ya ba de*, a language that was not even remotely familiar to my ears, echoed in the small entranceway, while men and

Shwedagon Pagoda.

women, both wearing long skirts called *longyis*,[1] bustled around, pulling at me and my baggage. I assumed they were trying to help me navigate among the various officials I needed to see in order to receive the necessary approvals to enter the country. I had never been so disoriented in my life. I was in Burma.

Somehow I made it through the airport with my own gear plus two large footlockers that I had brought as a favor to my colleagues at the Smithsonian's National Zoo. Chris Wemmer, director of the Conservation Research Center at the zoo,[2] had invited me to Myanmar, and I couldn't turn him down when he asked me to carry these trunks to Yangon for him. Usually I try to travel light, but not this time. In retrospect, I am amazed that the luggage arrived at all. In general I am excited and fascinated by first entries into new places. But with the added exhaustion from flying almost nonstop halfway around the world, this arrival was a real test of my fortitude. Fortunately U Myint Aung, a forester who had been sent to meet me by the Forest Department, was waiting on the other side of customs. After piling everything into a taxi, we set off for a guesthouse that had been recommended to me. Surprisingly, after the chaos of the airport (at least to my eyes), the streets of the city were relatively quiet. The rains had subsided, but the roads were still knee-deep in water. Bicycles, each with a minimum of two or three riders, and very overcrowded buses with passengers

The illuminated Shwedagon Pagoda and nearby Buddhist temples as evening approaches.

hanging off in all directions were the major modes of transportation in this city. Even though each driver was pounding on his horn, everyone seemed to know exactly where they were going, and every vehicle was moving in an orderly fashion. Still, I was grateful to be crammed inside a taxi rather than suspended from the side of one of those buses.

Yangon is a sprawling city, not a tall one. Several large lakes and many ultra-green parks connected by winding major thoroughfares provide the structure for this overgrown colonial town at the southernmost end of the Irrawaddy River. The city is in the tropical zone, and during the monsoon season the vegetation is lush and everything is wet. The residential and government architecture is basic British Empire colonial, with large windows, gabled roofs, and brick construction originating from at least several waves of foreign rule, but with a touch of ancient and contemporary Burmese style in parts of the woodwork and design. Very few buildings are new. Nothing is modern. Most dwellings are in need of some repair. And for those few buildings under construction, work had stopped long ago.

Burmese visitors and pilgrims on the terrace surrounding Shwedagon Pagoda.

Yet all of these architectural elements of Yangon are irrelevant in comparison to the overwhelming dominance of the Shwedagon Pagoda, the largest shrine to Buddha in the world and the holiest place in Myanmar, situated on Singuttara

Hill in the very heart of the city. Built nearly 2,500 years ago, the pagoda has been enlarged from an original thirty-foot-tall (9 m) structure to the current bell-shaped golden stupa towering over three hundred feet (100 m) in height. Each year tens of thousands of pilgrims visit this monument, which was built to house eight sacred hairs of the Buddha. The Shwedagon Pagoda is only one of the many shrines to the Buddha that are found in Yangon. The city is full of large and small Buddhist temples. It is a fundamental tenet of Buddhism that one must commit good deeds in the present life in order to be born into a better life in one's next incarnation. These good deeds often include spending large sums of money on building magnificent pagodas and temples. Near the Shwedagon is situated the Maha Vijaya Pagoda, the second-largest temple in the city, which was built by U Ne Win, the first supreme leader of the military regime that has ruled Myanmar since 1962.[3] For U Ne Win, balancing his repressive government policies on the one hand with the building of a massive Buddhist pagoda on the other must have been a complex task in his commitment of good deeds towards his next reincarnation.

After I got settled at the Highland Lodge, a guesthouse in the northern part of the city frequented by foreign biologists and conservationists, my first task was to arrange an audience with the director general of the Forest Department. The Forest Department is housed within the Ministry of Forestry. Because the Wildlife and Sanctuaries Division, which is part of the Forest Department, was to be my main point of contact for working in Myanmar, it was critical that I first see the director general, or even deputy director general U Than Nwai, to explain my plans. For some reason I thought that setting up such an introductory meeting and establishing an itinerary for my first trip to Myanmar would be simple and straightforward. Not so—it took nine days.

Burmese names for people, as with many aspects of the local culture in Myanmar, at first seem confusing. Is everyone's first name U? Are all persons named Aung related to each other in some way? Do people have first and last names? I quickly learned. The Burmese use *U* much as we use *Mr.* when referring to a man. They also employ *Daw* where we would use *Miss, Mrs.,* or *Ms.* It doesn't matter that *U* (pronounced "Oo") really means "Uncle," and *Daw* means "Auntie." It is proper to use *U* and *Daw* even in everyday conversation when addressing a friend or colleague. These two customary gender titles are necessary in part because Burmese names do not indicate a person's sex.

The practice of choosing personal names is also different from Western naming traditions in that one does not receive a family name at birth. Instead, given names are dependent upon the day of the week that a baby is born. If, for example, you were born on Monday, then two or three names from the list of "Monday-born" names would be selected for you. Separate lists of names exist

Buddhist worshippers at one of the small shrines at the base of Shwedagon Pagoda. These shrines are honored by people born on a particular day of the week.

for each day of the week, except Wednesday, which has two lists, one if you were born in the morning and one if you were born in the afternoon or evening. Therefore, not everyone named Yin or Aung or Htun is related, or even of the same sex. Additionally, each given name denotes some characteristic or trait that the bearer supposedly possesses, so the name is open to some interpretation, much as we infer personal features from the twelve signs of the zodiac. Occasionally exceptions do occur, such as Daw Aung San Suu Kyi, the well-known democracy advocate and Nobel Peace Prize winner in Myanmar. Suu Kyi is the name that she was given at birth because she was born on a particular day of the week. She decided to add Aung San to her name in recognition of her father U Aung San, the revered general and martyred national hero of Burma who led the country to independence from the British in the 1940s.[4] For most Burmese, however, adding the name of another family member to one's own name is not a common practice.

The day of the week of one's birth is important not only in determining personal names, but also in the religious practices of Myanmar. When a Burmese Buddhist approaches a pagoda, the day of the week on which he was born determines at which corner of the terrace he will pray. Each day of the week has been assigned a specific compass point, celestial planet, and symbolic animal, and pilgrims pray and leave offerings at the birth post marking their day of the week. Eventually, after checking a worn calendar that listed past dates and days of the week on which they fell, I received my own Burmese name, U Aung Lin, from my friends because I was Sunday-born and destined to be "victorious, successful, and bright." I wasn't so sure.

I was in Myanmar at the invitation of the Burmese Forest Department through the courtesy of my conservationist colleagues from the National Zoo in Washington. They had arranged my visit, but in addition to directly working with them on vegetation studies, I was here because many of the plants of this country were practically unknown to science. Botanists now estimate that as many as four hundred thousand species of plants may currently inhabit the earth, give or take fifty thousand.[5] Even after three hundred years of study we do not yet have an accurate account of how many species of plants are on the planet. We can only provide an estimate. In some places, such as Europe and North America, we know a lot about the indigenous plants; in other places our knowledge is still very poor. Places in the latter category include the Andes of South America, the rain forests of central Africa, and the monsoonal regions of tropical Asia, including Myanmar. When I stepped off the airplane that had taken me from Bangkok to Yangon, I was one of only a handful of Western botanists who had visited Myanmar since the 1940s. This land was a virtual terra incognita with respect to a comprehensive enumeration of its plant species.

An outdoor vegetable market in Yangon.

Traditional knowledge of the plants of Burma dates back over a thousand years, and local markets today are still full of wild species collected as foods, condiments, and medicines. Western botanical knowledge was brought to Burma by the British during the age of colonial rule, starting in the early 1800s, primarily because of their great commercial interest in timber. Due to the tenuous political, social, and economic situation in Burma following the chaos of World War II and the end of colonial rule in 1948, the growth of scientific knowledge of the local plants of the country was slow despite the efforts of the small cadre of field-oriented Burmese botanists who took up the task of documenting their flora. As a result many of the plant species of Myanmar are still poorly known to science, and many species are yet to be discovered and named.

The need for more knowledge about the plants of this country and thus the opportunity to make important botanical discoveries were among the reasons why I started my explorations in Myanmar. I knew that unlike many of its neighbors, such as Thailand, with less than 5 percent of its forest cover remaining, Myanmar had a large proportion of its virgin forest intact.[6] However, as I had seen with my own eyes in many other areas of the world, such as the Amazon Basin and Costa Rica, this situation could very quickly change. Would botanists such as myself and my colleagues in Myanmar be allowed to venture into pristine

areas to observe and collect the flora?
I had a singular opportunity to contribute
to a more global effort to discover and
document the remaining plants of the
planet before the forests, woodlands,
savannahs, and deserts were even more
degraded by human activity. If predictions
by some environmentalists are correct, we
may not have more than a few decades to
complete our inventory of the biodiversity
of Earth before 10 percent or more of the
species go extinct.[7]

For many developing countries, such
as Myanmar, much of the botany and
conservation activity are carried out in
the ministries and departments devoted
to maintaining and utilizing the natural
forests. Universities in the same countries,
unfortunately, often lack the resources,
facilities, staff, and even students required
to pursue active research on biodiversity.
It is usually left up to the forestry departments and environmental ministries to conduct such work. Ironically, in some cases
the same ministries in charge of preserving natural areas are also in the process of
exploiting them. Myanmar, with the largest
remaining natural reserves of teak in the
world, has been eyed for decades by greedy
timber companies all over Asia.

A teak forest near the border of Magway and Rakhine states in western Myanmar.

In this country of golden pagodas and abundant teak forests, a foreign
scientist is eyed with suspicion. After a five-day wait, I was fortunate to
be granted a brief audience with the deputy director general of the Forest
Department, who was at least partially welcoming to me. He grilled me about
my purpose in coming to Myanmar and scrutinized my credentials. In the end
he agreed to help me develop a program that would allow me to tour some of the
forest reserves and sanctuaries in the central valley of the country. In exchange
for this help, he wanted assurances that I would train his staff of foresters in
current botanical techniques, and of course I readily agreed. From the initial
planning stages for my trip to Myanmar, I had recognized that training local

scientists and naturalists was a critical responsibility for a foreigner working in any country. Local training was also the only chance that a long-term, in-depth understanding of the biodiversity of the region could be achieved. After my meeting with the deputy director general, I was sent to the office of U Aung Than, deputy director of the Wildlife and Sanctuaries Division, to work out the details. U Aung Than explained to me the process of devising a schedule, organizing the logistics, and getting the appropriate permission from the required ministries and the security office. I was placed once again in the hands of U Myint Aung, the park warden who had met me at the airport, and his friend U Ye Htut, also a park warden at another wildlife sanctuary. And I waited. Four days later my journal entry described my thoughts:

> *And the monsoons continue. Still in Yangon, waiting for the program to begin; still organizing. What I thought was looking like success now seems less promising. After going back and forth day after day from my guesthouse to the Forest Department with broken jeeps, downed power lines across the roads, delays, and avoidances, our program has slowly taken shape; it looks okay, but not yet complete. U Htun Paw Do, the new acting deputy director of Wildlife and Sanctuaries Division, gave me the news that Daw Yin Yin Kyi would be my liaison officer, but could not arrive in Yangon until tomorrow, so we wait again another day. . . .*[8]

To my astonishment and delight, Daw Yin Yin Kyi did arrive the next day. Remarkably, all permission letters were in hand, a vehicle was found that would take us where we wanted to go, and our gear was soon packed. First we would stop in the town of Toungoo to visit a working teak camp, then we would go to the Forest Research Institute at Yezin where Daw Yin Yin Kyi, the resident botanist, was based. From there we would take a brief trip to the mysterious Mount Popa, and finally we would have a stopover at the only botanical garden in the country, in the town of Pyin-Oo-Lwin outside Mandalay. It had taken me nine days after arriving in Yangon to meet the necessary officials in the Forest Department, to plan an acceptable itinerary for my introduction to the natural areas of the country, to be granted permission by the security police, and to meet my "liaison officer," Daw Yin Yin Kyi. Although to me the wait seemed interminable, later I learned that I was fortunate in needing only nine days to accomplish these tasks. Other foreign visitors told me that they had waited for weeks before being permitted to leave Yangon. I counted my blessings, said my good-byes to U Myint Aung and U Ye Htut, and with one last view of the Shwedagon Pagoda, I was off.

CHAPTER 3 # Ancient Cities and Sacred Mountains

"A little to one side but in full view was one of the loveliest pagodas. In the setting sun its colours, cream and fawn-grey, were soft like the silk of old dresses in a museum. It had a symmetry that was grateful to the eye; the turrets at one corner were repeated by the turrets at every other; and the flamboyant windows repeated the flamboyant doors below. The decoration had a sort of bold violence, as though it sought to scale fantastic pinnacles of the spirit and in the desperate struggle, with life and soul engaged, could not concern itself with reticence or good taste. But withal it had at that moment a kind of majesty and there was majesty in the solitude in which it stood. It seemed to weigh down the earth with too great a burden."

W. Somerset Maugham, *The Gentleman in the Parlour*, 1930

The Ananda Paya, one of the most stunning temples of Mon architecture in the ancient city of Bagan.

Mount Popa, an extinct volcano known as the Mountain of Flowers, rises over 4,900 feet (1,500 m) out of the hot and dry plains southwest of Mandalay.[1] These lowland plains have been cultivated by Burmese farmers for thousands of years. The rice paddies and sesame fields, each surrounded by a row of towering toddy palms, stretch for miles all the way to the banks of the Irrawaddy River. On the western flank of the mountain sits Toung Kalat, the volcanic plug that was rocketed out of the apex of the volcano over a million years ago and is now draped in Buddhist temples and a monastery. From the top of Mount Popa, looking toward the setting sun, you can see the tallest of the pagodas that sit along the edge of the river in the ancient city of Bagan.

Bagan and Mandalay are situated in the middle of the central valley of Myanmar, which is bounded by mountain ranges on the east, west, and north. Two of the three main rivers of the country, the Irrawaddy and the Chindwin, traverse the valley from north to south and form at their mouth a giant delta, which has ceaselessly pushed its way into the Andaman Sea for millions of years.

Rangoon, a city established more recently than either Bagan or Mandalay, lies along the edge of the delta.

Mount Popa from a distance.

Even before the British began to push their way into Burma in the 1800s, the scattered villages and settlements in the central valley were being pulled together by a growing web of religious, commercial, and political connections that would eventually coalesce into the most powerful kingdom in the history of this part of Southeast Asia.[2] The Court of Ava, ultimately centered in Mandalay, ruled the Third Burmese Empire, which encompassed the greater part of central Burma from the mid-1700s to the invasion of the British in the late 1800s. During this period the Third Empire, known as the Konbaung Dynasty, was at the height of its power and political control, ruling over two million people. The empire was bounded on the west by the peoples of the Arakan and Chin states, on the north by the Chinese and the mighty Himalayan mountain range, on the northeast by the Shan Dynasty, and on the southeast by the Mon-speaking peoples of Tenasserim. Such was the political and cultural situation in Myanmar in the late 1700s and early 1800s as the British Empire began to expand beyond its central authority in India. After the fall of the Konbaung Dynasty, never again would the Burmese enjoy such wealth, prosperity, and culture.

The nobility and rulers of the Konbaung Dynasty, although in solid control

CHAPTER 3

"In the distance I saw the pagodas for which it is renowned. They loomed, huge, remote and mysterious, out of the mist of the early morning like the vague recollections of a fantastic dream."

W. Somerset Maugham,
The Gentleman in the Parlour, 1930

of the Burmese-speaking people of the countryside, were not fully prepared for the arrival of the British and the modern Western world. The English, rapidly expanding their power in India in the early years of the nineteenth century, were clearly interested in the kingdom of Burma, which lay to the east across the Bay of Bengal. The Burmese, in their own way, were poorly informed about the manner of the British, or *thosaung kala*,[3] who had conquered their neighbors to the west. When the Burmese rulers decided that eastern Bengal rightly belonged to them and launched an attack to take control of this region, they did not anticipate and were not ready for the overwhelming response from the British that began the First Anglo-Burmese War in 1824. Although it took nearly two years, the British Expeditionary Force ultimately drove the Burmese armies back to the central valley with a decisive naval battle fought near Bagan. The Burmese defeat resulted in the ceding to the British of both the state of Arakan bordering the Bay of Bengal and the state of Tenasserim along the Andaman Sea, which together included most of Lower Burma. The outside world had forced itself into the Golden Land.

One of the earliest responses of the Burmese rulers to their defeat in the first war with the English was rather curious. They did not quickly strengthen their army, nor did they build higher walls around the capital city of Ava (near present-day Mandalay). Rather, they gathered together the top scholars of the land to write a new history of the country, in order to understand how they had lost the battle. The resulting *Glass Palace Chronicles* concluded that the Court of Ava, if it was to prevail, must consolidate its influence in the central valley by promoting a Myanma identity through a common language, culture, and religion.[4] Although they were to some extent successful in this consolidation, the second war between the Burmese and British empires in 1853 made it clear that more extensive reforms in government and society were also needed if Burma was to survive as a country. At the same time the world itself was in the midst of its first phase of what is today called "globalization," and the isolated structure and traditions of the Konbaung Dynasty were no longer tenable as the European colonial powers knocked at its door. The great King Mindon, who attempted to institute reforms in the Myanma military, industrial base, and transportation system, especially through the initiation of Western education for his officers, ultimately failed at this task. The British takeover of Mandalay in the Third Anglo-Burmese War in 1885, the resultant conquest of all Upper Burma, and the subsequent exile of King Thibaw and Queen Supayalat ended over a hundred years of the last and most powerful Burmese dynasty.

Where does the ancient city of Bagan fit into the precolonial history of Myanmar? The conquest by the British in the 1800s and the fall of the final Burmese Empire represents only a small part of the history of the rule of the Burmese people in Southeast Asia. The fall of Mandalay to the British in 1885 had been preceded by centuries of strife and warfare in Myanmar among the various tribes of the north, south, east, and west. The establishment of the First Burmese Empire at Bagan in 849 AD marked the beginning of the dominance of the Burmese people in this region.[5] Bagan, strategically situated on the banks of the Irrawaddy River, became the center of Burmese power and culture for over four hundred years, ending with defeat at the hands of the great Kublai Khan in 1287. During those years Bagan served as one of the major capitals of civilization in Southeast Asia, with an empire that encompassed the regions of the Mon, the Arakan, and the Shan and eventually extended into Thailand and even Laos during the Taungoo Dynasty in the sixteenth century.

Bagan, even today, is a wonder of ancient architecture and archaeology equaling if not surpassing comparable sites in Cambodia and Indonesia, such as Angkor Wat and Borobudur. The construction of thousands of religious temples began when King Anawratha was converted to Theravada Buddhism around

ABOVE: The Buddhist monastery perched atop the volcanic plug of Mount Popa.

OPPOSITE: Close-up of the Buddhist monastery.

PAGES 36–37: The misty summit of Mount Popa, the "Mountain of Flowers," at over 4,000 feet in elevation.

CHAPTER 3

ANCIENT CITIES AND SACRED MOUNTAINS

"*The mountain was smothered in mist,
which came sweeping heavily like wet smoke
over the ridge. It was a rather eerie sensation
following the narrow path into the dim,
dripping forest and out on to the open
hillside again, in the teeth of the wind,
always wondering what might loom round
the next corner.*"

Frank Kingdon-Ward,
Pilgrimage for Plants, 1960.

CHAPTER 3

1050 AD. Adopting the Mon style of pagoda design and architecture, Anawratha began a period of construction of magnificent temples, pagodas, and monuments to the Buddha that has continued for over a millennium. The most recent pagoda was completed in the last decade of the twentieth century.

Myanmar has had a long history of changing empires, relocation of capital cities, continual warfare between various ethnic groups, and repeated attempts by foreign powers to conquer the land.[6] In light of this history the present-day military regime is not out of character with past events. Perhaps one of the most difficult things to understand about Myanmar is how to reconcile its frequent warfare with its Buddhist values of peace, meditation, and rebirth. To compare on the one hand the First Burmese Empire, which militarily conquered the entirety of the land, with on the other hand the elaborate and extensive architectural treasures of Bagan built in devotion to the Buddha reveals a grand contrast between power politics and devout religion. Yet this same tradition goes on today as some of Myanmar's most strident dictators continue to build massive temples, such as the Maha Vijaya Pagoda in Yangon, which was financed and constructed by U Ne Win, the supreme military commander of Myanmar who initiated the current junta.

"The colonial state was born as a military occupation."

Thant Myint-U,
The Making of Modern Burma, 2001

In modern Myanmar, as in the past, the great majority of the population practices Buddhism, while Christianity prevails in parts of the west and north. However, incorporated into Burmese Buddhism is a unique form of spirit worship that grew out of the ancient rituals of animism, the belief that nonhuman objects have a soul or consciousness. The thirty-seven spirits, or *nats*, in Burmese Buddhism are representative of the spiritual nature of the trees, rivers, rocks, ghosts, and even Hindu gods.[7] *Nats* are always making mischief and require offerings of flowers or fruits to ensure that they will not upset the oxcart or let the goats destroy the vegetables. The presence of *nats* is an integral part of the everyday activities of most Burmese. And Mount Popa, just sixty miles (100 km) from Bagan, seems to be a mecca for these spirits. The Buddhist temples on Toung Kalat at the base of the mountain share their space equally with numerous shrines to the *nats*.

OPPOSITE, TOP:
Nat or spirit houses surrounding a sacred fig tree.

OPPOSITE, BOTTOM:
Nat shrines built by the people of Kachin State.

Photographs by James Henry Green, c.1920s.

I first traveled to Mount Popa at the end of the dry season, just after the arrival of a few early monsoon rains. The extinct volcanic cone rises out of the flattened plain and can be seen for miles as you approach. The green vegetation of the slopes of Mount Popa is in stark contrast to the scorched and dry rice paddies that surround it. This mountain serves as a critical watershed for the immediate area, and it is well protected not only by the Forest Department that maintains Mount Popa as a national park, but also by the *nats* that inhabit the forests, streams, trees, and rocks. This mountain has been a sacred home of the *nats* for a thousand years and has been visited by kings and pilgrims who

climbed to the summit to receive the blessings of these spirits. I went to Mount Popa to study the plants.

The banks of the Irrawaddy River near the city of Bagan.

Traveling with my friend and colleague Daw Yin Yin Kyi, head botanist at the Forest Research Institute, I found the forests of Mount Popa, especially the old-growth wet forest in the crater of the extinct volcano, to contain the first really exciting plants I had seen in Myanmar. Most of the mountain is a national park and in name it is protected as a wildlife sanctuary, but at the same time it continues to be used as a source of medicinal plants, firewood, and in some cases hunting grounds by the people from the surrounding villages.[8] Daw Yin Yin Kyi and U Uga, the chief warden at the park when I first visited, assured me that the sacredness of the area due to the presence of a Buddhist monastery —and the added protection of the *nats*—ensured that the bulk of the plants and animals would survive the locals' incursions into the park. A team led by U Uga, a short, strong, energetic fellow with a wry smile and a distinct military air about him, was working with the inhabitants of the thirty-six villages neighboring Mount Popa to interpret the conservation value of the biodiversity as well as the sacredness of the forests. Here at Mount Popa I found my first example of the impact of religious beliefs, both Buddhist and *nat* worship, on the conservation of a natural habitat in Burma. Within the forests it was not uncommon to come upon a small clearing or isolated stone outcrop that was the site of a small shrine to either the Buddha or the *nats*, or both. Although the land surrounding the mountain was completely degraded environmentally, I could still find species of wild gingers and orchids in the understory of the verdant forests all the way to the summit of Mount Popa.

CHAPTER 3

A vista of the hundreds of Buddhist pagodas and temples scattered across the plains at Bagan.

One day as we were leaving Mount Popa on our way to visit Bagan, the dusty road on which we were traveling dipped down slightly as we crossed a dry riverbed. I thought it was interesting how the local villagers had constructed the main pipeline, which conducted water away from the mountain to the surrounding towns. The heavy iron water pipes were supported by sections of large tree trunks, which were rather substantial in girth. Aside from the protected trees in the park at Mount Popa, very little such vegetation was found in this area. I assumed that these wooden supports must have been brought from many miles away. I asked the driver to stop the car so I could take a look. To my great astonishment, the pillars holding up the water pipes were tree trunks, but they had been turned into stone. Scattered along the bed of the river were hundreds of similar sections of rock-solid tree trunks. As I looked more closely, I realized that I was in the middle of an extensive petrified forest.

At that moment I had a vision of the vast forest of teak that many millennia ago covered the plains surrounding Mount Popa, which are now dry, dusty rice paddies and scattered villages. A gigantic explosion at some point in the past blew off the top of the smoldering volcano and deposited a thick layer of soggy ash over the land. Now, perhaps a million years later, this monument of mummified tree trunks was all that remained. The thousands of fossil trees in this petrified forest were not that different from the thousands of decaying stone temples, pagodas, and Buddhist shrines only a few miles away in Bagan. The petrified forest was a symbol of the abundant natural resources that once covered the land; Bagan represented a former complex empire of wealth, culture,

ANCIENT CITIES AND SACRED MOUNTAINS

LEFT: A panorama of the Bagan pagodas in the 1920s. Photograph by James Henry Green, c.1920s.

BELOW: The crumbling Tharabar Gate, entrance in the east wall to the city of Bagan.

OPPOSITE: The Htilominlo Paya, built in 1218, northeast of Bagan along the road to Nyaung U.

CHAPTER 3

and power. Each represented in its own way the secret but glorious history of Myanmar.

After returning from Bagan, I spent a few more days recording the plant species at Mount Popa by making pressed and dried botanical specimens that would be brought back for more careful study at a later date. Such specimens include samples of the leaves, stems, bark, flowers, and fruits of each species as well as detailed notes about the habitats and forest types in which the plants occur. It is not uncommon for botanists to also take photographs of the plants and preserve flowers in alcohol or tissue samples in silica gel for DNA analyses. These specimens provide a permanent record of what a botanist sees and discovers at a particular place and at a specific point in time. They provide a persistent stream of evidence of plant life on Earth, and are essential to understanding the classification and evolution of life.

From Mount Popa we headed east to Meiktila, and then due north toward Mandalay. The dry zone is parched in May, and the roads are dusty. We reached Mandalay at nightfall. The former capital city could not pose more of a contrast to the green rain-drenched ambience of Yangon. At the end of the dry season, Mandalay is extremely hot, and not the most attractive metropolis. The buildings and streets radiate intense heat, and everyone in the city appears to be waiting for the cooling rains. I was glad to depart early the next morning for the refreshing oasis of Pyin-Oo-Lwin, a small colonial hill town thirty-seven miles (60 km) from Mandalay. Formerly known as Maymyo, Pyin-Oo-Lwin is the site of Myanmar's only established botanical garden. The garden is run by the Forest Department, and U Uga, who had come with us from Mount Popa, discussed with me the possibility of establishing a future plant research and conservation center here. We spent the day touring the garden, meeting with officials, and brainstorming about a national botanical garden in Myanmar. My friend had big plans, and I wanted to help. Over the years the garden had degenerated into a town park for Sunday picnics by the local inhabitants. U Uga wanted my advice on the best course of action to restore it to an active botanical garden with horticultural displays, an educational agenda, and a productive research program. We talked late into the night. Before I knew it, it was time to depart once again for the Forest Research Institute in Yezin, halfway back to Yangon.

Yezin marks the transition between the hot and dry northern zone of the central valley and the wetter southern zone. The Forest Research Institute and the Institute of Forestry together occupy an attractive campus just north of the town of Pyinmana. It is here in Yezin that the next generation of foresters and agriculturists are being trained. The campus of buildings, designed in colonial styles mixed with more modern architecture, is surrounded by lush rice paddies and verdant experimental plots in which new crops and methods of cultivation are

ABOVE: One of the hundreds of temples built in Bagan between the eleventh and thirteenth centuries.

RIGHT: Thatbyinnyu Temple in the old city of Bagan was built in the middle of the 12th century by King Alaungsithu.

ANCIENT CITIES AND SACRED MOUNTAINS

TOP LEFT: A guardian spirit at the entrance to the Ananda Paya.

TOP RIGHT: The south-facing golden image of the standing Buddha inside Ananda Paya.

LEFT: A golden image of the seated Buddha.

being tested. This scene was slightly reminiscent of a typical agricultural college in the American Midwest, except for the water buffalo grazing in the fields, crimson-clad monks marching along the roads, and loudspeakers blasting Buddhist prayers from the local monasteries.

Daw Yin Yin Kyi, a deceptively frail-looking but at times surprisingly head-strong woman in her sixties, is chief botanist at the Forest Research Institute. She took me to her office next to a small, interesting herbarium of dried and pressed plants that is a representative sample of the flora of Myanmar. Botanists spend a lot of their time examining and studying these delicate specimens, which are found in herbaria around the world. For me, these collections provided new insights into the plant diversity that I would find in this country. In the collections I found specimens from many of the places I wanted to explore, including Mount Victoria in the Chin Hills and Sumprabum on the road between Myitkyina and Putao in the far north of Myanmar. From information recorded on the specimens, I could discern the time of the year when many of the species would be in flower, which is the most critical stage for collecting plants. Before we had to leave Yezin to return to Yangon, I spent a day converting the information on species and localities laid before me in the decaying and decomposing specimens of the herbarium into data on my laptop computer, which would then be readily accessible for analyses at a later date. These collections, some from the early part of the twentieth century, together with my discoveries at Mount Popa, constituted a small but growing core of knowledge of the plants of Myanmar.

The petrified remains of a forest that once stood at the base of Mount Popa.

I had now tasted a minute kernel of what I would eventually learn and experience. I wanted to know more, but I would have to wait until my next visit to the country. More rains were on their way.

CHAPTER 4 # The Arrival of the Monsoon

"Quite suddenly it burst upon us with awful fury, the wind blowing with hurricane force. Now the lightening blazed incessantly, flash following flash with such rapidity that we could see everything—bending trees, whirling leaves, and the dark outline of brooding mountains; and to the continuous roll of thunder, like heavy artillery, was added the shriller rattle of drenching rain as it beat furiously on the stiff palm leaves."

Frank Kingdon-Ward, *In Farthest Burma*, 1921

The sky suddenly became very dark, almost a deep purple. It had been one of the hottest days I had experienced so far in Myanmar, over 113 degrees Fahrenheit (45°C) and not a breath of moving air all day. We were returning to the city of Pyay from a plant-collecting trip along the eastern ridge of the Rakhine Yoma, the last mountain range in the west that slopes down to the Bay of Bengal. April was not a good time to search for plants. This month marked the end of the dry season; it had not rained since November, and most of the species we were interested in were still dormant, biding their time underground waiting for the first rains. Many of the gingers, the plants I had been studying, are adapted to such monsoonal climates with their distinct dry seasons and wet seasons. We did find a few ginger species that had broken dormancy. One ginger, *Kaempferia candida*, had just pushed its early nearly pure white flowers aboveground into the bright, hot sun. Before our discovery that day, this species had been last collected by Western botanists in the late 1880s. (We later found that it was commonly sold in the local markets as an ingredient for soups.) Still, we hadn't found many species in our search of the Rakhine Yoma.

As we drove down the winding road on the eastern slopes of the hills, the wind, almost a welcome whisper at first, started to rise. The thunder in the distance told us that something big was coming our way. Just as we reached the flat plain, the storm struck. Suddenly the trees along the sides of the road were

Looking west from Mandalay Hill across the flooded Irrawaddy River during the monsoon season.

49

bent to the ground by the wind. Branches, ripped from the trunks by gusts of over sixty miles (100 km) per hour, were hurled horizontally across the road in front of our vehicle. The blasts of wind picked up several approaching young boys off the seats of their bicycles and flung them to the ground while their bicycles flew over their heads. Then, as the temperature quickly dropped, hail started to open fire on the roof of our jeep. The road was soon covered with a layer of icy marbles. The storm was intensifying. I thought about crouching down in the front seat of the car for protection, but the scene fantastically unfolding outside compelled me to watch all that was happening. I felt like Dorothy in *The Wizard of Oz* when the tornado swept her up across Kansas. Finally, I came to my senses and told the driver to pull into an open area along the road that was relatively free from trees to wait out the squall. Then, as abruptly as it had started, the storm was over. I had just experienced the "start of rains storm."

Thirty minutes later we began to drive on. The first town we reached, called Okh-Shit-Byin, was just beginning to recover from the storm. All of the dogs were still barking, and sheet-metal roofs, which had blown off most of the houses and shops, littered the road. Our driver dodged the obstacles as we peered at the damage. The unwelcome, turbulent—but expected and well-known—messenger of nature who each year announced the beginning of the rainy season had just passed through the region. The monsoon had arrived. The intense rains would not start for another month or two, but the end of the dry season, with its hot days and nights, was now in sight. Despite the disruption and destruction of this storm, the "sharp squall" signaled the finale of the dry season, and for many in this parched land it was a call for celebration. We stopped at a roadside restaurant for a beer.

The monsoons affect a wide region of southern Asia, stretching from parts of Indonesia all the way to the west coast of India and north to Pakistan. Unlike the tropical rain forests of Southeast Asia, which are evergreen due to the high rainfall that occurs throughout the year, the tropical monsoon forests found in Thailand, Indochina, Myanmar, and India are highly seasonal, with distinct dry and wet periods.[1] In Myanmar the most severe rains take place from June to September, a period that accounts for 90 percent of the region's annual rainfall. Each year after the rains end, a cool dry season arrives, which is much welcomed throughout the area. This cool period is soon replaced by a gradual increase in temperatures from February to March, with the most intense heat arriving in April. The forest trees shed their leaves at this time, and non-irrigated agriculture activities come to a halt; a time of waiting begins. Extreme storms, such as the one I witnessed descending from the Rakhine Yoma, often mark the return of the monsoons. With the start of the rains, the forests come alive once again, and many of the local crops begin to sprout. Life is renewed.

OPPOSITE: Flooded rice paddies in western Myanmar.

PAGES 52–53: Teak trees with bright yellow flowers in undisturbed forests along the upper Irrawaddy River near Bhamo.

The monsoons, although a source of rejuvenation in normal cycles, can be exceptionally destructive when they are severe. During years when the rains are especially heavy—years which seem to be on the increase, according to reports in international newspapers—torrential rains can cause widespread flooding. These inundations wash away homes, crops, and livestock, displacing millions of people from their homes and villages and causing the deaths of thousands from drowning, landslides, and house collapses. In 2007 at least a third of the reported deaths during the monsoon season in India were from snakebite, as people, livestock, and wild animals were crowded into ever-shrinking refuges above the rising waters.[2] Destruction can be particularly ruthless along the floodplains of the Irrawaddy River in Myanmar, the Brahmaputra River in Bangladesh, the northeastern section of India, and the Terai plains of Nepal. The devastating cyclone that smashed into the delta region of Myanmar in 2008 killed over a hundred thousand people.[3]

BELOW: A flooded village partially under water during the height of the monsoons.

RIGHT: Storm clouds brewing over the Irrawaddy River near Shwegu.

CHAPTER 4

THE ARRIVAL OF THE MONSOON

As we left Okh-Shit-Byin, life in the town was already returning to normal as the sun reappeared and the tin roofs were hoisted back in place. A few hours farther down the road we reached Pyay, formerly known as Prome or Pyi, an ancient city that was originally ruled centuries ago by the Mon people of southern Myanmar. Pyay lies on the banks of the Irrawaddy River and, like most cities and towns in Myanmar, is dominated by an impressive pagoda. The Shwesandaw Pagoda in Pyay is modeled after the great Shwedagon Pagoda in Yangon and contains four hairs of the Buddha. Stopping in Pyay to see this pagoda, so reminiscent of the Golden Pagoda in Yangon, reminded me of my first visit to the country a year earlier and the challenges I encountered upon landing at the airport during the height of the monsoon. My second arrival in Myanmar had been much smoother. A new terminal for international flights had been completed at the Mingaladon Airport in Yangon, which made passing through immigration and customs almost a pleasure. This country was already beginning to change for me. I was optimistic.

ABOVE: A stormy sky over dry hills near Pyay.

OPPOSITE: Pagoda in Pyay.

Warned by my previous experience, I anticipated days of waiting for an audience with the director general of the Forest Department. I was startled to find myself, two hours after my second arrival in Yangon, seated in the office of my friend U Uga, formerly the warden at Mount Popa National Park and now director of the Nature and Wildlife Conservation Division of the Forest Department. We had a lot to discuss about both my plans for Myanmar and Uga's plans for me. He could not have been more encouraging. The work that I proposed, which was to initiate a new major inventory of the native plants of the country, was eagerly and enthusiastically endorsed. During the previous year at the National Museum of Natural History in Washington, after my first visit to Myanmar, I had spent hours combing the literature and studying hundreds of specimens to find out as much as I could about the plant species of Myanmar. The relatively small amount of scientific information available on the flora of this region made me realize the great opportunity I was being handed to investigate the plants of Myanmar. However, I also understood the amount of work that would be needed to achieve this goal. The challenge was daunting and would have been impossible if not for the encouragement of U Uga. He had a clear and long-range vision of the biodiversity and conservation activities that were necessary to catalog the plants and animals of his country, as well as to protect them

Kaempferia indica, a ginger that produces its flowers as the first rains begin in the monsoon season.

from the newly developing threats caused by economic expansion in Myanmar. He knew that I might be an important key to training his cadre of park wardens and their assistants in botanical inventory techniques. He also knew of my great curiosity about the gingers of Myanmar, and about the numerous new species yet to be discovered and described. We were a perfect combination.

Through the efforts of U Uga I was also able to meet Dr. Kyaw Tint, the new director general of the Forest Department. The "DG" was a slender, handsome man who spoke with passion and authority about the biodiversity of Myanmar. He was equally enthusiastic and eager to help make our plan succeed, and he quickly approved the concept and itinerary. However, in a solemn moment before I left the interview, he warned me in a stern but friendly manner that I should be careful not to mix science and politics in Myanmar. As I departed, I could not help but think that in order to succeed in any conservation endeavor, one inevitably had to do just that: reconcile the biological necessities with the political, social, and economic realities. I thanked him for his advice and left.

After a series of discussions over the course of a few days with U Uga and his staff, we agreed that I would take the lead on the publication of a new inventory of the flowering plants of Myanmar, in collaboration with Daw Yin Yin Kyi of the Forest Research Institute. I had visited the institute during my first visit to the country the previous year, and knew that the plant specimens in the herbarium's collection were vital and necessary to produce a new checklist. I also knew that the resources at Yezin were in no way sufficient to tackle the job. We would have to initiate a new plant-collecting program, as well as round up the information on plant diversity already available at the major botanical institutes in the United States and the United Kingdom, including the Royal Botanic Gardens at Edinburgh and Kew. The latter resources were important because it was the British who had conducted some of the earliest plant explorations in Myanmar during the colonial occupation in the 1800s and early 1900s. The first recorded notes on plant diversity in Burma are ascribed to a Lieutenant Pottinger of the British Foreign Service, who provided brief descriptions of the vegetation types, especially in the north of the country, at the turn of the eighteenth century. Unfortunately, all of his natural history collections were lost when he "got into trouble with the Maru tribe who murdered some of his followers, and he had to make a quick getaway."[5]

"Every year from February to May the sun glared in the sky like an angry god, then suddenly the monsoon blew westward, first in sharp squalls, then in a heavy ceaseless downpour that drenched everything until neither one's clothes, one's bed nor even one's food ever seemed to be dry. It was still hot with a stuffy vaporous heat. The lower jungle paths turned into morasses, and the paddy fields were great wastes of stagnant water with a stale mousy smell."

George Orwell, *Burmese Days*, 1934[4]

One of the most renowned twentieth-century British plant explorers was Frank Kingdon-Ward, who was born in England in 1885 and made his first plant-collecting expedition to Upper Burma when he was twenty-nine years old.[6] Kingdon-Ward, the son of a professor of botany at Cambridge University, left the university before completing his training at Christ's College to teach high school in Singapore, where he received his first introduction to the Orient. A plant collector extraordinaire, he epitomized the attitude of the colonial British in Asia, who believed that Burma and British India were part of the British Empire, and therefore everything in these lands was fair game for exploitation. Kingdon-Ward had an immense interest in plants and horticulture, and although he was not a fully trained botanist in the model of the scientists at Kew Gardens or the British Museum, he and others like him provided a steady stream of new plants from Asia for the gardens of wealthy Victorians in England and Scotland. The Himalayan regions of China, Burma, India, and Tibet, practically unexplored at the turn of the last century, were a rich source of native rhododendrons, camellias, magnolias, poppies, primulas, orchids, and many other plants for the booming horticultural trade at that time. The mountain climates of these tropical and subtropical regions were the source of novel and exciting plant species that could survive the mild winters of the British Isles. Rich bankers and merchants

CHAPTER 4

from London with giant estates in Cornwall and Devon were the patrons of the far-flung plant collectors and hired them to fill their expanding and exuberant gardens with the botanical bounty collected on long and often dangerous expeditions to the far reaches of the Empire. One such patron was Lieutenant-Colonel Sir Edward Bolitho, who inherited the Trengwainton Estate in 1925 and joined a number of others in financing Kingdon-Ward's expedition to Assam and Upper Burma in 1926. Kingdon-Ward returned with seeds of many species of rhododendron, such as *Rhododendron macabeanum*, which can still be seen growing in the gardens at Trengwainton today.[7]

Kingdon-Ward spent nearly forty years walking and stalking the mountains of eastern Asia in search of plants. He mounted nine expeditions to Burma and collected seeds and cuttings of hundreds of species, to be sent back to England for propagation and distribution. Many of his scientific botanical specimens are now preserved in the herbaria of the Natural History Museum in London, the Royal Botanic Gardens at Kew and Edinburgh, and the New York Botanical Garden. I have tracked down and pored over these

botanical collections, dissecting their flowers and pinpointing on present-day maps the exact localities where the initial collections were made. In addition to these specimens, Kingdon-Ward's nine books and hundreds of journal articles, written mostly for the general public, provide a chronicle of his journeys. I have read them all. In studying Kingdon-Ward's specimens and devouring the hundreds of pages of these volumes with titles such as In *Farthest Burma, Plant Hunting on the Edge of the World, Burma's Icy Mountains,* and *Return to the Irrawaddy,* I was preparing to tackle the challenge of exploring modern-day Myanmar.[8] What would the villages and places that Kingdon-Ward described in his books be like today? Would I be able to get to Sumprabum along the road north of Myitkyina, where he collected an especially unique ginger? Did any natural forests still exist on Mount Victoria, the tallest peak in the Chin Hills? Would I be able to find the species that he had discovered and described on that mountain before I was even born? I knew there were still new species to find in Myanmar. Kingdon-Ward's notes and specimens offered the clues that were going to lead me to them. I had the opportunity sanctioned by U Uga and the Forest Department to trace the paths of the botanists who had come before me, as well as to forge my own trails in this land of the Weeping Goldsmith.

As I left U Uga's office at the Division of Nature and Wildlife Conservation to head back to my guesthouse, I could not help but feel a bit displaced in space and time. Thoughts of gingers, colonial Burma, and Kingdon-Ward were mixed with the realities of modern-day Myanmar that faced me at every turn. The sky was dark, and it was raining hard. The monsoons were here, and so was I.

"For on the Hkamti plain there is no long dry season, and the forest is evergreen in spite of the chill winter nights; but as we go south, we get more and more into the region of the regular monsoons, where wet and hot dry seasons alternate. During the dry season, about March and April, just before the rains break, many trees shed their leaves for a brief period and burst into flower. . . . Although these miles and miles of jungle appear monotonous, yet looked closely into, the monsoon forest is exquisite, as though peering beneath the surface, one grew conscious of the real spirit of the forest behind its plain exterior. The temperate forest, changeful as a petulant child, may be admired as a whole; it is the details of the monsoon or tropical forest, in its limitless diversity, that attract."

Frank Kingdon-Ward, *In Farthest Burma,* 1921

The flowers of
*Rhododendron
macabeanum*, collected
in the Himalayas and
introduced into the
gardens of Cornwall
by Kingdon-Ward.

CHAPTER 5 # Across Two Rivers

"We left the high road and took a rocky path that wound through the jungle in and out of the hills. There was a heavy fog and the bamboos on each side were ghostly. They were like the pale wraiths of giant armies that had fought desperate wars in the beginning of the world's long history and now, lowering, waited in ominous silence, waited and watched for one knew not what."

W. Somerset Maugham, *The Gentleman in the Parlour*, 1930

The sun had set, and the twilight, such as it was on a very overcast day, lingered. As we dipped through the hills south of Pyinmana near the small town of Lewe, I caught a glimpse of a tall, slender herb topped by a cone of green leaves from which protruded long, white, tubular flowers. The plants filled a shallow hollow between two small hills covered with sparse scrubby vegetation. After years of collecting plants in the field, many botanists will develop the ability to identify species from a distance, and often from the window of a speeding vehicle. I had developed a particular eye for gingers and wild bananas, and could now quickly identify individual species of plants in what others might simply see as a blur of vegetation. As the car sped down the bumpy road and the light continued to fade, my mind raced through the thousands of plant species that I knew. These plants didn't fit any of them. After another few miles of bouncing around in the front seat of our aging jeep, I began to doubt that I had seen these botanical apparitions at all.

We had left Yangon early that morning in the pale light of dawn on our way up-country to the town of Yezin, home of the Forest Research Institute. Our plan was first to set up the logistics for the student botanical training course we were teaching at the institute and then, if all went well in Yezin, to travel across the country to visit Alaungdaw Kathapa National Park, one of the premier protected areas managed by the Forest Department. The road north out of Yangon was

A spectacular ginger, called *Hitchenia glauca*, with fragrant flowers that open in the evening. This plant was collected south of Pyinmana.

busy with buses and trucks of all sizes carrying people and things of all sizes. I was traveling with Debbie Bell, a colleague from the Smithsonian, and U Thet Htun, park warden at Moyingyi Bird Sanctuary, which is situated about fifty miles (80 km) from Yangon. U Thet Htun, who had been trained in botany at Rangoon University, was now a park administrator leading bird tours. Because of his background in botany, he had been assigned by the Forest Department as my liaison officer for this trip to make sure that everything went well during our travels. Born in Mandalay, he was a bit on the chubby side and rather quiet. For the initial part of our drive he was very low-key, seemed to be half asleep, and did not pay particularly attention to anything happening along the roadside. At first I was convinced that his job was to spy on me and make sure that I didn't encounter anything in Myanmar that the military rulers did not want me to see. However, he was friendly enough, and I enjoyed his company. Little did I know during this first trip that over the next several years that I would spend in Myanmar, he would become one of my closest partners in exploring the country. U Thet Htun would not only be my ally, but he would also watch out for my well-being under all types of circumstances. He called me "Dr. John" and rescued me more than once from potentially disastrous situations.

The new toll road between Yangon and Bago was impressive: well-paved, flat, and straight. I thought we would be in Yezin in no time at all if the road was this good all the way. Stopping for breakfast in Bago (at one time called Pegu, and the seat of political power in the fourteenth century, between the First and Second Burmese Empires), we paid a quick visit to the Shwethalyaung Buddha, a giant horizontal statue 180 feet (55 m) long and 52 feet (16 m) high. This colossal image represented the Buddha in the sacred reclining position, which is the posture that Buddha assumed just before attaining enlightenment. The statue was constructed over a thousand years ago, and after several centuries of neglect had been restored by the British in the late 1880s. To see the Shwethalyaung Buddha was a propitious sign that our journey to Yezin would be easy and restful. At least, this was my hope as the road began to seriously deteriorate almost immediately upon leaving Bago, and our driver weaved from side to side, dodging dogs, pigs, chickens, oxcarts, and local villagers. For the next 125 miles (200 km), the horrendous condition of the highway was not improved by the monotony of the endless surrounding rice paddies. Thankfully many pagodas and small towns along the way provided a welcome relief. The fourteen hours it took to reach Yezin were grueling.

A little over halfway between Yangon and our destination of Yezin lay the town of Toungoo. Toungoo is now a relatively quiet city, but for over two hundred and fifty years between the fifteenth and eighteenth centuries it was the heart of the Second Burmese Empire.[1] From this central location in Lower

OPPOSITE, TOP LEFT: A teak plantation near Toungoo under the management of the Myanmar Forest Department.

OPPOSITE, TOP RIGHT: Recently cut teak logs harvested from the forests along the Bago Yoma Crossing.

OPPOSITE, MIDDLE RIGHT: The entrance to the Bago Yoma Crossing, which cuts through some of the primary teak forests of central Myanmar.

OPPOSITE, BOTTOM: Crossing the Chindwin River by ferry with large rafts of teak ready to be floated downriver during the monsoon season.

CHAPTER 5

Burma the Burmese kings extended their dynasty south, north, and west to include the territories of the Mon, the Shan, and the Arakan as well as parts of Thailand in the east. Today Toungoo serves as a gateway to the hills of the Bago Yoma, a ridge running north and south along the western edge of the central valley and home to some of the richest teak forests of Myanmar. As a short side trip from the main highway we took a road to the east that leads into the state of Kayah and the mountains bordering Thailand, where an ethnic insurgency against the central Myanmar government has been active for years. We didn't get all the way to Kayah (I later found out that we did not have official permission to enter this insurgency area), but we did stop in a managed teak plantation about fifteen miles (25 km) from the center of the town. According to my escort of foresters, teak is notoriously difficult to grow in plantations over long periods of time and needs a natural understory of herbs and shrubs to profitably survive and grow. In neglecting the history of the cultivation of teak, which is the most valuable natural resource in Myanmar, the accelerated harvesting promoted by the military rulers and implemented by the Myanmar Timber Enterprise was not proving successful. Once back in Toungoo, we continued north, and it was just before we reached Pyinmana, as the light of day receded in the west, that I noticed the green-and-white flowers in the low hills along the roadside. It wasn't until we reached Yezin and I consulted the herbarium that I had any idea what these plants might be.

Botanists have been collecting plant specimens to document the world's green biodiversity for hundreds of years. The most prominent botanical institutes of Europe, Asia, and North America are all centered around their collections of preserved natural history specimens, which are the foundation of all research activities. These collections of dried plant specimens are called herbaria.[2] It has been calculated that the major natural history museums and associated scientific institutions of the world, located mainly in developed countries, together contain over 275 million plant specimens.[3] Each specimen has been individually collected in the field, pressed flat, thoroughly dried, mounted on stiff paper, labeled, and filed away in insect- and fungus-proof cabinets. These specimens are studied by plant specialists called taxonomists and provide an incalculable wealth of information about the hundreds of thousands of species of plants that exist today. Some of the specimens represent species that may now be extinct. These fragile exemplars preserved in museums are all that remain to record their existence.

Each specimen is accompanied by data on who collected it, where and when it was found, and usually notes about various characteristics of the plant itself. It is standard for the botanical name to be indicated, and sometimes local names are provided as well. In most herbaria the specimens are organized according to a recognized classification scheme so that one can easily find a particular species of

ABOVE: A bamboo raft with living quarters on board floating down the Chindwin River.

LEFT: Sailboat on the Chindwin River.

CHAPTER 5

equally diverse communities of passengers and crew fought for the few seats in the small cabin or stretched out along the deck on picnic blankets with baskets full of sweets and fruits to pass the time during the crossing. The most popular vendor cranked the handle on his sugar-cane press as he filled glass after glass with a thin, slightly jaundiced juice apparently to everyone's liking. Just as I was settling into river life, the steam whistle blew; we were approaching the west side of the Chindwin.

We had been met in Monywa by U Tun Nyo, the head warden at Alaungdaw Kathapa. Another graduate of the Forestry School in Syracuse, New York, he was very pleased that we were visiting his park. On the other side of the river we boarded his vintage Land Rover, piled in our supplies, and were quickly off to the Forestry Office at Yinmabin. The river was lined with giant stacks of teak from the forests of Magwe and the Chin Hills, waiting to be floated down the Chindwin as soon as the river rose to the right stage. We left the floodplain behind and headed across the dusty roads for a relatively quick ride to our next stop.

Yinmabin was a small, hot, and quiet town where we found a cool spot for lunch under a giant enterolobium tree. These trees, which lined the main street of the town, are members of the bean family and had been planted decades, if not a century, ago. They now provided much-needed shelter from the fierce midday sun. The final leg of our journey before we entered the park was from Yinmabin to Kabaing across a small isolated road through prickly thorn acacia scrub. Although it was the rainy season, the weather had been relatively dry for the last few days, and we were confident that we could easily drive to Kabaing and maybe all the way to the base camp, twenty-two miles (35 km) inside the park, before nightfall. Our optimism was too great and before we were even halfway to our destination, the rear axle of the Land Rover gave way under the load, and we broke down far from any town or village.

I am completely unmechanical when it comes to vehicles, so I struck off into the scrub to see what I could find, while my colleagues worked on the splintered rod. It was desolate land with low thorny shrubs and sandy soil. I found a few plants in flower, but this type of vegetation was not right for gingers. I did spot my first hoopoe, one of the characteristic and bizarre birds of Asia, with a spotted crest of feathers and distinctive pattern of flight, but botanically we could not have chosen a more boring spot to break down. Somehow my resourceful foresters fixed the broken axle well enough so that we could drive the Land Rover, albeit very slowly, over the bumpy road. We limped into Kabaing just as the sun was going down.

After a sleepless night fighting the mosquitoes in a dilapidated forestry cabin, we rose at dawn to continue our trek into the park. The dry weather had ended in the night, and the rain, which had pounded the tin roof of our cabin all night

long, had made the road impassable for the Land Rover. According to the foresters, we had three options: we could try to take a small tractor, which was used for
clearing tree falls, up the muddy slopes; we could commandeer the four elephants
assigned to the forestry camp as our means of transportation; or we could walk.
After some discussion, it was decided that we would do all three. First, we would
use the tractor to haul ourselves and our gear the first six miles (10 km), to where
the slopes became too steep to pass. There we would transfer our gear to the
elephants for transport to the base camp, while we walked the remaining sixteen
miles (25 km). When I asked why we didn't just use the elephants to carry us as
well, I was politely told that foresters were not allowed to ride on elephants. U
Thet Htun put it in a slightly different way: "Real foresters don't ride elephants,
Dr. John." Fortunately the rain had stopped, and even though the trails were
muddy, they were passable on foot. Debbie, who had become quite ill from food
poisoning during the night, was made as comfortable as possible nestled among

Elephants being loaded
at Alaungdaw Kathapa.

our gear on the back of one of the elephants, which slowly lumbered up the slopes. We, the real foresters, walked. Passing a line of large statues of the seated Buddha in the touching-the-earth position, we entered the park.

Finally, after many days in Yangon and Yezin talking to administrators and directors, and two more days of overland travel across the two great rivers of the country, I was where I really wanted to be: in the forests of Myanmar. The first part of the trail passed through rather uninteresting degraded growth, but the habitat quickly changed as we started up the slopes, passing into what the Burmese call *indaing* forest. *Indaing* forests are made up of a diverse group of trees in the Dipterocarp family, one of the most important groups of timber trees in Southeast Asia.[5] The trees are not very tall, and beneath them the understory is rather open, composed of grasses and other low herbs. We hiked through this forest type for a number of hours until we reached a higher elevation, where teak began to appear. Teak forests are true deciduous forests in which the leaves fall from the trees during the driest part of the year, much as they do in winter in temperate zones. In fact, the dried leaves and grasses on the forest floor pile

Buddha shrine at Alaungdaw Kathapa.

Elephant man.
Photograph by James
Henry Green, c. 1920s.

up during the dry season until a fire sweeps through and clears away the dry tinder. Adapted to the periodic burning, the trees rarely suffer from the flames. The nutrient-rich ash, combined with the early rains, stimulates new growth as the monsoons begin. It had been raining now for several months, and the large leathery leaves characteristic of teak were deep green. To my amazement the understory of this tall teak forest was waist-high in ginger plants.

Despite the long way we had to hike to get to our base camp at Thebeik Sae, I had time to collect a dozen different species of gingers in five different genera. The most precious was one of the first plants I saw as I climbed the lower slopes.

Collecting gingers (*Globba radicalis*) from the backs of elephants.

I had only read about this plant before coming to Myanmar, but I knew it was a mantisia the minute I saw it. Most of the plants were growing on a high, steep embankment, but it was not difficult to convince one of the mahouts to coax his elephant closer so he could reach a plant that still held its delicate yellow flowers.[6] Once I had the flowers in my hand, I had no doubt that it was *Mantisia radicalis* (now called *Globba radicalis*), first described in East Bengal in 1885 and now, as a result of my own collections, also known in Myanmar. Most of the plants had flowered a few months earlier, but I was lucky enough to find this last one with flowers in order to confirm its identification. As we trudged on, I found many more species to collect and record. After a long midday rest stop and the crossing of three rivers, we finally reached camp just before sunset. My feet were sore, but my plant press was full.

The field station at Thebeik Sae was rustic but quite suitable for our needs, and we quickly made ourselves at home. Debbie (who had recovered once we arrived in camp), U Thet Htun, and I spent the next several days exploring the various vegetation types in the park to see what species could be found in each.

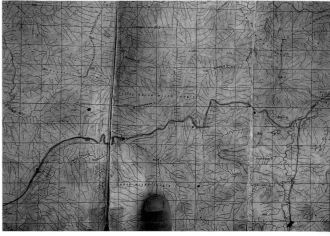

In addition to the *indaing* and dry teak forests, other habitats found in the park included semi-deciduous and pine forests as well as some extensive bamboo brakes. Although it rained hard each night, the days were clear, and we were able to complete our initial assessment of the flora in the short time we had. Near the station is the well-known pagoda after which the park is named, the Alaungdaw Kathapa Pagoda, a sacred Buddhist shrine that serves as a destination for pilgrims during the Tin Gan festival at the end of the dry season in early April. During the festival, thousands of visitors flock to the park and the pagoda to earn their merit by demonstrating respect for the monks and to celebrate the Buddha. Although it is maintained as a national park by the Forest Department, the sacred nature of the land at Alaungdaw Kathapa and the proximity of the pagoda have for centuries safeguarded the plants and animals that inhabit the forests. In rainy July, unlike during the dry season festival, few pilgrims visited the pagoda and monastery. Debbie, U Thet Htun, and I—along with the Assistant Park Warden

ABOVE LEFT: Hiking through a rocky ravine in Alaungdaw Kathapa National Park.

TOP RIGHT: A forester's antique map of the trails in the park.

ABOVE RIGHT: Chest-high in ginger plants as we search for new species.

OPPOSITE: A thick stand of bamboo that was burned at the end of the dry season.

U Aung Kyaw, two of his forestry guards, and two of the elephant drivers—sat and ate cakes, drank tea, and chewed betel nuts with the monks. I thanked them all for preserving and protecting the forests. I think they understood.

That evening I sat around the dinner table at the station with all the park staff for our final meal at Alaungdaw Kathapa. We drank Gordon's gin with lime and sugar, smoked some of my Danish cigars, and swapped stories about our past adventures in forests in both Myanmar and other countries. I casually remarked how cool the evening seemed, and how few mosquitoes there were. I suggested that malaria was probably rather rare in this part of Myanmar, as hardly any mosquitoes were present. The group of foresters, who by now had become my friends, all looked at each other. Then U Thet Htun remarked equally casually, "We *all* have malaria, Dr. John." He poured more gin into my glass. Later that evening I carefully tucked the mosquito net around my sleeping bag as I turned in.

The next morning before dawn, as the first light was just beginning to sift through my open window, I was gently awakened by soft bells approaching from the distance. It was the elephants. The mahouts had rounded up their charges and were slowly drifting into camp to load up our gear for the long march out of the park. I quietly arose with the early songs of the forest birds. U Thet Htun informed me that the old Land Rover, now repaired, had somehow navigated the muddy roads and would meet us halfway to the park entrance. This was good news. We left the station and, after crossing the three rivers on foot, found the vehicle waiting for us. We said our good-byes to U Aung Kyaw and his staff, transferred our gear from the elephants, climbed aboard the sputtering Land Rover, and wound our way down the slopes, slipping past the serene statues of the Buddha at the entrance.

An invitation to lunch at a local monastery outside Alaungdaw Kathapa National Park on our way back to Yinmabin.

Outside the park, on our way to Yimabin, we were invited to stop for lunch at the local monastery in the small village of Thidon. Somehow U Wi Sat Ta, the *pongyi*, or head monk in charge of the monastery, had heard that several foreigners were visiting Alaungdaw Kathapa. In the main hall we were treated to a gracious meal, surrounded by several hundred watching villagers. More than a few times the round table around which we sat and feasted was hoisted over our heads, and an entirely different cuisine was placed before us as a new table was set in place. It was hard to know how to express our gratitude for such hospitality and kindness. U Wi Sat Ta and I looked each other in the eye and exchanged

Globba radicalis, a lovely ginger that was found in western Myanmar.

words. Neither of us could comprehend the other's language, but each of us knew exactly what was being said. As we left the monastery, I spied a strangely familiar plant in the garden near the open gate and stooped to look. Never missing a gesture from his guests, the *pongyi* asked for a small knife, dug around the roots, and presented me with a piece of the plant. It had long green stems topped with a drooping cluster of bright white bracts enclosing golden orange flowers, each on a thin, pale green stalk. It was *padeign gno*, the Weeping Goldsmith.

CHAPTER 6 *Buddha's Garden*

"There is a moment just before sundown when the trees seem to detach themselves from the dark mass of the jungle and become individuals. Then you cannot see the wood for the trees. In the magic of the hour they seem to acquire a life of a new kind so that it is not hard to imagine that spirits inhabit them and with dusk they will have power to change their places. You feel that at some uncertain moment some strange thing will happen to them and they will be wondrously transfigured. You hold your breath waiting for a marvel the thought of which stirs your heart with a kind of terrified eagerness. But the night falls; the moment has passed and once more the jungle takes them back."

W. Somerset Maugham, *The Gentleman in the Parlour*, 1930

The sun setting over Yangon in the dry season, as viewed from Shwedagon Pagoda.

From my view on the broad terrace encircling the Shwedagon Pagoda, the sun was a deep red as it sct over Yangon. The paving stones of the pagoda had baked all day long in the relentless sun of April. They were far too hot for my bare feet, unaccustomed to walking without the protection of shoes or sandals. In contrast, hundreds of barefooted Burmese pilgrims were strolling the broad walkways encircling the gilded shrine that towered above. Walking in the customary clockwise direction around the pagoda, people of all ages, sizes, and ethnicities explored the various halls and pavilions scattered around the main terrace. The red glow of the sun was reflected from the many golden spires and bells that adorn the prayer halls and stupas. I had returned to Myanmar after a number of months in Washington. One of my first stops when I return to Yangon is always Shwedagon Pagoda.

Our work on a new inventory of the plants of the country was proceeding at a good pace. In an unusual turn of fortune, my colleague Daw Yin Yin Kyi had been allowed by the Ministry of Forests to visit the Smithsonian earlier in the year to work with me on the project. This visit to Washington was her first time in North America, and she was impressed by the massive government buildings and many museums lining the National Mall in the capital city. We had used the time during her stay to develop an outline of the plant checklist and to determine the scope of our work. I was now back in Myanmar to continue plant collecting and exploring. On my arrival this time, it was my hope that I would receive permission to travel to Natma Taung National Park. Inside the park is Mount Victoria, one of the tallest mountains in the Chin Hills in western Myanmar

"It was nearly nine o'clock and the sun was fiercer every minute. The heat throbbed down on one's head with a steady, rhythmic thumping, like a blow from an enormous bolster."

George Orwell, *Burmese Days*, 1934

and the site of many early plant collections by Frank Kingdon-Ward. A very rare ginger named after him, *Globba wardii*, is only known to occur at Natma Taung. Plant species such as this one, which are found only in a very restricted area and nowhere else, are called endemics. Myanmar is full of endemics, and one of our goals was to document as many of these rare species as possible, with the intention of designing conservation plans to preserve the species and their habitats. Fortunately, Mount Victoria had already been declared a national park and was being protected from further human encroachment and development.

To my great regret and disappointment, after several days of waiting in Yangon I was denied permission to visit Mount Victoria, ostensibly due to "security" reasons. Some unrest and possible insurgent activity by the Chin ethnic minority in this part of Burma had been reported, and the directors of the Ministry of Forests and the police recommended against any foreigners traveling to the area. The real reason for denying permission remained a question to me. Whatever the motive, my colleagues in the Forest Department would not let me travel without official sanction. This was a clear example of the restrictions placed on conducting biodiversity research in Myanmar due to the political realities. The seemingly arbitrary nature of being granted or denied permission to travel to a region of the country by the minister and security police had nothing to do with the scientific value, or in my case the botanical richness, of a locality; the decisions were purely political. At least this time the authorities would allow me to visit two other important wildlife sanctuaries that I had never seen. One, called Shwesettaw, was south of Natma Taung, and the other, called Shwe-U-Daung, was north of Mandalay. I couldn't object.

Shwesettaw Wildlife Sanctuary, due west of the Irrawaddy River below its confluence with the Chindwin River, is in the eastern foothills of the Rakhine Yoma. On the other side of this low range of hills lie the coastal swamps of the Bay of Bengal. We arrived at Shwesettaw in the intense heat of the late afternoon after a long drive from Mount Popa. The plains on either side of the Irrawaddy are extremely dry and parched at this time of the year. We easily drove across a number of sandy, dry riverbeds, which would be impassable once the monsoons started in a few weeks. South of Bagan is the city of Yenangyaung, in one of the

A field of oil wells at Yenangyaung in Myanmar.

oil-rich regions of Myanmar. Here we passed hundreds of pumping stations and oil rigs that dotted the landscape. Each was tethered in a crisscrossing web of metallic conduit to a central pipeline that fed the oil to waiting ships on the Irrawaddy. It was not a hospitable place. At Magway we stopped for supplies before taking a ferry across the river to the small town of Minbu. From there we reached the sanctuary by a rambling road through highly degraded land.

Despite the heat and two hours of driving through this harsh territory, we were encouraged by the warm welcome we received from the park warden, U Maung Maung Tint, and his two range officers, Daw Thin Thin Kyi and Daw Lay Lay Khaine. The wildlife sanctuary, which stretches along the Man River and well into the hills to the west, contains a combination of bamboo, *indaing*, and mixed deciduous forests. The warden and his staff were conducting a plant inventory of these forests and were happy to see a botanist arrive. Although teak is not found in the sanctuary, close relatives of this economically important species as well as many other trees and shrubs are common here.[1] More important for the Division of Nature and Wildlife Conservation was the large population of the endangered Eld's deer, called *thamin* in Myanmar, in the forests. A more thorough knowledge of the plants occurring in the area would be of great help in managing these threatened animals. In addition to my companion U Thet Htun, I had brought along Mike Bordelon, manager of the botany research greenhouses at the Smithsonian. I wanted to start building up a living reference collection of gingers and other plants from Myanmar, and Mike knew a tremendous amount about propagating and growing plants. His help, as I had anticipated, turned out to be invaluable.

Shwesettaw Wildlife Sanctuary is the location of a famous pagoda that bears the same name. The Shwesettaw Pagoda sits along the low-lying banks of the Man River and attracts pilgrims from all over the country, who visit primarily during the months of March and April to see two of Buddha's footprints, each now sheathed in a thick layer of gold leaf. Similar to what I had seen at Alaungdaw Kathapa National Park, the undisturbed and relatively intact forests at Shwesettaw were the result of the sacred status of this region, through which the Buddha had walked centuries ago. I was beginning to appreciate the close relationship between Burmese Buddhism and the conservation of critical habitats in Myanmar. Immediately after we arrived at Shwesettaw, we were taken by our hosts to visit the pagoda.

Outside of Minbu no private accommodations are available near the wildlife sanctuary, and we were invited to stay at a guesthouse run by the Forest Department. A number of years ago a large cluster of commercial guesthouses were scattered along the riverside near the pagoda to serve the hundreds of visitors that came to the sanctuary during the New Year festival. But in the early part of the rainy season in 1996, all of these buildings, and a great many pilgrims, were swept away in an unexpected flash flood. Today, only temporary stalls that sell food and souvenirs are located along the river. Our guesthouse was placed high on a hill overlooking the forest sanctuary.

ABOVE: Temples and guesthouses lining the Man River near Shwesettaw Wildlife Sanctuary.

OPPOSITE: The golden Buddha at Shwesettaw Pagoda.

We spent several days scouring the forests in the wildlife sanctuary, but to our dismay we found few plants in flower. For botanists, it is imperative to find specimens with either flowers or fruits, which are critical for accurate identification. We found neither. It was just too late in the dry season, and almost every plant was still dormant. One could easily understand why the plants remained dormant: it was oppressively hot and dry. The sun beat down; the temperature rose above 113 degrees Fahrenheit (45 C) by late morning without even a faint breeze. It became impossible to continue our work. By mid-afternoon neither Mike nor I could move. My journal reads, "Hot, hot, hot! Over 115 degrees F. These are Burmese Days. We are hiding out in any shade we can find, stretched out on a woven mat waiting for any wisp of air."[2]

That evening our hosts dismantled our beds and moved them out of the stuffy rooms of the guesthouse onto the porch. The night before it had been so hot in Mike's room that the wax candle beside his bed had melted even though he had not ignited the wick. Now outside the building under our mosquito nets, we listened to the stillness of the night. Just before dawn, I finally fell asleep.

Even our Burmese colleagues found the heat to be extreme, although they have found a number of ways to cope with the intensity of the sun. Daw Thin Thin Kyi and Daw Lay Lay Khaine met us the next morning with their faces attractively coated in a thick white paste called *thanakha*. This natural sunscreen is derived from the shaved bark of a tree in the orange family.[3] Burmese women and young children gently grate the bark on a small, flat moistened grinding stone. The resultant fine white paste is tenderly applied to the face or any exposed surface of the skin to prevent sunburn. It is common to simply massage the paste into the skin. Upon application it provides a cooling sensation and will be effective as a sunblock for a good part of the day. In addition to using it as a sunscreen, some women apply *thanakha* as a beauty cosmetic, creating attractive patterns of delicate swirls or intricate brushstrokes on their cheeks, nose, and even their ears. I have heard that a new commercial *thanakha* product, which is preground and packaged in bar form, can be purchased in the larger cities of Myanmar. Except when they are small boys, men rarely use *thanakha*.

In the kind of countryside we experienced around Shwesettaw, small sections of *thanakha* branches, along with a large selection of other natural products that are used as cosmetics, herbals, medicinals, and foods, can be purchased in the local markets. In contrast to the local natural habitats, where we found few flowering plants at the end of the dry season, the markets were teeming with plant products. The description in George Orwell's *Burmese Days* of the things he saw in the 1920s during one of his visits to a market in Kathar, north of Mandalay, still serves as an accurate account of what one might see today:

OPPOSITE, TOP: A woman with an elaborate pattern on her cheek created with a natural cosmetic called *thanakha*.

OPPOSITE, BOTTOM: The preparation of *thanakha*, showing the tree bark, water cup, and grinding stone.

*The merchandise was foreign-looking, queer and poor.
There were vast pomelos hanging on strings like green
moons, red bananas, baskets of heliotrope-coloured
prawns the size of lobsters, brittle dried fish tied in
bundles, crimson chilis, ducks split open and cured like
hams, green coconuts, the larvae of the rhinoceros beetle,
sections of sugar cane, dahs, lacquered sandals, check
silk longyis, aphrodisiacs in the form of large, soap-like
pills, glazed earthenware jars four feet high, Chinese
sweetmeats made of garlic and sugar, green and white
cigars, purple prinjals, persimmon-seed necklaces, chickens cheeping in wicker cages,
brass Buddhas, heart-shaped betel leaves, bottles of Kruschen salts, switches of false
hair, red clay cooking pots, steel shoe for bullocks, papier-mâché marionettes, strips of
alligator hide with magical properties.*

George Orwell, *Burmese Days*, 1934.[4]

Fruits, vegetables, spices, mushrooms, roots, medicines, tea, meats, fowl, fish, animal parts, cookware, farming supplies, *longyis*, clothes, shoes, baskets, and small
toys are ever-present for purchase in almost any market throughout Myanmar.

The typical Burmese cigars, described as "green and white cigars" by Orwell

and locally called cheroots, can be purchased in large bundles in any market.
Cheroots come in a number of sizes and contain a nearly tobacco-free concoc-
tion of herbs wrapped in a thin flexible leaf taken from a single species of small
forest tree. I have also seen older women along the Irrawaddy smoking fat, foot-
long cheroots wrapped in dried corn husks. Cheroots and the characteristic odor
of the smoke they produce are common throughout the country.

Next to smoking cheroots, chewing betel nuts is the most prominent habit
practiced (mostly by men) in Myanmar. Betel nuts are the large, hard seeds of
a special palm cultivated in the countryside.[5] When mixed with a small amount
of calcium (usually in the form of crushed shells or lime) and wrapped in a spicy
leaf from the betel pepper vine, the palms nuts produce a slight intoxication
and feeling of well-being as they are crushed and masticated. In Myanmar it is
common to add some cardamon, caraway, coconut, and even cured tobacco to
the "quid" to impart extra flavor and increase the potency. Chewing betel nut
is a common practice at any time of the day, is prevalent in any social circle, and
is no secret, as it turns the saliva of the user bright red, leaving a telltale crimson
stain on the lips, gums, and teeth. The reddish blotches that spatter walls, side-
walks, and street corners in villages and towns mark the aftermath of a good
chew of betel nut, which causes the user to periodically spit out the extra saliva

generated by the nuts. I have ruined a number of shirts by ineptly discharging my betel quid out the window of a fast-moving vehicle. Baskets of betel nuts and the heart-shaped pepper leaves in which they are wrapped are sold at local markets, but it is more common to purchase a ready-made betel nut chew with all of your favorite ingredients from a street-side vendor.

The distinctive and idiosyncratic presentation of merchandise in Burmese markets is almost as impressive as the diversity of the products being sold. In the city of Lashio in the state of Shan, for example, the central market covers over an acre of space. Women in colorful *longyis*, dainty blouses, and cheeks painted with eddies of *thanakha* squat in the center of careful arrangements of shallow metal pans and bamboo baskets, each overflowing with a different delicacy for the buyer: green and red chilis, peeled garlic gloves, white fava beans, sliced green mangos, small dried whole fish, tamarind pods, toddy sugar cubes, diced gleaming papaya, and bundles of eggplant, morning glory leaves, bitter gourds, winged beans, and cilantro. Down the aisle are giant mounds of durians, ginger roots, melons, onions, pineapples, and large dipterocarp leaves for wrapping food. Neighboring market stalls are lined with row after row of delicately woven baskets piled high with rice. Each vendor has a simple weighted scale or standardized container for measuring out the exact amount of grain or number of fruits for the customers. Some haggling over prices may occur, but in general everyone knows what to expect to pay.

One of the most attractive displays can be found at the banana stands, where bunches of fruit in bright yellows, reds, greens, and purples are available. The banana merchants never heap their produce in piles, as is often seen in markets of the Western tropics. In Myanmar, each large bundle, or hand, of bananas is carefully hung by rope or twine from a wooden framework to best show off the curved architecture of the thickly-bunched fruits. The bananas are grouped together by their colors in a symmetrical, aesthetically pleasing design, as if being readied for the arrival of an artist with brush and watercolors in hand. On the tough central stem of each heavy cluster of fruits is a tiny number or logo tattooed in colored ink on the vegetable skin, indicating the grower who brought each of these works of art to the market. Nothing is left to chance in sorting out the sales at the end of the day.

No market is complete without flower merchants. It is customary for the flower stalls to be grouped together in one common area to allow customers to compare the quality and variety of the flowers. The Burmese people use flowers in many ways and for many occasions, but most frequently as offerings to Buddha. No Buddhist shrine, temple, or pagoda is ever without some type of flower decoration. During festivals, the colorful assortment of flowers increases by a considerable magnitude, but even between celebrations, flowers and other

OPPOSITE, TOP:
Baskets of chopped and sliced betel nuts, along with the betel pepper leaves in which they are wrapped before chewing.

OPPOSITE, BOTTOM:
The rice market.

"As is usual in the East the sellers of the same things congregated together. The stalls were merely tiled roofs on posts, speaking well for the clemency of the climate, and the floor was either the trodden earth or a very low wooden platform. The selling was done for the most part by the women; there were generally three or four of them in each stall, and they sat smoking long green cheroots. But in the medicine stalls the vendors were very old men, with wrinkled faces and blood-shot eyes, who looked like wizards. There were piles of dried herbs and large boxes of powders of various colours, blue, yellow, red, and green, and I could not but think he must be a brave man who ventured upon them. . . . There were pills so large that I asked myself what throat was ever so capacious as to be able to wash them down with a drink of water. There were small dried animals that looked like the roots of plants that had been dug out of the ground and left to rot, and there were roots of plants that looked like small dried animals. . . . Trade was brisk that morning, and they were kept busy weighing out drugs, not with flaky weights we use at home but with large pieces of lead cast in the form of the Buddha."

W. Somerset Maugham, *The Gentleman in the Parlour*, 1930

offerings are abundant. In addition, every Buddhist household has a small shrine upon which floral gifts are regularly bestowed. For this reason, the markets are full of cut flowers. Gladioli, daffodils, chrysanthemums, and irises are common, many of them grown in the more mountainous regions and brought down to the markets in the plains. It is also common to see wild gingers collected and brought to the markets for the same purpose. It was in the flower market in Bago that I first discovered the ginger that the Burmese call "the weeping goldsmith," which appeared to have particular significance as an offering in monasteries and at pagodas, although on my initial encounter I did not yet know exactly why. In the countryside, where the large flower markets are not readily accessible, it is not uncommon for local farmers to select their own species of wildflowers to place in their small family shrines.

Back in the countryside, our time at Shwesettaw Wildlife Sanctuary had come to an end, and we headed back across the Irrawaddy River toward Mandalay. We had received permission from the Forest Department to visit Shwe-U-Daung Wildlife Sanctuary, one of the oldest sanctuaries maintained by the Ministry of Forests. If we were lucky, we could reach Mandalay in a day's travel, spend the night there, then go on to the wildlife sanctuary the next day. Some of the early monsoon rains had started in the central valley, and I was concerned that it might be difficult to cross the dry riverbeds we had easily traversed on our trip south. Fortunately for us, the heavy rains had not yet arrived, and crossing was not a problem.

OPPOSITE, TOP: A beautiful and well-organized banana stand in a market in Yangon.

OPPOSITE, BOTTOM: Three large stalks of bananas for sale in the fruit market.

PAGES 100–101: Shwe-U-Daung Mountain, north of Mandalay.

CHAPTER 6

CHAPTER 6

Shwe-U-Daung, the tallest mountain in central Myanmar, is located about 120 miles (200 km) north of Mandalay, at the western edge of the Shan Plateau. The mountain, which reaches almost ten thousand feet (3,000 m) high, is near the town of Mogok. *Mogok* is the Burmese word for "ruby," and some of the largest gem mines are found in this region. Because of these gem deposits, the area is generally off-limits to foreigners. The extent of police control of this area became clear to us when, after spending a night in Mandalay, we tried to pass a military checkpoint near the river port of Thabeikyin on our way to Shwe-U-Daung. We were informed that the permission we had received from the Forest Department was not good enough to allow us to pass to the wildlife sanctuary. Permission was also needed from the police in Mandalay. We all piled back in the Land Rover and returned to Mandalay, where after another two days we were finally granted the appropriate permission from the Police Department. U Thet Htun was surprised that it took only two days; I was convinced he had performed magic on my behalf.

Thabeikyin was a likable small town on the banks of the Irrawaddy River. No accommodation was available in the wildlife sanctuary, so we located a small, semi-comfortable guesthouse in Thabeikyin, overlooking the river, where we could stay while we were exploring the mountain. My mosquito-filled room had a single window that looked out over the river, which was narrower here than in places of previous crossings farther south at Monywa and Magway. Above Mandalay fewer ships and sailboats ply the waters of the river, which had only recently started to rise with the early monsoons. In Thabeikyin, with my river view, I was awakened each morning by steamships whose captains felt obliged to sound their horns as they passed the town.

To my great delight U Aung Kyaw, whom I had met during my first trip to Alaungdaw Kathapa Park, was now the park warden at Shwe-U-Daung Wildlife Sanctuary. U Aung Kyaw was a dedicated forester who had spent a good part of his professional life separated from his family, on assignment to remote nature reserves and forestry camps. He had boundless energy and was always running

CHAPTER 6

A lonely hut on the slopes of Shwe-U-Daung.

ahead of us down the forest trails. I was thrilled that he agreed to be our guide, and we quickly set about planning a trek into the forest sanctuary. As in every other forest reserve I had explored, Shwe-U-Daung is a mixture of forest types. U Aung Kyaw told me that we would encounter some degraded areas but would also see extensive deciduous forests with large tracts of bamboo, true evergreen wet forests where the plants never lose their leaves even during the dry season, and possibly a pristine semi-cloud forest if we reached the top of the mountain. He confirmed that a large number of ginger species could be found in the sanctuary. Mike, U Thet Htun, and I were ready to go. Perhaps because we were in an area officially off-limits to foreigners, U Aung Kyaw had been instructed to include a small military escort as a proper security precaution. I had been on collecting trips with soldiers carrying rifles before, but I did not like the idea. I didn't have a choice this time.

The rains had begun, so many of the streams were full and it was necessary for us to cross them either by wading up to our waists or crossing on makeshift log bridges. The best thing about the dry season is that the land leeches are dormant as well as the plants, but as soon as the rains come, these blood-sucking friends emerge. Now as we hiked into Shwe-U-Daung I would have to stop periodically to pull several of these annoying creatures out of my socks and from beneath my shirt. I never got them all, and I would wring my own blood out of my clothes at the end of the day.

We spent a good part of the first day penetrating the secondary forest that surrounded the core of the sanctuary. Even in these overgrown and disturbed habitats we found gingers, although most of them were common species that we had seen before in other parts of Myanmar. We finally reached the natural forest habitats, including both deciduous and bamboo forests. Signs of the presence of wild elephants were common, and U Aung Kyaw recorded these sightings in his notebook. More important for us was the welcome observation that many of the herbaceous plants in the forest understory had broken dormancy with the early rains. Here in the less disturbed habitats we encountered more interesting species of ginger, in flower or at least with young leaves sprouting above the soil layer. Mike spent most of his time digging up plants for the experimental garden while I took notes and photographs and made pressed specimens of those plants with sufficient flowers. Toward the end of the day the rains became more intense, and we decided to retrace our steps back to the entrance to the park. We would continue our explorations on the following day.

The sun was shining brightly when we entered the evergreen forests the next morning. We had started early and begun our hike from a different portal into the sanctuary. After a few hours of walking through the same type of deciduous forests we had seen the day before, we came to a cleared area where rice paddies and other crops were being farmed by a small family of local Burmese. It was very hot, and the farmer asked if we would like to come into his cottage for some water and a brief respite from the sun. He was quite surprised to see foreigners so deep inside the sanctuary, but he knew U Aung Kyaw and was quite friendly to us. I myself was surprised to see dwellings and crops being cultivated inside a wildlife sanctuary, but the wardens sometimes allow such activities in order to teach the local villagers how to respect and sustainably use the remaining forests and natural areas.

After removing our boots we climbed a crude ladder to enter the farmer's modest thatched hut. The coolness of the interior was unexpected. Seating myself against the central wooden column that supported the roof, I noticed the unpretentious family Buddhist shrine fastened to one of the side beams. Several upright stems of what appeared to be a rather elegant ginger with tufts of pink, white, and green bracts had been carefully placed as an offering inside a carved bamboo vase next to a smoldering stick of incense. As my eyes adjusted to the lower light inside of the hut, I more carefully scrutinized the flowers and realized that I had never seen this plant before. It vaguely resembled a new genus of ginger that I had described a few years earlier from Thailand.[6] The farmer sensed

my interest. U Thet Htun asked him where he had come across these plants, and he replied that they were common deep in the evergreen forests, about a two-hour's walk from his farmhouse. Despite the coolness of the cottage and the hot, glaring sun that awaited us outside, we scurried back down the ladder, threw on our boots, and were off.

We hiked for nearly two hours, and after fording several more streams, we finally reached the tall evergreen forest. Reminiscent of the welcoming interior of the farmer's hut, the forest was cool under the thick canopy of tree leaves. There, spread out before me in a sea of green foliage on the forest floor, were hundreds of the flowers that had been in the farmer's bamboo vase. Each one was composed of a stem of several deeply ribbed leaves and a long, erect stalk with a cluster of shiny emerald bracts at the apex, topped by a whirl of pink or white. Bright yellow flowers burst out of each of the green bracts. A small stream gently trickled nearby. It was a lovely sight—Buddha's Garden in the forest.

ABOVE: A small Buddhist shrine in a local hut where the author first discovered a new species of ginger.

RIGHT: *Smithatris myanmarensis*, a new species of ginger, growing naturally in the forests on Shwe-U-Daung.

Everyone was struck by the beauty of the flowers, and especially the serenity of the place where they were growing. Mike and I exchanged grins. We had never seen a more tranquil natural garden; certainly nothing that had been created by the hands of humans could compare. The biggest smile was on the face of the farmer who had led us to the spot. We all set to work writing notes, taking photos, and making specimens. Although we had a long way to go to get back to Thabeikin before dark, no one was hurrying. In fact, none of us wanted to leave. Finally U Aung Kyaw broke the trance and urged us to finish our work. As we stepped out of the evergreen forest and headed back down the trail toward our guide's cottage, I noticed that the rifle slung over the shoulder of one of the security guards was adorned with a single pink-and-green ginger taken as an offering from the forest. This small gesture seemed to be a fitting end to our days at Shwe-U-Daung. A few years later, I described and named this plant from Buddha's Garden as the new species *Smithatris myanmarensis*, honoring both a famous Scottish botanist, who had been a specialist in gingers during her career, and the country where the flower was found.

ABOVE: A Myanmar soldier, who works with the Myanmar Forest Department, helping to collect plants at the end of the day.

OPPOSITE: The white form of *Smithatris myanmarensis*

"... but I had scarcely reached the bank when I stopped suddenly in amazement. Was I dreaming? I rubbed my eyes, and looked again. No! Just above the edge of the snow, a vivid blush pink flower stood out of the cold grey earth. ... But what could it be? Yet so fascinating was it to stand there and gaze on this marvel in an aching pain of wonder that I felt no desire to step forward and break the spell. Indeed, for a minute I was paralyzed with an emotion which perhaps only those who have come across some beloved alpine prize in Switzerland can faintly appreciate. I can recall several flowers which at first sight have knocked the breath out of me, but only two or three which have taken me by storm as did this one. The sudden vision is like a physical blow, a blow in the pit of the stomach; one can only gasp and stare. In the face of such unsurpassed loveliness, one is afraid to move, as with bated breath one mutters the single word 'God!'—a prayer rather than an exclamation. And when at last with fluttering heart one does venture to step forward, it is on tiptoe, and hat in hand, to wonder and to worship."

Frank Kingdon-Ward on finding a new species of Primula. *Plant Hunting on the Edge of the World*, 1930

CHAPTER 6

CHAPTER 7 *The Choir of Cicadas*

"A heavy thunderstorm by night in the hill jungle is an awesome sight. Flashes follow each other with great rapidity all round the hills, like gunfire, and peering through the driving rain you see the maddened trees suddenly lit up, and then blotted out; a moment later they are lit up again, fainter this time, as the flash is farther away; then darkness again. Very faintly do they show up yet a third time within the space of a minute—now the flash is miles and miles away and there is no answering roll of thunder. But all the time the wind is howling and the rain drumming on the hard, leathery leaves, till gradually the noise dies down and presently the stars are sparkling in a limpid sky."

Frank Kingdon-Ward, *In Farthest Burma*, 1921

Pilgrims arriving at Alaungdaw Kathapa National Park to celebrate the Thingyan Festival and the start of the New Year.

Bad news. My friend and mentor in the Forest Department, U Uga, was out. Not quite out of the Forest Department, but out of his post as director of the Division of Nature and Wildlife Conservation. Something had happened that I was never able to discern, and he had been transferred laterally out of the most important division of the department. I was told that such shuffling of administrators happens all the time in the government of Myanmar. Nonetheless I was worried. U Uga had a vision for the effective conservation of Burma's natural resources that was very compatible with mine. Did his exit mean that all of our planning for a new inventory of the plants of Myanmar, and for the development of the botanical garden at Pyin-Oo-Lwin, was now in jeopardy?

It was April, and once again the dry season was drawing to a close in Myanmar. I had arrived in sweltering Yangon only the day before with my team from the Smithsonian. In addition to Mike and Debbie, who had previously accompanied me on early visits to the Golden Land, I had invited Ida Lopez to join us. Ida, who had been working as my research assistant at the museum for several years, had heard one too many stories about Myanmar and wanted to see the country for herself. She was part of the growing team of botanists at the museum working on the new plant checklist of Myanmar, and I had decided that it was the right time to catalog all of the specimens in the herbarium at Yezin. I would need as much help as possible, and Ida was an expert in such things. We spent a few days in Yangon showing Ida the city and then were off up-country. After the grueling fourteen-hour drive from Yangon to Yezin, which I had by now endured many times, we were ready for work.

At the Forest Research Institute, Daw Yin Yin Kyi had also developed a small group of assistants to help with the project. U Aung Zaw Moe and Daw Mu Mu Aung knew their botany and, together with our crew, set about creating a computerized catalog of the roughly seven thousand specimens in the herbarium. Between the herbarium data and the records of the specimens we had collected during our own expeditions, as well as the many specimens that Kingdon-Ward and other botanists had collected during expeditions in the 1800s and 1900s, we were developing a substantial database of information on species diversity. Much of the work I had done was conducted outside Myanmar. I had now studied and cataloged important Burmese specimens kept at the Natural History Museum in London, the Royal Botanic Gardens at Kew and Edinburgh, Harvard University, and the New York Botanical Garden. Colleagues from institutions in a number of countries had also heard that we were working in Myanmar and were sending us information from their files about the plants of the country. Slowly and sometimes painstakingly, we were increasing the number of the plant species known from Myanmar by a considerable magnitude. Our endeavor had become global.

Early one morning, Mike, U Thet Htun, and I departed the Forest Research Institute for Alaungdaw Kathapa National Park. I was determined to find some of the species of ginger that we had missed on our previous journey to the park. We abandoned Ida and Debbie in the relative cool of the herbarium to work on the specimen inventory, and according to my field journals we "left Yezin heading north through the blazing, furnace-like heat of the dry zone surrounding Mandalay; then west across the drought-constricted Irrawaddy through Sagaing and Monywa, then across the Chindwin. Nothing new. Fourteen hours of burning road and arid countryside."[1]

The villages along the way baked under the hot sun; the fields were dusty and abandoned. Yinmabin was nearly a ghost town. When we finally reached Kabaign, where we had spent the night on our earlier trip, the forest on the other side of the village was nearly unrecognizable. What had been a lush green understory and canopy of leafy trees was now a blackened and smoldering heap of ashes. The trees still stood tall, but their trunks were scorched, and the ground layer was completely burned. I was startled and discouraged, but learned from U Thet Htun that it was common for fires, either natural or intentionally set, to rage through these deciduous forests during the dry season, burning all of

The forest floors of the monsoon forests burn during the dry season, through naturally occurring or man-made fires.

the old vegetation but not killing the plants themselves. The ash may even replenish the fertility of the soils. We drove on with bandanas covering our faces to keep out the smoke.

Because it had not rained for months, the road was easily passable all the way to the base camp at Thebeik Sae. We passed many people wearing colorful straw hats or carrying large baskets stuffed with various goods, including food and clothing, on their heads as they walked the entire distance of the road. The small rivers were now low enough to ford without difficulty in the Land Rover.

But even more astonishing on this visit than the smoldering forests and well-traveled road through the park was the vast village of bamboo huts, provisional restaurants, and hundreds of people camped at our destination. What had been a secluded forestry retreat was now a New Year's holiday adventure park of pilgrims celebrating the Thingyan Festival at the Alaungdaw Kathapa Pagoda. Screaming children, people chattering away on the backs of elephants, and smoky wood-burning stoves all added to the festive atmosphere of the camp. We were approaching the Water Festival,[2] during which everyone marks the end of the dry season by gently sprinkling cups of water over each other's shoulders and heads as a symbol of good luck in the coming year. I now understood why all of the villages and towns along the road on our drive to the park appeared to be abandoned. Everyone was here, to pay respect to the monks and the pagoda and to celebrate the New Year. Overshadowing all of the noise from the pilgrims was the high-pitched, incessant, deafening whine of the summer cicadas, giant flying insects that clung to each tree trunk and branch in the forest. Discouraged at the level of noise and the number of people, I thought to myself that the situation here was no different than in Yangon.

The next morning we prepared for a hike into the surrounding hills. With U Htay Win, the senior range officer at Alaungdaw Kathapa, I studied an ancient map of the park. The map was not particularly detailed, but it did show the major hills, creeks, and streams. Most of the areas we were headed for were simply labeled as "dense mixed jungle" (or "fairly dense mixed jungle"!). I was particularly excited about exploring a pine ridge called Min Dun Hung Dan, about a day's walk from our base camp at Thebeik Sae. We packed enough supplies for

three days, loaded them onto two of the work elephants at the forest camp, and started out. As at Shwe-U-Daung Wildlife Sanctuary, U Htay Win and U Thet Htun insisted that two security forest guards with rifles accompany us on the trek. This time I didn't care, especially because Alaungdaw Kathapa was also a tiger reserve. I was more interested in getting as far away from the hordes of pilgrims as I could. The dry terrain made hiking relatively easy, and we had covered a good distance by mid-afternoon. Yet the same dry terrain meant that most of the gingers and other plants had not yet broken dormancy, so our collecting was restricted to shriveled rhizomes and dried stems that Mike assured me were alive, and could be grown back at our greenhouses. I was particularly keen to find a very strange type of ginger that bears the botanical name of *Hemiorchis* ("half orchid"), because its flowers closely resemble those of orchids. Our suspicion that this species might be here was based on several specimens I had seen in the herbarium at Kew Gardens, which had been collected many years before in this general region of Myanmar. No one had recorded its presence since that time. I knew that the flowers, which are only an inch or so across, appear from underground stems at the very end of the dry season, a month before the leaves unfold.

The mahouts and forest guards selected for our campsite that night a very peaceful spot along a small streambed that still contained some water. We would

ABOVE: A giant strangling fig sheltering a field camp. Photograph by James Henry Green, c.1920s.

LEFT: One of our nightly field camps at Alaungdaw Kathapa National Park.

CHAPTER 7

string our mosquito nets from a framework of bamboo poles and sleep on an open tarp under the stars. Mike, U Thet Htun, and I decided to climb to the pine ridge before dark. The forest through which we walked at the base of the ridge was a mixed deciduous forest with old teak and fig trees, mostly leafless at this time of year. The climb to the top was not difficult, but in the heat of the afternoon we were soon drenched from sweat and welcomed the cool breeze that greeted us at the summit. We spent a few hours exploring the unique semi-dwarf forest of pines and gnarled hardwoods that sparsely covered the hills. We collected a species of tree in the daisy family and some flowering crape myrtles, but found few flowering herbaceous plants and no gingers. Still, the pines constituted an interesting forest formation, and it was well worth the hike to record it. As we descended the slopes, I noticed that the winds were starting to rise, and the sky, which had been a searing blue all day long, was taking on a more sinister dark tone. Before we got halfway back to the camp, the clouds opened up and the first rain of the monsoon season began to fall. We were soon soaked through and through. Today was the exact date of the annual Water Festival in Myanmar, and Mother Nature had been kind enough to "shower us with luck" by dumping huge buckets of icy rain on our heads and on every other being in the forest. We had not carried our rain gear with us up to the ridge, and soon began to shiver under the cold rain. By the time we made it back to the camp, we were drenched with tremendous good fortune. That night, instead of a tranquil sleep under the stars, as we had earlier anticipated, all eight of us, including Mike, U Thet Htun, U Htay Win, the two mahouts, and the two security guards, slept together under the tarp as the rain poured down.

The sun rose early on the following morning as we awoke to a clear day. The cicadas, which had quieted down when the rains started the preceding evening, once again began their whining chant as we broke camp and headed down the riverbed. During certain times of the day the cicada choir was so loud that it was nearly impossible to carry on a conversation with someone standing immediately next to you. And when the choir stopped, even for a minute, the silence was equally deafening. These large relatives of aphids are about two inches (5 cm) in length, and at this time of the year they cover the branches of the trees, especially in the teak forests. Cicadas are plant-sucking insects, piercing smaller branches with their needle-like mouthparts and tapping into the vascular system of the plant like a miniature sugar maple tapper. The sap from the tree flows into the body of the insect. Unfortunately, the insect's sap spigot has no "off" position for the sap spigot, and when its body is full, the excess sugary liquid just drips out the other end of the bug. A "rain" of sugar water from the cicadas starts to fall from the forest canopy as the day heats up. Although there's nothing dangerous about it, the constant sticky drizzle from above is a distinct nuisance.

For six hours we hiked along the dry creek bed, encountering few plants of interest. However, we did see signs of gaur and panther, and found more samples of petrified wood among the stones lining the creek. I began to wonder if we had made a mistake coming back to Alaungdaw Kathapa in April. Perhaps we should have waited until later, when the monsoons were well underway and the native plants had started to sprout. It was just too dry at this time of the year for almost all of the species we wanted. After a few more hours we decided to set up camp for the night and found an appropriate site at the edge of the forest. Mike and I wandered off into the scrubby forest to find some shade in which to process our few meager specimens.

Just as Mike was about to take off his pack and sit down on the cement-hard soil, I yelled and pushed him to the side. Mike, startled by my tone, gave me a puzzled look. He then realized that there were only two reasons why I would act in that fashion: either he was about to sit on a poisonous snake,[3] or he was about to sit on something more precious. He looked down, and at his feet was a tiny red-speckled shoot about four inches (10 cm) tall, with three yellowish green flowers clustered at the top. It was *Hemiorchis*, the "half-orchid" ginger we had been stalking for two days. Mike and I shouted for joy. The flowers were beautiful, and, as observed by the botanist who had originally named the plant over a

Hemiorchis, one of the wild gingers we were searching for at Alaungdaw Kathapa National Park.

hundred years ago, they closely resembled orchids with their pale green petals, yellow petal-like stamens, and deep yellow labellum, or lip, with a striking red center. No leaves had yet emerged from the long, deeply buried underground stems. We spent the next few hours in the final light of the day taking notes and photographs, making specimens, and digging rhizomes. We found a few more plants of *Hemiorchis* in the immediate area, but nowhere else. We had chosen a fortuitous spot to pitch our camp.

It had been a long day, but we had discovered a very important piece of the taxonomic puzzle of the gingers. *Hemiorchis* was a very special plant, as we only fully appreciated when we were able to study it more carefully back in the herbarium and greenhouses at the Smithsonian. That evening we sat around the fire while we ate our rice and some tasty cooked wild greens that the older forest guard had collected along the creek earlier in the day. I had noticed him pulling the bright green unfurling leaves off a small tree, but had not paid much attention until that evening. The foresters know a lot about the local plants and animals, and I always trusted their knowledge. At the end of the meal we toasted the success of our day with the last of our Mandalay rum before we all piled under the tarp with our Burmese buddies once again as the rains started to fall.

The flowers of *Kaempferia rotunda*, an early-blooming ginger, breaking its long dormancy period.

The third day arrived with a blazing sun and exceptionally high humidity, due to the heavy rains in the night. Our objective was to head back over the ridge and down to the base camp at Thebeik Sae. The elephants and their mahouts set out early while we followed at a more leisurely pace. Still, it was tough going because of the heat and the uphill climb. Along the route we entered a somewhat flat area with an open understory that was carpeted with the lavender-and-white flowers of *Kaempferia rotunda*, a common but magnificent ginger. The sheer number of flowers with their bright colors, set off against the charred background of the forest floor, made the scene even more stunning. We were amazed at the amount of natural variation in the lavender tones of the different flowers: some plants were almost pure white with a hint of blue, others a deep, dark purple. Farther up the trail we also collected a few dormant plants of what I suspected was *Globba*, another ginger that I had picked off the steep and rocky roadside embankments on my earlier visit to the park a few years before. By mid-afternoon we were once again passing the Alaugdaw Kathapa Pagoda, which was still packed with pilgrims and visitors. We were back.

The forestry crew at the base camp informed us that the road out of the park remained passable despite the rains, which had now started. We decided to pack up our gear, clean ourselves up a bit, and have a quick meal before heading back to Kabaing and Yinmabin that evening. Although the late lunch was by no means sumptuous, it was nice to be sitting around a table under a roof rather than squatting on the ground with a tarp over our heads. The meal was simple: rice, eggs, hot peppers, some unknown meat for the guards, and a large plate of what appeared to be the same cooked wild greens that we had eaten earlier, picked this time by the younger forest guard on our way back to the pagoda. Someone located a few beers at one of the pilgrim restaurants to complement our lunch. We were satisfied, and ready for the long dusty trip back to Yezin.

Searching for gingers along a dry streambed in Alaungdaw Kathapa National Park.

We loaded our gear and ourselves into the Land Rover, the driver and I in the front, Mike, U Thet Htun, and U Htay Win crowded into the back seat. We had only traveled a few miles when a great wave of fatigue hit me. I started to lose focus, everything became a little blurry, and an intense light-headed sensation overtook me. I at first thought that I was simply exhausted from the heat, the hike, and the beer. Then I looked over my shoulder at my three friends in the back seat and realized that we were all feeling the same way. U Htay Win's eyes were rolling, and Mike and U Thet Htun were a pale shade of green. At that moment the driver stopped the vehicle at one of the three rivers we had to ford. I jumped out to guide him across. I could barely stand up. Something was very wrong. None of us could talk clearly. I looked at the driver, and he seemed okay, although he had the same greenish tinge as the others. Somehow I guided the driver and the vehicle across the stream to a small shelter that had been erected on stilts in case the river rose during the rainy season.

We decided to stop here until we all felt a little better. I barely made it up the steep ladder into the shelter before I vomited over the side railing. The driver was next, followed by U Thet Htun, then U Htay Win. The cabin was swaying; our legs were weak. We all lay down and moaned and tried to keep from passing out. Mike somehow avoided gagging like the rest of us, but lost control of his legs. We lay prone on the floor of the shelter for over an hour as our heads spun.

Finally, U Thet Htun, who had recovered a bit, hoarsely whispered that we had better get going if we were to get down the mountainside before the rains made the road impassable. The driver said he could handle the vehicle, so we stumbled down the ladder, all sick as dogs, piled back in the Land Rover, and drove off.

At Kabaing, two hours later, we stopped at a small restaurant for water. It was difficult to get out of the car. The owner called for the local "doctor," who could do nothing but take our blood pressure. Although the continual feeling of weightlessness and loss of body control worried me, I had to laugh as each of us had his blood pressure recorded here in the middle of nowhere. By the time we reached the Forestry Office in Yinmabin, Mike and I were feeling a little better. My dreams that night were powerful and vivid, but I slept.

In the morning, we all had recovered. With our wits about us, we deduced that we had not been poisoned by bad or spoiled food, but had simply eaten something at our final meal in the park that was poisonous itself. Then I remembered the greens that the young forest guard had collected on the side of the trail and that had been cooked with our eggs. None of us, including his mentor, the older guard, had seen the actual plant from which he had gathered the leaves. I now believe that he had mistakenly picked a look-alike species that was similar in appearance but quite different in its hallucinatory effects from the plant collected on the previous day by the older, more experienced guard. This mistake was an easy one to make, but nearly a fatal one for us. Our Burmese hosts were somewhat embarrassed by this event, but we tried to laugh and joke about it once we realized what had happened.

Mike, U Thet Htun, and I made it back to Yangon later that week. Our plant collections had not been as extensive as I had hoped, but we had discovered the half-orchid ginger and a few other important species. Some of these plants we would not be able to fully identify until Mike brought them into flower in the research greenhouses in Washington. Yet as botanical warriors who had successfully explored and survived a trek through the "dense mixed jungles" of Alaungdaw Kathapa during the hottest time of the year, we were thankful to return in relatively good health to tell Ida and Debbie about our discoveries. Our two colleagues, with the help of Daw Yin Yin Kyi and her assistants, had accomplished their mission in Yezin as well by completing the catalog of a large section of the herbarium. We had all made progress in our undertakings, but had experienced Burmese traditions in very different fashions. Ida and Debbie and their friends at the Forest Research Institute had celebrated the Water Festival with a big party that ended with everyone drenching each other with garden hoses. Mike and I on the same day had spent our New Year holiday trying to keep dry under a waterproof tarp in the company of the elephant drivers. We weren't sure who had most enjoyed the celebration.

CHAPTER 8 *Paradise in Maymyo*

"First of all Mandalay is a name. For there are places whose names from some accident of history or happy association have an independent magic and perhaps the wise man would never visit them, for expectations they arouse can hardly be realized. Names have a life of their own. . . .The very name of the Irrawaddy informs the sensitive fancy with its vast and turbid flow. The streets of Mandalay, dusty, crowded and drenched with a garish sun, are broad and straight. Tram-cars lumber down them with a rout of passengers; they fill the seats and gangways and cling thickly to the footboard like flies clustered upon an over-ripe mango. . . .Here are no narrow alleys nor devious ways down which the imagination may wander in search of the unimaginable. It does not matter: Mandalay has its name; the falling cadence of the lovely word has gathered about itself the chiaroscuro of romance."

W. Somerset Maugham, *The Gentleman in the Parlour*, 1930

Imagine that a powerful empire invades a foreign land under the pretext of liberating the local populace from authoritarian rule; quite apparent, however, is an underlying, merely selfish economic motive. The overwhelming force of the invaders results in a rapid defeat of the defending army and the expulsion of the defeated ruler in less than three weeks. Envision how the chaos created by the occupation allows the destruction of the cultural repositories of the conquered land. Next imagine that the invaders completely destroy the existing government infrastructure and criminalize the ruling party to such an extent that no competent experienced civil servants remain to take over the basic running of the country. Finally, picture the complete lack of knowledge and appreciation by the occupiers of the language, culture, religion, and social customs of the defeated peoples, which leads to an immediate and passionate hostility toward the invading force. Then ask yourself, Should the invaders be surprised at the growth of a strong insurgency movement against the occupiers?

Although this situation sounds very similar to the invasion of Iraq in the

View from the pagoda on Mandalay Hill of the moat surrounding the Burmese Court of King Thibaw.

early twenty-first century, a similar scenario played out in Burma in the middle nineteenth century during the military conquest of the last Burmese king by the British.[1] The alleged inhumanity of King Thibaw, who slaughtered dozens of his competitors in the royal family when he assumed the throne in 1878, outraged British citizens and led to the invasion of the Burmese Court of Mandalay on November 11, 1885, by the British Expeditionary Force. Within sixteen days after the invasion began the Royal Palace surrendered, and two days later King

The moat in Mandalay, with the Burmese Court on the left and Mandalay Hill in the distance.

CHAPTER 8

Thibaw and Queen Supayalat were ushered aboard a steamship docked at the edge of the Irrawaddy and exiled to southern India for the rest of their lives. The real driving force behind the invasion was not the so-called brutality of Thibaw, but rather the aggressive commercial expansion of the British in Asia in the late nineteenth century. At that time the British aspired to increase their control of the markets in both Lower and Upper Burma in order to gain a "back door" to the lucrative trade with China. The immediate reason for going to war involved a clash over timber rights between the Bombay Burma Trading Company, run by the British and the Burmese government.

When Thibaw took control of the Burmese court in 1878 after the popular King Mindon became too ill to remain on the throne, two rival factions within the ruling class had already developed. On one side were the "royalists," headed by Thibaw and his wife Supayalat, who wanted to retain the privileges of the royal family. On the other side were the "reformists," led by the Kinwon Mingyi, an influential top government official who had been groomed by Mindon. Mindon had struggled during his reign to establish a new ministerial structure to modernize the Burmese government and move it away from an absolute monarchy, so that it could deal more effectively with the rapidly changing outside world. These new "scholar bureaucrats," influenced by Mindon and under the leadership of the Kinwon Mingyi, in an effort to destroy the power of the monarchy, advised Thibaw to arrest most of the royal family and have them slain. The British, in a supposed public reaction to this brutality, overthrew a government that was in fact struggling to modernize itself against a failing and ineffectual monarchy.

Law and order in Mandalay broke down immediately and completely when the British occupying force entered the city. The insensitivity of the British invaders to the social customs of the Burmese and the subjugation of the Burmese way of life quickly turned most of the citizens of Mandalay against the British. On the first night of the occupation, the expeditionary forces took control of the main palace, and converted it to their headquarters, which included an Anglican chapel and an officer's club. The royal library was burned to the ground, and respected monks were turned out of the monasteries that surrounded the palace. The interim government set up by the British completely excluded the Mandalay nobility and the royal Burmese agencies as it searched for alternative leaders who had earlier been exiled by the Thibaw government. By their own choice and actions the new foreign rulers had to confront the difficult chore of erecting, from the ground up, a new government infrastructure by which to administer the conquered land. Although the king they had exiled was not especially respected by many of his subjects, the cruelty, thoughtlessness, and brutality of the British quickly turned the population against them, and authoritarian rule had to be enforced.

OPPOSITE: A Shan
woman from Mogok.
Photograph by James
Henry Green, c.1920s.

ABOVE: Stone
carvers in the city of
Mandalay.

Some historians believe that British colonial rule, which did not end until
1948, as well as the early mistakes the British made by not setting up strong
Burmese-run government institutions, contributed to the establishment of military rule in Myanmar today.[2] The long history of monarchy followed by the foreign occupation paved the way for the present-day military generals' rigid control
of the country. Furthermore, the great ethnic diversity of the country has never
been reconciled, even by the Burmese themselves during the brief period following independence from Britain and before the solidification of control by the
military coup in the 1960s. The rule of force has regrettably, but inevitably, been
necessary to hold such a weakly coherent country together, from the time of the
first Burmese empires in the eleventh century through the era of British rule in the
nineteenth and twentieth centuries through the present. Today, ethnic Burmese
nationalism continues to hinder any significant coalescence of the different
minorities into a unified nation. One of the few significant signs of change has
been the official renaming of the country from Burma to Myanmar. Myanmar, or
Myanma, is an old name for the region promoted by the Court of Ava during the
height of its reign in the mid-1880s, when it was being challenged by the British.
At the time of the British invasion, seven primary ethnic groups prevailed: the
Burmans, the Mon (now largely assimilated into Burman culture), the Shan, the

Karen, the Kachin, the Chin, and the Arakanese. Even though the majority of the population is currently Burman, the same seven ethnic groups persist to this day, with each group concentrated in a different region of the country. Each of those regions today corresponds to a "state" named after the primary ethnic group—e. g. Chin State, Shan State, Kachin State (the remainder of the country is divided into seven political "divisions" with no ethnic significance, e. g. Mandalay Division, Bago Division, Sagaing Division). Right or wrong, the name Myanmar recognizes a single country rather than elevating a specific ethnic group, in this case the Burmans, over the six other minorities that make up the union.

One carryover and symbol of the days of the British occupation is the town of Maymyo. Now called Pyin-Oo-Lwin, this small but bustling town is on the western edge of the Shan Plateau, about two hours due east of Mandalay on the main road that goes through Lashio and eventually to China. Maymyo served as a holiday retreat for the ruling British, who frequently escaped to this hilly resort town, especially during the sweltering days of summer when Mandalay became unbearably hot. At an elevation of 3,280 feet (1,000 m), this small settlement is refreshingly cool throughout the year. The streets are lined with colonial-style brick cottages and guesthouses built in the early 1900s, most of which are remarkably intact after the bombardment of World War II. In the early part of the last century Maymyo supported a small British force, but now it is the location of one of Myanmar's largest military garrisons. Many members of the current ruling junta maintain houses in this pleasant resort setting.

The cool climate of Pyin-Oo-Lwin makes it an excellent place to grow both temperate and tropical plants. Such an ideal location for cultivating ornamentals was not lost on the British, who in 1917 established the Maymyo Botanical Garden in the typical English style, as a series of lakes and pools, arboreta, winding lanes, flower beds, and open vistas to be enjoyed by the visiting government and military officials and their families.[3] The botanical garden at Pyin-Oo-Lwin still stands today and is the oldest and most established botanical garden in Myanmar.

For me, Pyin-Oo-Lwin and its botanical garden evoked love at first sight. I have never decided what attracted me the most. Perhaps it was the old colonial presence of the town, which seemed to be marooned in a time long forgotten, or perhaps it was the cool air of over 3,600 feet (1,100 m) and the respite from the heat of Mandalay, or perhaps it was the small gilded pagoda in the middle of the garden lake. Pyin-Oo-Lwin was something special for me in this country, which I had come to know, value, and respect. My earliest memory of the garden was a view from a vista looking out toward the two lakes and a solitary Burmese gardener in his checkered *longyi* cutting the grassy hillside slopes. He methodically traced slow circles with his arm as he swung a long scythe in vertical loops over his head. He was not using a lawnmower; he was not using a weed-eater.

OPPOSITE, TOP: Main street in the colonial hill town of Pyin-Oo-Lwin.

OPPOSITE, BOTTOM: Multiuse motorized transportation in Myanmar on the road between Mandalay and China.

PAGES 128–29: A horse-drawn cart—here, between the towns of Katha and Naba in Upper Myanmar—is a common means of transportation.

It was simply a man and his arm and his scythe in rhythm, unhurriedly inching down the slope in the smoky glare of the early morning. Over the years I have kept this vision in my memory as I have watched Pyin-Oo-Lwin change.

During my first visit to Pyin-Oo-Lwin in the company of Daw Yin Yin Kyi, the director of the garden, a park warden in the Forest Department, had no time to meet with a foreign botanist. On my second visit a year later U Uga, then warden at Mount Popa National Park, accompanied me. This time a new director, U Aye Lwin, met with me, and we had a long discussion about the history of the garden and its future outlook. U Uga was aware that I had a reasonable amount of experience with botanical gardens, and he was determined to pick my brain for ideas on how to transform Pyin-Oo-Lwin from its current role as a Sunday park for town residents into a full-fledged botanical garden. The garden had significantly deteriorated during the war with the Japanese and the struggle for independence from the British. But the basic design and structure had endured, and both U Uga and

The entrance to Kandawgyi National Botanical Garden in Pyin-Oo-Lwin.

CHAPTER 8

I could see the potential that Pyin-Oo-Lwin still retained. Long into the evening we debated the best way to begin the restoration of this hidden treasure at the edge of the Shan Plateau. The town and garden had two major geographic assets: they were easily reachable from Mandalay, and they were properly positioned along the increasingly active travel route to China. By the end of our discussion I felt it inevitable that this garden would not only survive but would develop into a major force for the Burmese people's appreciation of nature, as well as the conservation of the country's plant life. This time U Uga shared my vision.

Over the next year I spent a considerable amount of time developing a concept of how the garden at Pyin-Oo-Lwin could be renovated and advanced. U Uga pushed me to provide him with a plan and justification for each step. A full-fledged botanical garden should have programs of horticulture, botany, education, research, and conservation; however, it was too much to ask for this garden to develop all of these aspects at once. My early recommendations concentrated on a detailed prescription for getting the grounds and plantings in shape:[4]

- *A concerted effort at maintenance (weeding, mowing, edging, pruning, etc.) of lawn, flowering beds, and plots is urgently needed.*
- *Make better use of formal display beds of annuals and perennials to add color and form.*
- *The palm collection should be upgraded with new and diverse species.*
- *The Fruit Tree Garden needs to be pruned, labeled and made more accessible to visitors.*
- *Reopen the vista from the top of the rise overlooking the ponds and lake by judicious pruning and removal of some trees.*
- *Add an aquatic garden by cleaning and planting the two upper "silting" ponds.*
- *Upgrade the Rose Garden with species roses or eliminate it altogether.*
- *Prepare a new and revised map of the entire Garden for future development planning and for distribution to interested visitors.*

These suggestions were just a few of the ideas I threw back at U Uga. He could not get enough of my thoughts and pressed me further for ideas on education, research, and management.

- *Educational activities at a botanical garden should encompass at a minimum plant labels and educational display signs; at a maximum, formal exhibits, courses, and workshops on botany and horticulture should be provided to the visitors. A central educational facility should be constructed.*
- *A new Research Center must be established at Pyin-Oo-Lwin in order for any important progress to be made in the national botanical inventory.*

This task will require an on-going collections program that systematically surveys all regions of the country covering all of the major habitat types.

- *A master design plan is needed for establishing perennials and shrubs to enhance the plant species' richness and aesthetic value, especially in the central open areas around the ponds. These new plantings should include both horticulturally and botanically interesting species in order to educate as well as provide a pleasing environment for the visitor. A medicinal plant and ethnobotanical garden emphasizing Myanmar species should also be developed.*
- *It is critical to bring in a professional landscape architect with experience in both tropical and temperate garden design to plan this next phase. The climate of Pyin-Oo-Lwin allows a great variety of material to be grown at the Garden, which will allow a skilled landscape architect to create an outstanding design that includes both native and exotic species.*

Two years lapsed before my next visit to Maymyo. Once again a new director of the garden had been appointed. U Ko Ko Gyi met me at the entrance to the garden. I was astounded. The gardens had been transformed. The plantings had all been pruned, cleaned, and trimmed. The vistas had been opened. A new education building had been erected and exhibits on plant conservation installed inside. A new map of the garden was on display and included an additional piece of recently purchased property. U Uga had by this time risen to become the director of the Division of Nature and Wildlife Conservation in the Forest Department. Pyin-Oo-Lwin was now under his jurisdiction, and he had worked miracles. U Uga had seen the potential of the garden and had acted aggressively when he had the opportunity.

Sometimes good things are short-lived, however. Only a few months after my visit, I learned to my dismay that U Uga had run into some major difficulties with others in the department and had been suddenly moved out of his position as division director. I was shocked and troubled. So far the great strides that had been made in the development of the garden were all a result of his efforts; with the departure of my friend from his position of authority, I was unsure of the future.

A year later, to my great surprise and relief, I learned that the director general of forestry had always had a great interest in developing the garden at Pyin-Oo-Lwin, as had the minister of forests. The former Maymyo Botanical Garden designed and built by the British in 1917 now had been officially resurrected as the Kandawgyi National Botanical Garden of Myanmar. During my absence a master plan had been created with the help of a Japanese landscape architect, a Singaporean construction firm, and a Myanmar development company. New roads, walkways, a magnificent entrance with a waterfall and elephant sculpture,

The waterfall and Buddhist shrine at Dat Taw Gyaik near Pyin-Oo-Lwin.

CHAPTER 8

a rock garden, and a jungle boardwalk were all under construction. An admission fee was now being charged. My colleague U Thet Htun also had been assigned to work at the garden. In a short time he had drawn up a preliminary list of the Latin and common names of the trees and shrubs in cultivation and was beginning the reorganization of the former bamboo garden. When I went back to the recommendations that I had made to U Uga several years earlier for the development of the garden at Pyin-Oo-Lwin, I realized what tremendous changes had been made since my first visit. My thoughts went back to that solitary gardener I had seen single-handedly scything the lawns.

CHAPTER 8

OPPOSITE, TOP: U Thet Htun, my friend from the Forest Department, and his family in Pyin-Oo-Lwin.

OPPOSITE, BOTTOM: The series of lakes and landscapes at Kandawgyi National Botanical Garden.

RIGHT: A giant wild banana, *Ensete superbum*, growing on an outcrop of limestone rock.

One of the improvements that had not yet been made concerned the professional training of the foresters. From my earliest conversations with the director general of forestry, we had discussed a workshop for training park wardens, guards, and other staff in plant collecting and inventory methods. The time had come for us to implement a training course. With the assistance of Debbie Bell, several other botanists from the Smithsonian, and Daw Yin Yin Kyi, we planned a two-week course that would include lectures, hands-on herbarium work, and plant-collecting experience in the field. With a revitalized national botanical garden, enthusiastic leadership in the Forest Department, and a group of students willing to learn about their native plants, we were ready to go. We set the time of the workshop for November, when the temperatures would be cooler. I delegated to Yin Yin Kyi and her colleagues in the Forest Department the task of selecting the participants. After the workshop had been advertised for a few months, the final selections were announced: U Aung Zaw Moe, Daw Thida Mundt, Daw Tin Tin Mu, U Kyaw Win Maung, Daw Kyu Kyu Thin, and Daw Mu Mu Aung came from the Forest Research Institute; U Aung Naing Oo and U Tin Htun from the Institute of Forestry; Daw Aye Min Than from the Central Forestry Development Training Center; U Thet Htun, Daw Too Too Mar, U Shein Gay Ngai, and Daw Khin Thu Zar Kyaw from the Nature and Wildlife

Collecting plants on Mount Popa with Burmese students during the Smithsonian's botanical workshop in 1997. Debbie Bell is seated second from left; the author is standing in the back on the right.

CHAPTER 8

"Was there no matter for his derision in the spectacle of a horde of officials who held their positions only by force of the guns behind them trying to persuade the races they ruled that they were there only on sufferance? They offered efficiency to people to whom a hundred other things were of more consequence and sought to justify themselves by the benefits they conferred on people who did not want it. As if a man in whose house you have forcibly quartered yourself will welcome you any more because you tell him you can run it better than he can!"

W. Somerset Maugham, *The Gentleman in the Parlour*, 1930

Conservation Division, and U Myo Khin and U Nyo Maung from the University of Yangon. And as the primary instructor, even with my previous study of the Burmese language, I had to remember all of these names.

I was hopeful that training young foresters to make good botanical specimens and to carefully document the plant diversity of their parks and wildlife sanctuaries would greatly help our efforts to complete an inventory of all the species of Myanmar. I was especially pleased that wardens from some of the major wildlife sanctuaries would be attending the training session, including U Shein Gay Ngai, who was stationed at Natma Taung National Park, otherwise known as Mount Victoria. I was still determined to climb Mount Victoria to find the species first collected by Kingdon-Ward. Getting to know U Shein Gay Ngai during the two weeks of the course was the encouragement that I needed to again start hounding the director general for permission to go to Chin State. U Shein Gay Ngai warmly invited me to visit his park and told me that the best time to find the gingers in flower was in the cooler season, right after the rains ended. I wasn't so sure about the timing, but I was resolved to get there somehow.

The training went well. The Burmese wanted to learn, and their motivation was impressive. For each of the participants Debbie and I had prepared a fat notebook loaded with information on botany, taxonomy, and herbarium management.[5] We started the workshop with a series of lectures on basic botany, the use and importance of plant collections, modern schemes of classification, and methods of identification. Despite the many power outages, schedule changes, and interruptions, we were able to finish the two days of lectures and discussions on time. Next were two field trips, first to a forest reserve at Sein Yay, southwest of Yezin, and then a visit to Mount Popa National Park, where I had collected many times before. Enthusiasm was very high among the students, and I was pleasantly surprised at their collective knowledge of the plants. All they needed was encouragement and an opportunity to use their skills. Daw Yin Yin Kyi, who was in charge of logistics, made everything work as planned. I was learning a lot about the people as well as the plants.

The two weeks went by quickly, and by the end of that time my first class of students had collected hundreds of plants, had learned how to identify and classify

species, had been trained in the skills of pressing, drying, labeling, and mounting specimens, and had put to use the information contained in the collections in the herbarium. We all felt proud of ourselves as the workshop came to a close, and we celebrated with a final dinner and party at the Forest Research Institute that went well into the night. I was impressed with our success, Daw Yin Yin Kyi was pleased with her students, and U Win Kyi was satisfied that the workshop had accomplished its purpose. Botany was coming alive once again in Myanmar.

One of the star participants in the training workshop who rose above the rest, was U Myo Khin, a junior lecturer at the University of Yangon. He was a large, plumpish, slightly slovenly fellow, and at first I found him rather arrogant. He seemed to have a chip on his shoulder about sharing knowledge and was not very open to accepting information from westerners. He challenged me every step of the way. I tried to avoid him for the first few days of the course, which was not a very good strategy for a teacher. But as I watched him studying and discovering new plants during our walks in the forest, my impression of him began to change. He was a keen observer and thinker about the natural world. I realized that he already knew, even if not in a formal way, more about the botany of his country than I would ever learn. He, in turn, began to appreciate my open-ness to learning about the forests we entered. By the end of the course we had become mutually respected friends and colleagues.

Burmese students pressing plant specimens and recording notes during the Smithsonian's botanical workshop.

Over the next few years, whenever I was in Yangon I found myself interacting more and more with U Myo Khin in the small herbarium at the university. We would spend hours swapping stories about the new facts and details we had learned about the plants of Myanmar. He was excited about the future of botany in his country, despite the lack of resources at the university and the never-ending political and economic turmoil. Finally, after overcoming a mountain of bureaucracy both in Myanmar and the United States, I arranged for U Myo Khin to travel to Washington to visit the Smithsonian. For him this was the chance of a lifetime. For me it was an opportunity to train a future devotee of Burmese science, natural history, and botany. But he never made it to Washington. One day before he made his final travel arrangements, he took ill, and within three months he died of a brain tumor. When I learned of his death a great sadness descended upon me. I could not comprehend that this untimely death would rob Myanmar of such a valuable and thoughtful scientist, and rob me of such a valuable colleague. Irrationally, I also could not help but blame his country, which was beginning to mean so much to me, for being so cruel and heartless as to allow Myo Khin to die with such suddenness. I realized, despite my repeated visits and many friends in Myanmar, that I might never really understand this land and its people. Many months passed before I could bring myself to return.

CHAPTER 9

Up the Chindwin River

"*Exploration means days of boredom punctuated with moments of ecstasy. No bogus novelty will serve to induce these moments: it must be 'the real thing', on however small a scale. But the discovery, when it comes, and the experience, when it is reached, have all the excitement that exploration ever had in the days when it was still possible to discover oceans and continents.*"

Frank Kingdon-Ward, *Plant Hunter's Paradise*, 1937

The driver sighed. "Hla ba de," he murmured while staring at the beautiful young Burmese woman strolling along the side of the road. "Thei? Hla ba de," I casually replied from the front seat, and continued, "Cun do` twei` ba jin ba de."[1] A large grin spread over the driver's face. He was looking at me, not at the young woman. U Thet Htun, who was sitting in the back seat as we barreled down the road, wore an equally large smile, as if he were a father who had just heard his child utter its first word. With these simple phrases, I had completed my first Burmese conversation in Myanmar. A few years earlier, during my second trip to the country, I had admitted to myself how utterly lost I was in conversations among my Burmese colleagues. I couldn't even politely order a beer or a bowl of rice when I was on my own in a restaurant. I decided at that moment that it was imperative to learn some of the local language. If I was going to work in Myanmar, I was determined to learn to speak at least passable Burmese.

Burmese, like many other languages of Southeast Asia, is a tonal language. Each monosyllabic mixture of consonant and vowel can be pronounced with several different inflections or tones.[2] The thirty-three consonants (curiously the thirty-third consonant has "no suitable equivalent in English!" according to my language teacher) and sixteen vowel sounds are combined with four primary tones (low, high, constricted, and glottal stop) to compose the varied words of the Burmese language. It was obvious that I could not learn this language on my

A sailboat plying the waters of the Chindwin River.

own, so I called the Embassy of Myanmar in Washington, D.C., to ask if they knew anyone who might be interested in tutoring me. Fortunately, they did. For the next nine months Daw Kyi Kyi Myint Thaw, an expatriate Burmese living in Virginia and former professor of English at Rangoon University, came to my office once a week for a grueling lesson in Burmese.

Good reasons exist as to why Myanmar is so isolated from the West. To start with, the Burmese people could not be more different than westerners in their culture, social interactions, religious views, and language. I was already learning about the first three facets of Burmese life as I spent more and more time in the country with my forestry colleagues. Daw Kyi Kyi Myint Thaw demonstrated exceptional patience in trying to teach me about the fourth element: speaking the language. Not only did I have difficulty articulating the language's sounds, but I had to overcome the ache of trying to make my lips, tongue, and throat interact in completely unfamiliar ways. Then I was forced to contort the logical side of my Western brain to accept the Buddhist concept that everything tangible in life comes to an end, and therefore it follows that the verb *to be* does not exist in the Burmese language. Furthermore, no matter how many verbs there are in a sentence, they are all at the end, and each does not necessarily need a subject. Finally, after months of frustration and effort, I forced the back of my tongue to close my throat and correctly pronounced *ngâ pyi*, the word for an awful fish paste added to every recipe in Burmese cooking. My teacher smiled when she heard me pronounce this particularly difficult word. She was proud of her American pupil, and ready to send me off to Yangon.

This time I arrived at the Forest Department not only with a few Burmese words on my lips, but also with a copy of the first draft of the checklist of the plants of Myanmar. I had recruited several new Smithsonian participants in the project, principally Ellen Farr and Bob DeFilipps, and our progress on compiling the inventory of species was greatly accelerating. Ellen, who was the information technology guru in the Botany Department, set up an efficient computerized database of names and places to keep track of the ever-expanding catalog of plants. Bob loved the concept of exploring little-known places and the plants that might be found in these areas, so he agreed to serve as the compiler of all the information, which was now coming into the project from many different directions. In addition to my own new collections of plants from Myanmar and the contributions from other botanists at the Smithsonian, experts from botanical institutes around the world, who specialized in various plant groups and had heard of our checklist, constantly sent me additional data. The project had rapidly become electronic and global. Our inventory of species quickly exceeded the number and scope of all the earlier and now obsolete versions of the checklist of Burmese plants. And the information continued to grow.[3]

An ancient riverboat on the Chindwin.

The driver of our Land Rover, who had spied the pretty woman along the roadside, was speeding down the road between Mandalay and Monywa. I had taken this road many times before. In the past, when we reached Monywa we had taken the ferry across the Chindwin River and headed either west or south toward the wildlife sanctuaries at Alaungdaw Kathapa or Shwesettaw. This time when we arrived at Monywa, our plan was to head north, not along but actually on the river. Many parts of Myanmar are not accessible by road, and the main rivers of the country serve as important commercial and communication routes, especially during the rainy season when the currents run deep. River transport has always been a fundamental fact of Burmese life. When the British conquered the court of King Thibaw in the final Anglo-Burmese war in the 1880s, they sent their expeditionary forces up the Irrawaddy River on a large flotilla of naval ships to defeat the Burmese army at every fortification along the river. Rudyard Kipling's famous poem describing the "road to Mandalay" was not about a road at all, but about the mighty Irrawaddy River, "where the flyin'-fishes play."[4]

Although roads and highways now play an ever-increasing role in uniting distant parts of Myanmar, the country's three major rivers—the Irrawaddy in the central valley, the Salween (or Thanlwin) in the east along the border with Thailand, and the Chindwin to the northwest—are vital transportation routes for

much of the population. The Irrawaddy starts in the far north, where its head-waters drain the Himalayan region of northern Myanmar. The Salween begins in Yunnan Province in southwestern China and runs parallel to the Gaoligong Shan mountain range before entering Myanmar in Shan State, one of the main opium-growing areas of the country. The Chindwin River flows out of the Hukawng Valley of northern Myanmar, where it gathers the runoff from the eastern slopes of the mountainous areas of northeastern India. All of these great rivers serve the populations of people who live along their banks and on their floodplains by providing lines of communication and transport during the monsoons, as well as fertile ground for cultivation when the waters recede during the dry season.

We were on our way to the Htamanthi Wildlife Sanctuary, about 250 miles (400 km) up the Chindwin River and about 30 miles (50 km) east of Nagaland in India. Once again I had petitioned U Kyaw Tint, director general of the Forest Department, to allow me to mount an expedition to Mount Victoria or Sumprabum; once again permission had been kindly denied. I wasn't quite

A village of bamboo "gypsies" along the Chindwin River.

CHAPTER 9

sure why. U Khin Muang Zaw had been appointed as the new director of the Nature and Wildlife Conservation Division in the Forest Department to replace my friend U Uga. U Khin Maung Zaw was a tall, well-trained forester; although I greatly respected him, I was still not sure of the level of his commitment to the conservation of Myanmar biodiversity. Both he and U Kyaw Tint were impressed with my newest draft of the plant checklist, and they continued to praise my efforts to improve the Kandawgyi National Botanical Garden in Pyin-Oo-Lwin. They were also very pleased with the training workshop we had conducted the previous year, and indicated that our botanical guidance was beginning to have some effects on the productivity of their foresters.

Lately, though, U Kyaw Tint had been wrangling with some of the international conservation organizations working in Myanmar over permits, permissions, and priorities. For the first time I detected a hint of frustration with foreigners in his conversation with me, even though he did not say anything specific. U Kyaw Tint had to walk a very fine line between the limits imposed on him by the ruling ministers and military leaders of his country and the demands of sympathetic but often aggressive Western environmentalists, who wanted unlimited access to wildlife areas that were usually off-limits to foreigners. Sometimes I felt that he just wanted all of us to go away, even though it was his job to protect the same habitats that we were also trying to conserve.

In Myanmar, as in other Southeast Asian cultures, more is often implied by what is not said than what is actually said. The Burmese do not like to deliver negative news and thereby displease others; if the news is not good, often a tangential reply is given, or no reply at all, and always with a smile. The negative news for me was that I could not yet go to Mount Victoria. However, the disappointment was softened by the pronouncement that we would be allowed to go to Htamanthi Wildlife Sanctuary, in a region of Myanmar that had been little explored for plants. I had heard from my colleagues at the Smithsonian that Htamanthi was inhabited by many animals and still had good stretches of undisturbed evergreen forest. These

"Occasionally one passed a raft of teak-logs, with a little thatched house on it, going down-stream to Rangoon, and caught a brief glimpse of the family that lived on it busy with the preparation of a meal or cosily eating it. It looked a placid life that they led with long hours of repose and ample leisure for the exercise of idle curiosity. The river was broad and muddy, and its banks were flat. Now and then one saw a pagoda, sometimes spick and span and white, but more often crumbling to pieces; and now and then came to a riverside village nestling amicably among great green trees. On the landing stage was a dense throng of noisy, gesticulating people in bright dresses and they looked like flowers on a stall in a market-place; there was a turmoil and a confusion, shouting, a hurry and scurry as a mass of little people, laden with their belongings, got off, and another mass of little people, laden too, got on."

W. Somerset Maugham, *The Gentleman in the Parlour*, 1930

reports sounded promising. To get there, we could either fly to the town of Khamti, north of the reserve, and take a boat downriver, or drive to Monywa and take one of the frequent public river transports up to the park. Because flights are scarce and risky in the rainy season, we chose to go up-river from Monywa. But it may have been the wrong choice.

Monywa is a small, comfortable town. When we arrived, it was too late in the afternoon to secure a place on one of the numerous "speed" boats that ply the river in both directions. Over the last few weeks many people had been waiting for the monsoons to arrive so that the river would be deep enough to accommodate the larger boats. Now that the rains were here, everyone wanted to travel. While U Thet Htun was busy arranging our passage for early the next morning, I took the free time to explore the two main pagodas of Monywa. The Thanbokde Pagoda is impressive, with over ten thousand (though some say only six thousand) statues of Buddha of various sizes adorning the walls both inside and outside the ornate building. Nearby is the Bodhitahtaung Pagoda. The *bo* tree or pipal, a type of fig commonly cultivated in Myanmar, is recognized as the tree under which the Buddha received enlightenment, and this pagoda is landscaped

OPPOSITE: The Thanbokde Temple in Monywa, famous for its ten thousand images of the Buddha.

ABOVE: At the Bodhitahtaung Pagoda in Monywa, statues of Buddha sit under pipal trees, a type of sacred fig.

with over one thousand *bo* trees, with more planted each year.[5] A giant, brightly-painted, reclining Buddha[6] with a gold gown, blue pillow, and red toenails had also been placed on a hill above the pagoda and could be seen for miles around by anyone approaching Monywa by road or river.

Before sunrise the next morning we checked out of the small guesthouse where we had spent the night. Most of the boats departed from the bank of the river in the center of town. When we arrived at the riverside, all of our field gear in tow, nearly a hundred vessels were jockeying for position along the stone-paved riverbank, ready to pick up passengers and cargo. Almost all of the boats shared the same basic design: a painted metal hull, long and narrow, sitting low in the water, with a low wooden roof covering the two passenger compartments, one forward and one aft. In the forward compartment, a lower berth for sitting

passengers had two rows of seats separated by a thin walkway, while the upper berth was an unadorned flat surface upon which passengers simply reclined for the voyage, or where cargo was stored. The rear compartment had only a single double row of seats. Passengers reached a particular seat by filing down a narrow outside walkway running the length of the craft while holding onto a railing attached to the roof. Upon finding your seat, you entered the compartment through a window. The pilot and crew handled the vessel from a small booth in the bow; a small wooden box with a hinged side door that served as the WC was appropriately positioned at the stern.

U Thet Htun found the boat on which he had reserved our seats. I steadied myself as I crossed the narrow gangplank, then climbed through a window to take a seat in the rear compartment. The seats were wood, and they were hard. U Thet Htun was next to me. Mike entered last. We were off.

The river trip from Monywa to Hommalinn and then to Htamanthi was more complicated than I had anticipated. I was told if all went on schedule, we could get to the wildlife sanctuary in two days. We would then spend several days exploring the park and collecting plants before returning down-river. The agenda was tight and allowed little room for alterations. This visit was a preliminary effort to determine the feasibility of a long-term plant inventory program at

PAGES 148–49: The giant reclining Buddha in Monywa, called Shwe Ta Liaing.

ABOVE: Picking up passengers along the Chindwin River.

CHAPTER 9

Htamanthi that would parallel the animal conservation work currently underway there. I was optimistic that we would succeed.

We made good time traveling upriver on the first day. Our goal was to reach the town of Mawlaik (formerly known as Kalay), halfway to Htamanthi, by nightfall. The first seven hours of travel were uneventful. I became a bit concerned when the propeller of the boat was damaged on a new sandbar that the pilot hadn't seen. However, the damage was quickly repaired, and we made our first stop to discharge passengers at the small town of Kalewa. There I made the mistake of getting up from my seat to allow two local women to exit through my window. Before I could regain my place, two tough-looking off-duty soldiers who had been crammed into a single small seat in front of me rushed to the open spot and began to fight with each other over my seat. The situation became rather awkward as I tried to reclaim my seat; the two soldiers were not about to budge. At that point it began to rain exceedingly hard, and everyone hurried to lower the plastic curtains above the windows as the water began to pour in.

Boats at Kalewa on the Chindwin River. Photo by James Henry Green, c. 1920s.

Fortunately, U Thet Htun intervened; he showed the soldiers my ticket, and they begrudgingly squeezed back into the seat they had originally occupied. The motor started up, and the vessel began to once again move upriver. So this was river travel by public transport.

Fifteen minutes later, the previously damaged propeller worked itself loose from its shaft, and all forward motion immediately ceased. We began to drift downriver with the current. It was still raining hard. The pilot decided that he could not make the repairs without additional help, so we drifted back to Kalewa. It was clear to me that we were not going any farther that day, so Mike, U Thet Htun, and I disembarked with our gear into Kalewa. My initial dismal impression of this small river town during a torrential downpour may have been influenced by the unexpected interruption of our journey and the weight of the field gear on my back. The buildings appeared old and dilapidated; the tin roofs were rusty; the muddy streets were nearly impassable on foot. We found a small guesthouse as the last gray light of the afternoon disappeared. After a cold shower and a mediocre dinner, I spent the rest of the night swatting mosquitoes and trying to sleep in a small cubicle not much larger than a wooden coffin. I thought the dawn would never arrive.

Luckily our boat had been repaired in the night. Before sunrise I breathed a sigh of relief when we were off once again. I was not sad to see Kalewa recede far behind downriver. As the sun rose and the air freshened, it was good to be back on the river. North of Kalewa, the terrain began to change. Here *indaing* forest lined the river, and a sawtooth ridge of mountains appeared to the west. These jagged slabs of forest-covered limestone, one piled on top of the next like a row of toppled dominoes, revealed the land's ancient geologic past. Present-day mainland Myanmar was a large land mass drifting in the Indian Ocean until about forty million years ago, when it was thrust by the shifting continents into the southern coast of Asia.[7] The rows of serrated hills are a result of that geologic collision. I had not seen land formations like this sawtooth ridge in any other part of Myanmar, and I was anxious to see what plant species were present in the rocky crevasses of the low mountains.

ABOVE: A Kalewa street corner. Photo by James Henry Green, c. 1920s.

OPPOSITE: The sawtooth hills along the Chindwin River above Monywa—a distant view (TOP) and a close-up view (BOTTOM).

At midday we passed the city of Mawlaik, where we had planned to spend our first night. We had not gone much farther upriver before the motor of our boat gave a final loud groan and quit for the last time, still many miles south of Hommalinn. The pilot poled the boat over to a sandy beach, where all of the passengers and our belongings were put ashore to wait for another vessel. At this point I became discouraged, realizing that we might never reach Htamanthi. After a while, another boat pulled in to the sandbar and took us aboard. This craft was even slower than the first one, and by nightfall we had only traveled a short way farther up the river. We disembarked at Paungbyin for the night. The rain had stopped, but all of the guesthouses were full in this small but pleasant town. Ever-resourceful U Thet Htun found an open second-story loft owned by a prominent local merchant, who allowed us to stretch out our sleeping bags there. We slept under the glow of the burning incense of the household Buddhist shrine.

Paungbyin was still far short of our destination. Even if we could get a fast, reliable boat to Hommalinn, it would take at least two more days to get to the wildlife sanctuary at the rate we were going. I made the decision that, rather than proceed upriver even farther into the "heart of darkness," we would hire a boat the next day to take us back downriver, and collect plants in some of the forested areas we had already seen along the way. We had heard that a new road had been constructed from Kalewa to the frontier town of Tamu, on the border with India in the state of Manipur. I concluded that we had a better chance of finding some interesting plants by traveling these roads than by spending more days on unreliable riverboats. The next morning we found a private boat and pilot. At an exorbitant rate, by local standards, we paid the boatman and started back down-river. We were able to stop at several accessible forested localities, and our pilot only grounded the boat on sandbars two or three times along the way.

As I had suspected from the unique geology of the region along the Chindwin River, the forests were full of interesting plants, especially gingers. Many of the species were familiar, but some were new and others unexpected. We found two marvelous species in the genus *Globba*, which had originally been described from India and classified in a different genus. I had found a similar plant during my first trip to Alaungdaw Kathapa, not far from our present position. The common name of one of these species means "dancing lady," because the yellow and lavender flowers resemble petite ballerinas with bowed heads and outstretched arms. The local people also called this plant *chauk pan*, which means "rock flowers," owing to its tendency to grow on wet rocks in deep wooded areas. We found wild bananas, a rare species of cycad (a relative of plants that were around when the dinosaurs roamed the earth), and many species of turmeric and other gingers. One of the most interesting species was a member of the prayer plant family (Marantaceae) in the genus *Halopegia*. This genus

OPPOSITE, TOP:
Collecting plants on the steep banks above the river.

OPPOSITE, BOTTOM:
Globba radicalis, a ginger collected on the road between Kalewa and Kaley.

includes only two species: one in Myanmar and one in Africa, thousands of miles away. Such cases of closely related plants with long-distance separate distributions between continents have puzzled scientists for centuries.

Our team spent a number of days collecting plants and exploring the region around the town of Kalewa, where we had spent the first awful night on the trip upriver. From Kalewa we traveled by jeep along the new road west toward India. The highway was freshly paved, but guarded by many military checkpoints. I was told that the Indian government had funded the highway to promote cross-border commerce between the two countries. On the other side of the Chindwin, we took the road southeast toward Monywa. In contrast to the paved road to India, this narrow track that headed into the hilly interior of Myanmar was a muddy mess in the rainy season. In the first twenty miles after we

left the river, we passed at least five stranded buses and trucks that had broken down as a result of the horrendous condition of the road. The drivers and their mechanics were busy repairing tires, axles, and drive shafts. The passengers of the buses seemed resigned to and prepared for the many days it would take to reach Monywa, a little over two hundred miles (320 km) away. This road was probably a main thoroughfare during the dry season, when the river was too low for boat travel and the mud had turned to dust. If I had not had my own experience with river travel during the past several weeks, I would have wondered why these people did not travel by boat instead of making this arduous overland journey.

After a few days in Kalewa, where we had found a much nicer guesthouse to reside in than the place we had spent our first night, we took an early morning boat back to Monywa and then a public bus to Mandalay. After the rigors of the Chindwin River, the hotel in Mandalay seemed palatial.

Since that first attempt, I have never tried to return to Htamanthi Wildlife Sanctuary. I have been told that it is easier to get there during the dry season, when the airplanes are reliable. But for us, the dry season is not a good time to collect plants. Travel during the rainy season has its own challenges, as we had found out on the Chindwin River. Still, I am determined to get there someday.

BELOW: A tributary river that empties into the Chindwin, near Kalewa.

OPPOSITE: A wild banana, *Musa laterita*, common in Myanmar. Leaflike pinkish red bracts enclose the yellow and green flowers.

CHAPTER 9

CHAPTER 10 *Dust, Jade, and Prostitutes*

"In the market was to be found everything to eat, to wear, and to furnish his house that was necessary to the needs of the simple Shan. There were silks from China, and the Chinese hucksters, sedately smoking their water pipes, were dressed in blue trousers, tight-fitting black coats and black silk caps. They were not lacking in elegance. The Chinese are the aristocrats of the East. There were Indians in white trousers, a white tunic that fitted closely to their thin bodies and round caps of black velvet. They sold soap and buttons, and flimsy Indian silks, rolls of Manchester cotton, alarm clocks, looking-glasses and knives from Sheffield. The Shans retailed the goods brought down by the tribesmen from the surrounding hills and the simple products of their own industry."

W. Somerset Maugham, *The Gentleman in the Parlour*, 1930

The Irrawaddy River at Myitkyina, Kachin State, in Upper Myanmar.

It was February and the height of the dry season in Kachin State in Upper Burma. We stopped our dilapidated jeep to pick up two forest rangers and two soldiers and then continued on toward Pidaung National Park. The access road to the park passed through rather degraded forest. There was no point in stopping to search for plants in these scruffy habitats. The pale gray dust that coated the road was about four inches (10 cm) deep and had the consistency of extra-finely-ground flour. As we sped down the track, our jeep kicked up a dense trail of powder that stayed hanging in the still air behind the vehicle. An old flatbed truck coming toward us was followed by an equally thick screen of dust that was so dense we couldn't see more than a yard in front of us after it passed. We quickly closed all the windows in the jeep to keep out the dust, but the numerous gaping holes in the floorboards provided an open conduit that pumped the fine powder into the vehicle's passenger compartment. Everyone was coughing and wheezing. By the time we reached our destination about forty-five minutes down the road, the entire vehicle, all of our gear, and each one of us was completely covered in the pulverized remains of the dusty road. When Mike and U Thet

Htun got out of the car, they both looked like hundred-year-old men with dusty gray hair and beards. I hesitated a moment as I imagined what my lungs looked like after breathing this pervasive dust for an hour. All the mud of the monsoon season had turned to a fine dust—and the worst was yet to come.

Pidaung National Park, established by the British in 1918 as a game preserve for hunting wild gaur, elephant, and tiger, is the oldest wildlife sanctuary in Myanmar. Over the last century the forest has been severely altered, and weedy plants and secondary growth now cover most of the area. No large mammals remain. However, the reserve covers a broad area, and we were hoping that we would find a few patches of primary forest with some interesting plants. The vegetation in Upper Burma in the foothills of the Himalayan mountain range is quite different from what I had seen in other parts of the country. Myitkyina, the main city in Kachin State, can be reached from Bhamo by road during the dry season, or by air for most of the year. It is the entrance to the wildest regions of Myanmar, particularly the Hukawng Valley to the northwest, bordering

A government launch on the Irrawaddy River, near Myitkyina, North Burma. Photograph by F. Kingdon-Ward, c.1940s.

India, and the area to the north beyond the small outpost of Putao that leads to Hkakabo Razi, the tallest mountain in Southeast Asia. Frank Kingdon-Ward spent a good part of his life exploring for plants in this mountainous region, where he collected specimens to send back to his wealthy patrons in England and Scotland. Now it was my turn to see how the habitats so vividly described by Kingdon-Ward in his many books had changed since he first visited Myitkyina almost one hundred years earlier.

I had arrived in Yangon with little fanfare. For the first time, none of my Burmese colleagues met me at the airport. I was unsure if this was a good or bad sign. Their absence made me a little nervous, as in each previous visit it had been clear that the security police did not want us to go anywhere without our escort from the Forest Department. Perhaps the political situation was relaxing, and our presence was not as much of a threat to the ruling military junta as it had seemed when we first came to Myanmar a few years back. I had heard some talk of at least a partial reconciliation between the military generals and Daw Aung San Suu Kyi, the Nobel Peace Prize winner and leader of the pro-democracy movement in the country. Perhaps this thaw in the political standoff had made everyone a bit less paranoid about our work. Mike and I easily passed immigration and customs and were soon deposited by a very friendly taxi driver at our home base at the Highland Lodge. For the rest of the day we settled in, paid our respects at the Shwedagon Pagoda, and worked on our jet lag. Before I left Washington I had been in contact with U Khin Maung Zaw, the new director of the Division of Nature and Wildlife Conservation in the Forest Department, and expected everything to be ready for us to travel up-country to Myitkyina as soon as we arrived. But of course this was Myanmar, and it took several days to get permission and make all the necessary arrangements before we set off on a flight first to Mandalay and then to the converted military airport at Myitkyina.

Myitkyina lies on a flat plain along the Irrawaddy River, just below the confluence of the Mali Hka and the 'Nmai Hka, the two rivers that flow out of the Himalayas to form the Irrawaddy. The Mali Hka flows straight south from Hkakabo Razi, whereas the 'Nmai Hka sweeps to the east along the mountain range bordering China—called the Gaoligong Shan—before it tumbles into the Mali Hka twenty-five miles (40 km) north of Myitkyina. Kingdon-Ward and his Burmese colleagues mounted nine expeditions to this part of Myanmar between 1914 and 1953.[1] Always traveling on foot, he was the first Western botanist to see many of these areas and brought back key horticultural species, some of which are still cultivated today. Many of the species he collected were new to science. His knowledge of the Himalayas in Myanmar, Tibet, northeastern India, and southwestern China was deep and broad. Myitkyina was his access point to the mountains of northern Myanmar; this small town was where he started and

ABOVE: The Mali Hka, the western branch of the Irrawaddy River, with miners dredging for gold.

LEFT: The confluence of the Mali Hka and the 'Nmai Hka, where the Irrawaddy River forms, above Myitkyina.

where he finished each expedition. In his first book, *In Farthest Burma* (1921), Kingdon-Ward described his return to Myitkyina after eight months exploring the "Triangle" between the Mali Hka and 'Nmai Hka:

Suddenly a bugle close at hand rang out "Last Post" and I sprang up with a start. The high bank of the Myitkyina shore rose above us, and a moment later we were alongside. Without waiting for anything I leapt ashore to stretch myself, stiff with cold and cramp—we had been thirteen hours in the boat. Here were the grass lawn, the roads and shaded bungalows just as of old; everything seemed to be wrapped in slumber; but I must wander through the familiar scene like a restless spirit revisiting its beloved haunts, drinking in the scent of roses.[2]

He had started out from Myitkyina in late April 1914, marching east along the 'Nmai Hkaand and then north across the 27-degree latitude line before turning west, where he forded the mighty river and made for Putao, at that time called Fort Hertz. From there he headed south, skirting west of the Mali Hka, stopping in Sumprabum for a final search for new plants in the surrounding cloud forest, and eventually arriving back at Myitkyina on Christmas Eve.

Raft on the Mali Triangle Bank. Photograph by James Henry Green, c.1920s.

During those months in the mountains of Upper Burma, Kingdon-Ward encountered not only unknown plants and places but a multitude of peoples living in the most obscure and isolated regions: Shan, Kachin, Maru, and Lisu villagers, mountain Buddhist monks, and Chinese traders. In his book he provides a rare glimpse of the lives and cultures of these people of "farthest Burma." He also provides us with a picture of the attitude of the British towards the far reaches of their empire. He describes a squad of Burmese soldiers: "The Asiatic is not less brave than the European; but in the long empty spaces of the night his nerves strain and snap like parting hawsers, and he crumples up. For he fears silence more than anything in the world."[3] And the downfall of the fierce Hkampti Shan warriors: "The days when they were great hunters and fighters are gone, never to return. About the year 1860, in an evil moment, a Buddhist priest came from Burma and converted the Shans of the Hukong [sic] valley to Buddhism, and they forsook hunting and fighting, forbidden to take life."[4] Or the fate of the Kachins: "The fact is, the Kachins realize they will have to give up their thievish, domineering ways, and abandon slavery, for even their jungles can no longer hide them from the prying eyes of the sircar. As you watch the unaccustomed white men passing through your deep forests with their elephants and ponies and their thousands of mules, and hear the tramp of armed men following on, Kachins, you must understand that the time has at last come for you to submit to the dominant race."[5]

Kingdon-Ward paints a very mixed picture in his portrait of Myanmar under British rule. He combines a certain disdain for the local people with a tender appreciation of the rivers and mountains, forests and plants. Contrast his comments above on the peoples of the mountains with his exhilarating experience during the rage of a monsoon storm: "Quite suddenly it burst upon us with an awful fury, the wind blowing with hurricane force. Now the lightning blazed incessantly, flash following flash with such rapidity that we could see everything—bending trees, whirling leaves, and the dark outline of the brooding mountains; and to the continuous roll of thunder, like heavy artillery, was added the shriller rattle of drenching rain as it beat viciously on the stiff palm leaves."[6] Or the glory of seeing a meadow of primulas, orchids, and poppies:

> Our route took us down the rocky bed of a narrow stream, the almost precipitous banks of which were smothered with flowering shrubs and small trees of cherry, birch, maple, and rowan, with bamboos and rhododendron higher up. As for the giant herbs springing from either bank, they met and embraced overhead, bridging the narrow defile, so that we passed beneath arches of purple meadow-rue or brushed through tangles of yellow Corydalis and white plumes of Astilbe. . . . By the water's edge were beds of orange-spotted monkey-flower, and balsam with pendent crimson bugles, saxifrages,

primulas and lilies, mixed with bushes of hydrangea, currant and hairy-leafed
raspberry. It was bewildering, this rampant growth of struggling, long-limbed
flowers in the dim-walled bed of the bubbling beck.[7]

This explorer of unknown lands, who at times was sarcastic, racist, and imperialistic, could also show his emotions, perhaps expressed most touchingly in the final pages of his first book, when he suddenly realized that the expedition was over and he must return to England: "and as I looked eastward for the last time before turning away to the railway station I felt a dreadful home-sickness stealing over me. In that moment everything—rain, fever, hunger, unending weariness of body and spirit, even infinite torment of flies—was forgotten, except that I loved the mountains."[8]

Medicinal gingers being sold in a street market in Myitkyina.

And here I was in Myitkyina, at the confluence of the Mali Hka and the 'Nmai Hka, almost a century after Frank Kingdon-Ward had launched his first expedition to the mountainous north. But things had indeed changed in the country. The British had abandoned their colonial Burma; the Japanese invaders had arrived and departed; World War II, which had further devastated the country, was over; and General Aung San, who had rallied his people first against the British, then against the Japanese, to establish a flourishing, independent, and free country, had been assassinated by his former Burmese colleagues. The repressive military government that took over after General Aung San had been eliminated from the leadership was now firmly in place. Much had happened in this country since Kingdon-Ward first arrived, but Myitkyina still remained the gateway to the wildest region of Myanmar.

For me as a botanist, being allowed by Secretary One[9] to finally visit Myitkyina and explore the surrounding region was a dream come true. Although American zoologists from the Wildlife Conservation Society based at the Bronx Zoo in New York had been here before me,[10] it was now my turn to follow the paths of Kingdon-Ward to see what interesting plants were still to be found. My first impression was not especially positive.

When U Thet Htun, Mike, and I stepped off the
plane, everything in Myitkyina seemed to be burning. The thick smoky haze characteristic of the dry
season lay across the city. At this time of the year,
it is not uncommon for the dried vegetation on
the forest floor to burn, in fires either intentionally
set by local people or due to natural causes. The
last rains had fallen four months earlier, and the
dry brush in the understory was easily set ablaze.
Most of the trees had lost their leaves as part of the
natural annual cycle of wet and dry seasons. These
parched leaves lay ankle-deep in the forests, forming perfect kindling. Along the streets of Myitkyina
the planted shade trees had also dropped their
leaves, which the townspeople dutifully swept into
piles and burned. The fumes added from thousands
of wood and charcoal fires used for cooking, plus
the acrid exhaust of diesel fuel from the numerous
trucks and buses, produced a smoldering atmo-
spheric cocktail on par with the worst Los Angeles
smog of the 1960s. This entrance to Myitkyina was
not quite the dream I had anticipated.

Myitkyina and Kachin State were also distinguished from other parts of Myanmar I had visited

CHAPTER 10

by the absence of the normally ubiquitous pagodas and Buddhist shrines. A new statue of the Buddha in the reclining pose had recently been built, and a few small temples were present outside the town center, but churches far outnumbered Buddhist monasteries. Kachin State and parts of Chin State were converted to Christianity by missionaries decades ago, and although Buddhism is still present, most of the people now embrace Christianity. The basic tenets of Buddhism, to respect life and to do good for others in anticipation of the next reincarnation, are in stark contrast with the concepts of original sin and repentance professed by Christianity. Somehow this Western religion seemed to me to be out of place in Myanmar.

Later that evening, U Thet Htun had some business to attend to in the town, so Mike and I struck out on our own to find dinner. I was looking forward to the opportunity to use my improving Burmese language skills by ordering dinner for us at a small local restaurant. The Mya Ayeyar Restaurant in the Shan Su quarter of Myitkyina offered me the challenge. We found an outdoor table on the patio, and with a smile, a nod, and my best Burmese grammar I was able to order us a sumptuous meal of soup, steamed rice, noodles, tofu, and fried vegetables. And of course, two tall Myanmar beers to celebrate our first day in Myitkyina.

Sitting at a table on the other side of the patio was another group of westerners enjoying their dinner in the smoky haze that had settled over the town. I was a bit surprised to see them in this restricted part of Myanmar. After finishing our meal, we stopped by their table to introduce ourselves and found out that they were French, Russian, Thai, and Dutch medical doctors working with Médecins sans Frontières (Doctors without Borders). They were in Myitkyina trying to prevent the next outbreak of malaria, which usually appears with the arrival of the monsoons, and to stop the spread of AIDS and HIV infections, which were approaching epidemic proportions in this part of Myanmar. According to the doctors, intravenous narcotics use and prostitution were the main causes of the spread of HIV. Evidently the prevalence of drugs and the growth of the sex trade were tied to the local jade and gem mining industries near Myitkyina; the mining operations had brought money and a significant share of "rough characters" to the area. The lack of medical care and the reluctance of the military government to recognize the problem had allowed both of these diseases to increase significantly in the last decade. I had encountered the presence of malaria throughout Myanmar, but this was the first time that the AIDS problem was so obvious. Later that evening, when Mike and I decided to experience the Rose Flower—one of the local disco bars, which are not common in the country—we were approached several times by female "escorts" who wanted to dance with us. The women of Myanmar, especially the Kachins, are known for their beauty, and these dancers were no exception. Mike and I had already accepted their offers when, fortunately

OPPOSITE, TOP:
The dry, degraded forest near Pidaung National Park.

OPPOSITE, BOTTOM:
An evergreen forest in Pidaung National Park with a tall dipterocarp tree, *Shorea assamica*.

or unfortunately, U Thet Htun reminded us that the time was late and we needed to get an early start the next morning. As I departed from the bar, I had to wonder what Kingdon-Ward did on his first day in Myitkyina in 1914.

In our limited time in the area surrounding Myitkyina, I wanted to accomplish three things. The first task was to explore Pidaung National Park and see what remained of the natural forest. The second task was to travel north to the confluence of the Mali Hka and 'Nmai Hka and attempt to visit the village of Sumprabum, where Kingdon-Ward had collected a very poorly known ginger called *Stadiochilus*. And the final task was to drive to the southwest, to the area surrounding Lake Indawgyi, one of the largest lakes in tropical Asia, where I had been told we would find intact semi-deciduous and evergreen forest in the surrounding hills. Although this would be only a small taste of the natural areas in this part of Myanmar, it would be a good start on sampling the vegetation.

The next morning, after enduring the hour-long deluge of dust, we arrived at the Pidaung wildlife reserve. As I had anticipated, most of the forest was highly degraded, and numerous settlements were located around the park and even inside the supposed protected area. Most discouraging were the numerous charcoal pits that dotted the area, where local village people had cut the forest trees and turned them into charcoal to supply their cooking stoves. Myitkyina is north of 25 degrees latitude, so it is technically out of the tropics, but the plants in the lowland area were still clearly tropical in nature. Our first stop was in a typical monsoonal forest, where most of the trees had lost their leaves at this point in the dry season. Here, very few plants were in flower, and all of the gingers were dormant. I was beginning to feel that maybe visiting Kachin State during this season would not be botanically productive. However, a few miles down the road, as the elevation increased, we found a small area of evergreen forest. Here tall trees in the genus *Shorea*, a member of the dipterocarp family that is important as a source of timber, dominated the forest. These trees retain their leaves during the dry season, and many of the plants in the forest, including the gingers, were still green. Mike and I readily went to work measuring plants, recording notes, and making specimens. Although few of these plants

had any flowers, we collected living material that would later be grown in our research greenhouses. We were reminded of the prevalence of illegal drugs in the Myitkyina area when Mike was pricked by a discarded hypodermic syringe while he was digging up some plants. Several years afterward, when Mike with loving care was able to bring one of the living specimens into flower at the Smithsonian, I was able to compare it to all the other gingers I knew from that part of Asia. This one turned out to be something very different and completely new to science. I eventually ascertained that its closest relative had been found in Bangladesh, 370 miles (600 km) to the southwest.[11] I had proven that new species of plants did still exist in this part of Myanmar, and we were on the right track toward discovering other interesting plants.

After spending most of the day crisscrossing the evergreen forest in search of other plants, it was finally time to head back to Myitkyina. As I was poking around one last grove of trees, I came across a small, makeshift cemetery in the forest, with four fresh graves. The little graves covered with red soil seemed to be for children who had recently died, perhaps of malaria. In the cool shade of the dipterocarp trees a wooden cross marked the head of each grave, and next to each cross was a tiny pair of sandals.

The next day we drove north toward the meeting of the Mali Hka and the 'Nmai Hka. In 1937 Kingdon-Ward traveled this route on his way to the Himalayas for the third time.[12] He walked all the way from Myitkyina to Fort Hertz, a distance of about a hundred and fifty miles (240 km), with an entourage

OPPOSITE: A giant dipterocarp tree in Upper Burma.

RIGHT: A grave in northern Myanmar.

Photographs by F. Kingdon-Ward, c.1940s.

"At Myitkyina the Irrawaddy, at 1000 miles from the sea, is an imposing stream 600 yards wide even at low water, with a gentle current. In the flood season the breadth at peak load, increases to 800 or even 1000 yards and the current flows at 4 or at peak load, increases to 800 or even 1000 yards and the current flows at 4 or 5 miles an hour, probably faster in the centre. Meanwhile it has risen some 30 feet."

Frank Kingdon-Ward, *Burma's Icy Mountain*, 1949

of ponies, oxcarts, and Kachin porters carrying his gear. One of his first stops was the mountaintop British outpost at Sumprabum. For me Sumprabum was important; this site was the only known locality of a very special ginger called *Stadiochilus*. From specimen records at the Royal Botanic Garden in Edinburgh and at the Forest Research Institute in Myanmar, I knew that this plant grows on rocks and has large reddish-pink flowers.[13] It had been collected by Kingdon-Ward and a later botanist in the vicinity of the "misty mountain," which is what *sumprabum* means. I was determined to find it in order to more accurately describe its flowers and to collect tissue samples for sequencing its DNA, thereby ascertaining its correct classification within the ginger family.

Unfortunately my friends in the Forestry Department had not obtained permission for us to go all the way to Sumprabum from Myitkyina during this trip. Nevertheless, I hoped that we might get a special permit from the local military authorities. In July 1937 Kingdon-Ward took eight days to travel the fifty miles (80 km) from the confluence of the rivers to Sumprabum. When he arrived, it was raining and cold. Now in February it was hot and dry as we drove north in our battered jeep along the dusty road. Perhaps I did not have to go all the way to the misty mountain to find *Stadiochilus*. We might be lucky and discover plants in the forest and hills that surround the point where the two rivers come together. After several hours of searching, however, it was clear to me that this rare plant would only be found at Sumprabum. But how to get there?

I hung my hopes on our forester guide, U Khin Maung Hla, and his boss U Zaw Mat, the director of the Forestry Office in Kachin State, to convince the military to let us go. But it was not to be. The authorities were worried about sending foreigners into an area where insurgents and bandits were known to be present. Furthermore, a scientist from the Wildlife Conservation Society had illegally visited this area near Putao the previous year, while searching for wild deer populations. He had angered the Minister of Forests when he persuaded a military helicopter to take him to a place that was strictly off-limits to foreigners.[14] The local military commander in Myitkyina was still smarting from the reprimand for that episode, and he was not about to give another foreign scientist permission to enter this area. I was very discouraged and angry that we were so close to finding this plant, but would not be able to reach it, though it was only fifty miles (80 km) up the road. The Myanmar military junta was strict about

OPPOSITE: A new species of ginger, yet to be officially named, that the author discovered in the evergreen forest at Pidaung National Park.

FLORA OF NORTH BURMA

Sumprabum 3000′–3500′. 3. March
1953.

Hedychium.
an epiphyte. flowering January
(we saw it out of reach, in
several places; flowers pinkish
purple. an unusual colour)
Ovary hairy.

F. KINGDON-WARD   22003

F.K-W   F.K-W   F.K-W

22003   22003   22003

access to certain parts of the country by non-Burmese, and I knew by now that when they said no, they meant no.

While I was still sulking about this disappointment, U Thet Htun had another idea. We could hire a local forester to find the plant for us. We had a good description of the species, and even a locality where the plant could be found. The forester could go to Sumprabum using public transportation, collect the plant, and bring it back to us in Myitkyina, where we could study the specimens firsthand. It would not be ideal, but it was worth a try. U Thet Htun arranged everything. If all went well, the forester we hired would be back from Sumprabum by the time we returned from our trip to Indawgyi Lake. I felt more optimistic that I would see this ginger before I left Myitkyina.

Mogaung, southwest of Myitkyina, is a crossroads for travel in Kachin State. Kingdon-Ward stopped here on his train journey from Mandalay to purchase jade ornaments. Myanmar's most important jade mines are located sixty miles (100 km) from Mogaung near Hpakant, one of the sites of HIV concern for the doctors from Médecins sans Frontières. True jade is known from only two sites in the world: Myanmar and Guatemala. The scarcity of the mineral makes it all

OPPOSITE LEFT:
A botanical
specimen of the rare
ginger *Stadiochilus
burmanicus*, from the
herbarium at the Forest
Research Institute.

OPPOSITE RIGHT:
A page from one of
Kingdon-Ward's plant
collecting books, with
notes on a specimen
of *Stadiochilus*
that he found near
Sumparbum in
1953. Note that
he mistakenly
identified the plant as
Hedychium.

the more precious, and the value of Myanmar jade is high. Mogaung also marks the gateway to the Hukawng Valley to the northwest, now the site of a new national park and wildlife sanctuary established to protect the largest population of Bengal tigers in the country. The road, also known as the Ledo Road, runs from Mogaung through the Hukawng Valley and crosses the border with India, eventually reaching the city of Margherita in Assam. This five-hundred-mile (800 km)-long road, together with the "Burma Road," was constructed by the Allies during World War II as a supply route from India to China.[15] It traverses some of the roughest terrain in all of Myanmar. Built by thousands of Burmese under the direction of British and American engineers, it was also the route taken by many villagers during their flight from the Japanese occupiers. Today the road is full of large potholes and covered in many places by landslides and overgrown vegetation; during some parts of the year it is impassable.

We took the road that travels southwest from Mogaung toward the town of Hopin, where we would meet U Sein Tun, the park warden at Indawgyi Lake. After a tedious drive across miles of dry rice paddy and dusty villages, which lie between the Gangaw Taung and Mangin Taung hills, we crossed a low pass in the hills and saw the lake below us. We soon arrived at a local township guesthouse on the edge of the lake. As I brushed the thick dust from my clothes and gear, I noticed that the moon, nearly full, was rising across the lake to the east. It was a good sign.

The next morning I recorded in my field journal: "The roosters awake first, the fishermen are already out on the lake, the pale orange moon quickly sets in the west, the mist over the water diffuses the new light from the rising sun, coots, ducks, and grey-lag geese announce their presence as a slight breeze picks up. The day has begun."[16] Unfortunately our first day at Indawgyi Lake was rather unproductive. In an effort to find a tract of obscure evergreen forest, we took a four-hour boat ride to the headwaters of the lake, then hiked another five hours through old pastures and cultivated fields, only to find more old pastures and cultivated fields. The sun was extremely hot. Our destination was a dry streambed where U Sein Tun thought we might find some interesting plants. But during the dry season all the plants were either leafless or dormant. We finally gave up and retraced our path back to the boat. On our way back across the lake, we stopped the boat at a pagoda built above the water on thick stilts. There we met two of the village "chiefs" from whom we needed permission to visit a special forest reserve. My Burmese language skills were not yet good enough to follow the entire discussion, but from what I could understand, our hosts were more concerned about what we were going

". . .and a good road from [Fort] Hertz to Myitkyina presents no insuperable engineering difficulties. . ."

Frank Kingdon-Ward, *In Farthest Burma*, 1921

to eat for lunch the next day than the problem of permits and the logistics of finding the site.

It was the end of the day, with the sun low in the sky, as we left the pagoda and traversed the boardwalk heading toward our boat, tethered at the end. In the shallow waters at the edge of the lake I noticed a rather indistinct strap-leaved plant growing under the water with a spiraling, corkscrew stem rising to the surface. As I looked closer, I realized that this plant was *Vallisneria*, also called eelgrass, or *nga-shint-myet* in Burmese. I had never seen it before, even though it is not uncommon in both temperate and subtropical waters. This plant, which spends its entire life underwater, has one of the most bizarre flowering strategies in the entire plant kingdom. The male and female organs are formed in separate flowers underwater at the base of the plant. During the evening of the full moon the ripe male flowers are set free from the plant and rise to the surface of the water on a raft of tiny bubbles. The petals of the floating flowers form miniature boatlike structures, with the open anthers sitting inside. The female flowers are positioned at the ends of the long corkscrew stems I had

The Shwemyinzu Pagoda situated on an island in Indawgyi Lake.

CHAPTER 10

observed. At the same time that the male flowers are released from the plant, the spiral stems, which have been held under tension, elongate, pushing the female flowers to the surface of the water as well. The slightest breeze causes the male flowers to sail across the water to the female flowers and touch their tiny anthers, which are bursting with pollen, to the receptive stigmas, thereby enacting pollination. Once the female flowers are pollinated, the corkscrew stems retract and pull the female flowers back underwater, where the submerged fruits and seeds slowly develop.[17] These plants are found in lakes in many parts of the world, but I had to come all the way to Indawgyi Lake in Myanmar to find this wonder of nature. As we headed back in our boat, I saw that the surface of the lake was covered by thousands, perhaps millions, of tiny flowers that had all set sail at the same time. The full moon was rising as we pulled into the shore near our guesthouse. Later that evening, as I crawled under my mosquito net with the moonlight shining in my window, I thought of the beautiful dance of nature that was taking place across the lake that night.

After a few days living at the guesthouse along the edge of the water, I had become very attached to Indawgyi Lake. It was large and full of wildlife, especially birds. Each morning, the mist would rise to reveal the fishermen scattered across the lake, with the hills far across the horizon silhouetted by the rising sun. This morning we were off to explore an evergreen forest in the Nanyinkha Forest

RIGHT: Eelgrass, *Vallisneria spiralis*, growing underwater in Indawgyi Lake.

PAGES 176–77: Fishermen on Indawgyi Lake, in Kachin State.

Reserve in the southwestern sector of the lake region. Somehow eight of us, including U Sein Tun's entire staff, were piled in the small vehicle as we chugged down the dusty road. After a few hours of driving and walking, I found myself in a beautiful tall forest of dipterocarps and other very large trees. The understory was filled with gingers, begonias, bamboos, bananas, lilies, and many other herbaceous plants. Large woody vines called lianas, with thick, contorted, and twisted stems, hung between the trees. Occasionally a great hornbill, one of the largest and most impressive birds of Asia, with a bulbous, inflated beak, would fly overhead. This unspoiled forest was just what I had been looking for; we encountered many new species of plants there for the first time. We spent a glorious day exploring the forest, and by the end of the afternoon our plant presses and notebooks were full. As I sat on the ground in a small clearing, putting the final specimens in my press, I knew that this serene spot would be our last stop and the farthest point we would reach on this trip. Tomorrow we would head back across the dust-covered road to Myitkyina, then back to Mandalay and Yangon. Soon I would be back once again in Washington. I looked up one final time at the tall trees surrounding me to store this verdant scene deep in my mind, knowing that I would have the need to recall it again at some time in the future. Every plant-collecting expedition has its "farthest point," at which you know that it is time to turn around. The journey back may be arduous, but you always know that your direction is toward home. I had reached that point here in the evergreen forest at Indawgyi Lake.

When we returned to Myitkyina, we received the bad news that the forester U Thet Htun had sent to Sumprabum to find the ginger for us had not been successful. It took him two days by bus from Myitkyina to get to Sumprabum, and

Jungle scene in Upper Myanmar. Photograph by James Henry Green, c.1920s.

CHAPTER 10

Collecting gingers in the evergreen forest at Indawgyi Lake.

two days to get back, so he had only two days to search for the plant. The village that had marked the locality of the plant in the earlier specimens was no longer there. The forester had radioed back to U Khin Maung Hla for help and instructions, but there was nothing left to do, so he returned empty-handed. In 1937 it had taken Kingdon-Ward eight days during the wet season to get to Sumprabum by foot; now, over sixty years later, one still needed two days by bus in the dry season to go the fifty miles (80 km). I was, of course, disappointed that our Plan B for finding the ginger had failed. Several years later a Burmese colleague in the Division of Horticulture sent me a photograph of a plant that he had collected in the Hukawng Valley. The plant had large reddish pink flowers and was found growing on a rocky cliff. To my amazement, he had discovered a second population of *Stadiochilus* about forty miles (60 km) due west of Sumprabum. I had hopes of eventually finding this species myself someday.

In Kingdon-Ward's last book, called *Return to the Irrawaddy*, he describes his final trip to Upper Burma in the early 1950s. In the book one can clearly sense his nostalgia for the Burma he knew before the end of British rule. Although the logistics were difficult in the early days of exploration, Kingdon-Ward had never encountered any problems entering the country and planning his expeditions. By contrast, in 1952, four years after independence, he struggled to obtain an entry visa from the Burmese embassy in London. When he finally received the visa and arrived in Rangoon, he was furious because he was not allowed to leave the city. Eventually everything worked out, and he flew to Mandalay by airplane and drove to Myitkyina by car. The expedition was a success, and as in the past, he discovered many interesting and new species of plants. In the final paragraph of the book he described his last impression of the town before departing: "Myitkyina, no longer the sleepy little riverside village it had been during the war, was now a bustling town, and riddled with thieves."[18] When Kingdon-Ward took that last trip to Kachin, I was just one year old. Years later when I visited Myitkyina, I did not find it riddled with thieves, but it was certainly not a "sleepy riverside village."

When I returned to Yangon, a message was waiting for me from U Khin Maung Zaw. The director general of the Forest Department, U Kyaw Tint, had suddenly retired, and U Shwe Kyaw, whom I had met a few years earlier when he was director of the Forest Research Institute in Yezin, had been appointed as the new director general. He wanted to see me before I departed for Washington. I didn't know how to interpret this sudden change in administration. I was quite fond of U Kyaw Tint, who had been very supportive of my botanical work in Myanmar. I didn't quite know what to expect from his successor.

Later that afternoon I was ushered by U Khin Maung Zaw into an audience with U Shwe Kyaw. The director general wanted to know everything about my work. He had many questions about the checklist of plants: How far along were we? How did we determine which species were present in Myanmar? How much had Daw Yin Yin Kyi contributed? Had other botanists and foresters in Myanmar seen and approved of the work? He also asked where we would publish the volume. In the United States? In Myanmar? How many copies would be printed? Would we include color plates? I provided the most up-to-

The sun rises on a still morning over Indawgyi Lake.

CHAPTER 10

date answers I had. He also was quite interested in my thoughts on the further development of the Botanical Research Center at the Kandawgyi National Botanical Garden in Pyin-Oo-Lwin. Many questions and many answers. We talked for nearly two hours.

The conversation eventually turned to my plans for exploring new regions of Myanmar. At this point I started to get the uneasy feeling that U Shwe Kyaw was not one to push the envelope on obtaining permission for me to visit any distant places generally off-limits to foreigners. He recounted several times the problems that the Forest Department had had with other foreign scientists who bent or occasionally even broke travel rules. I came away from our meeting with the distinct sense that this director general would not be as forthcoming with logistical help as his predecessor. Although I would not characterize his attitude as distinctly anti-foreigner, it certainly was not as welcoming as I had hoped. The situation greatly worried me, as the future of our progress on exploring Myanmar depended on the support of the director general and his staff in the Forest Department.

On the final day in Yangon before my departure, a friend had arranged a visit for me to meet the deputy minister of education. I had visited the University of Yangon during earlier trips to Myanmar, but with the death of U Myo Khin, my student protégé from our botanical workshop, I had not recently been back to work in the herbarium in the Botany Department. I was somewhat surprised at the warm welcome I received from the deputy minister and the director general for higher education, who joined us in our meeting. They were both very interested in developing a new program in biodiversity at the university, and possibly an exchange of students with the Smithsonian. Although they did not have many resources to offer, they were more than willing to seek permission for our team to visit some of the places that my Forestry colleagues had always claimed were totally off-limits to foreigners, such as Mount Victoria. My ears were on fire. Had I finally found the path to Natma Taung? As our discussion continued, I began to think that some of my problems might be solved by working with the Ministry of Education rather than the Ministry of Forests. We ended our conversation by making plans to work toward a mutual agreement of understanding on a new program in biodiversity. I left the university with thoughts of climbing Mount Victoria.

CHAPTER II *The Arakan Capital at Maruk U: Through Bamboo Hell*

"Then leaving the open spaces we passed through secluded hills and forests of bamboo. A bamboo forest is a graceful thing. It has the air of an enchanted wood and you can imagine that in its green shade the princess, heroine of an Eastern story, and the prince her lover might very properly undergo their incredible and fantastic adventures. When the sun shines through and a tenuous breeze flutters its elegant leaves, the effect is charmingly unreal: it has a beauty not of nature, but of the theatre."

W. Somerset Maugham, *The Gentleman in the Parlour*, 1930

OPPOSITE TOP:
Vista looking north along the Rakhine Yoma from Natyegan.

OPPOSITE BOTTOM:
Pagoda silhouettes at Mrauk U.

The sun was rising, and a cool breeze was blowing across the summit of the Rakhine Yoma. To the east lay the central valley of Myanmar, to the west the Bay of Bengal. I had just spent a rather uncomfortable night on a very hard wooden floor in a partially constructed (or destructed) bamboo hut at Natyegan, the "Lake of the Spirit" monastery, which had been abandoned years earlier. The day before, Mike and I had made a mad dash with our guides across the dry zone from Bagan south to Magway, then east across the Irrawaddy River to Minbu and up the mountainside. We had arrived at Natyegan shortly after dark in search of the "guesthouse" noted on the itinerary prepared by our hosts from the University of Yangon. When the vehicle finally pulled to a stop, I was still hot from the broiling November sun of the lowlands, I needed a bath after collecting a thick layer of caked dust from the road, and I was hungry. The darkening deep blue sky was dotted with the faint light of the first stars. I saw nothing at Natyegan but a few rickety buildings, which I was told had once been an active monastery. There was certainly no guesthouse. I was on the verge of getting angry.

In Myanmar it is not polite to get angry. So I forced a smile and cracked a joke about the excellent accommodations. The two assistant professors, U Tin Maung Ohn and U Ko Tin, shyly laughed as well. What else could we do?

Someone had misled us (purposely?) about the existence of a guesthouse on this lonely mountain pass. We eventually found the caretaker of the run-down buildings, who let us into the bamboo hut, where we set up camp for the night. After a makeshift meal of noodles and nuts, plus a couple of shots of Mandalay rum, things were looking better. Just before wrapping myself in my sleeping bag for the night, I took a short walk up to the ridge. The magnificent star-filled sky had lit up the valley below us. From this vantage point all of Myanmar appeared serene and at peace.

This trip was the second I had made with my new colleagues from the Botany Department at the University of Yangon. My frustration with the Forest Department had grown as a result of the constant changes in administration, the increasingly difficult communications, the dwindling logistical support, and particularly the exasperating travel restrictions imposed by the minister of forests. As a result of my initial meeting with the deputy minister of education, a memorandum of agreement had been signed between the Ministry of Higher Education and the Smithsonian to foster better interactions between the University of Yangon and our museum. Since that time I had given a number of lectures and hosted a workshop at the university. Now I was on the top of a ridge along the Arakan Mountains on the border between Magway Division and Rakhine State. When I had worked with the Forest Department, I had never been given permission to cross over to Rakhine. Tomorrow, not only would I cross into Rakhine State and pass through the ancient city of Mrauk U, but I would travel all the way to Sittwe, the current provincial capital, situated on a tongue of land sticking out into the Bay of Bengal.

The land of Rakhine, formerly called Arakan, was for centuries a country to itself before being conquered by the Burmese in 1785.[1] The region is bounded on one side by the Bay of Bengal and on the other by a tall mountain range that for millennia served to isolate the territory from the Burmese empire. The isolation and geographic position of Arakan had resulted in a strong Indian and Bengali influence on its culture. Although it was originally a Buddhist enclave, today many of the inhabitants are Muslims. Arakan was one of the sections of Lower Burma that was acquired by the British after the first Anglo-Burmese war in 1826.

Similar to the influence of the Indian subcontinent on the former politics and historical cultures of Rakhine, the plants of the region also showed affinities to the lands to the west. For this reason I figured that the vegetation of Rakhine State should be somewhat unusual, and I wanted to sample it firsthand. One of my particular interests was to initiate a search for a few plants that had been reported from this area during the latter part of the nineteenth century. Kingdon-Ward had never visited this part of Burma, so I did not have his notes or specimens to guide me. However, I had studied other botanical literature pertaining to India, Bangladesh, and Myanmar, and I suspected that we might locate some species in Rakhine found nowhere else in the country.[2]

Spending the night on the mountaintop made me think of my family back in Washington. Before I departed from my office at the Smithsonian, I had been reading some of the letters sent to Kingdon-Ward by his wife and daughters during his many years exploring Burma. While at the Natural History Museum in London, I had come across these letters squirreled away in a wooden box in the herbarium. One handwritten note from his daughter Pleione (who was named after a British flower) sent in 1937 reminded me in many ways of my own daughters:

> *My Darling Frank: . . . Yesterday Mart found a moorhen's nest. It was in the water so if we* had *wanted to frighten the little mother, we couldn't have. . . . As soon as it has been arranged, we are going with James to Snow White & the seven dwarfs. . . . You know (or don't you?) that there are some sweets called "Milky Way." These have cards like coupons in them (50) of famous film-stars. We are having a race to see who will collect the series first. . . . May is in flower. We are trying to make our feet hard, so are running with bare feet. With love from Pleione.*[3]

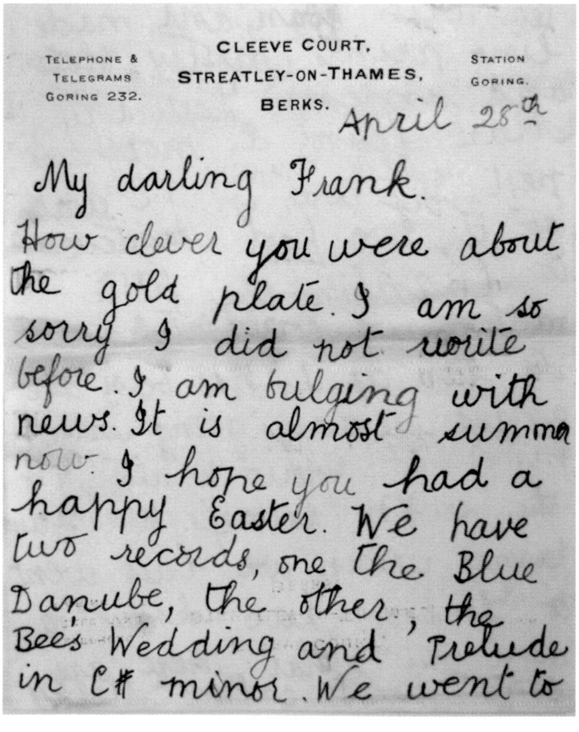

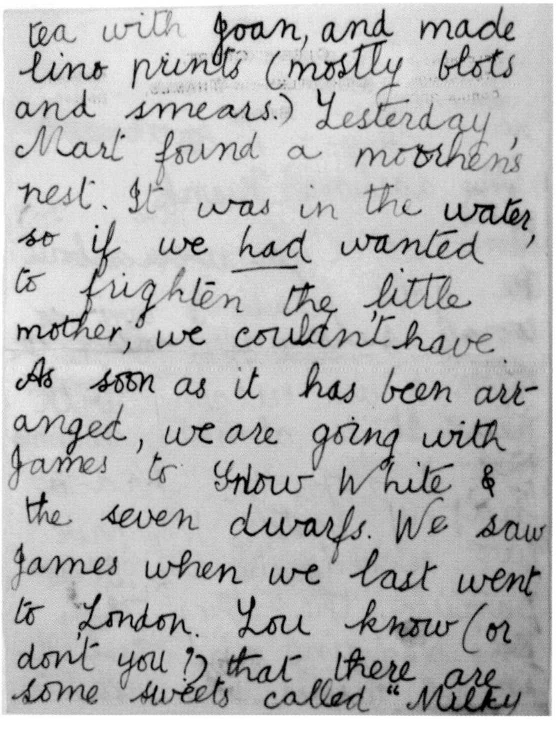

Knowing where Kingdon-Ward went in Burma, and knowing some of the things he must have experienced, it was difficult for me at first to imagine him as a father. But here was proof in these handwritten letters from his children. After

BELOW AND PAGE 186: A letter to Kingdon-Ward from his daughter Pleione.

Telephone & Telegrams Goring 232.
Cleeve Court, Streatley-on-Thames, Berks.
Station Goring.
April 28th
My darling Frank.
How clever you were about the gold plate. I am so sorry I did not write before. I am bulging with news. It is almost summa now. I hope you had a happy Easter. We have two records, one the Blue Danube, the other, the Bee's Wedding and Prelude in C# minor. We went to

tea with Joan, and made lino prints (mostly blots and smears.) Yesterday Mart found a moorhen's nest. It was in the water, so if we had wanted to frighten the little mother, we couldn't have. As soon as it has been arr-anged, we are going with James to Snow White & the seven dwarfs. We saw James when we last went to London. You know (or don't you?) that there are some sweets called "Milky

CLEEVE COURT,
STREATLEY-ON-THAMES,
BERKS.

TELEPHONE & TELEGRAMS
GORING 232.

STATION
GORING.

Way." These have cards like coupons in them (50) of famous film-stars. We are having a race to see who will collect the series first. The Ferdinandos have a little brother born on Monday. We went to Bucklebury to tea with Miss Hedges, who has one of the prettiest houses I ever saw. She said she had always wanted to keep house, and when she

was quite little she had £1 given her, and she bought about 7 chairs with it. She has a maid called Daisy, who keeps every single thing so beautifully tidy and neat. Miss Hedges can actually do a _Times_, mark you, crossword. May is in flower. We are trying to make our feet hard, so are running with bare feet. With love from Pleione.

reading these notes, I could imagine the great explorer climbing to the heights of Kokoborazi in the far north of Myanmar with a letter in his pocket from Pleione about Snow White and the seven dwarfs.

Expeditions to the Himalayas in the early twentieth century required plant hunters such as Kingdon-Ward to be away from their families and friends for six to twelve months at a time. Travel was by ship, train, and foot. Now an overnight flight across the Pacific enables me to arrive in Yangon from Washington in forty-eight to seventy-two hours. My field trips in Myanmar usually lasted three to six weeks. Still, that can seem quite a long time to be away from your wife and children, away from your home. When she was very young, my first daughter (also named after a flower never really understood where I went on these trips. She once confided to her mother that she thought I simply went to the airport, where they had dropped me off, and purchased photographs of plants and far-off places there before I came home several weeks later. Sometimes I wish it had been that easy. In my own field journals I find passages that I have written about my daughters while at locations like Natyegan:

And throughout this trip I have visions of my ladies: Whitney—dancing and spinning and leaping and stepping, a smile for me, an angry stare, an intense caring for others. Laetia—preoccupied with many things, always absorbing knowledge, sometimes a struggle, but eventually a triumph. And LLC—my favorite, my total preoccupation,

CHAPTER II

my source of strength and guidance and support, and my lover forever. These are my
ladies who I carry with me around the world. I owe them everything, my life, my love.[4]

I, too, carried letters around in my pocket.

The morning, after our stay in the half-open bamboo hut, we quickly packed up our gear. We wanted to get an early start as we crossed the ridge and headed down the western slopes toward a small town called Ann, where we were scheduled to spend the night. Before we left the higher elevations, we passed through a beautiful evergreen forest replete with gingers and other plants, such as impatiens, begonias, and wild peppers, many in full flower. At this elevation in the cloud forest some plants grow as epiphytes in trees, and we had to look up to the highest branches as well as down on the forest floor in our search for interesting species. In this one spot we discovered some of the most exciting gingers in Myanmar, including hedychiums, curcumas, zingibers, globbas, and even a *Rhyncanthus*, perhaps one of the most unusual gingers in the country, with striking yellow-orange flowers emerging from plants clinging to the trunks of the tall-

Rhynchanthus longiflorus, an epiphytic ginger growing in the treetops in the cloud forest near Natyegan.

est trees. Mike and I were overjoyed to find it; the professors from the university were not quite as excited. One of the plants I found, which commonly grew in the trees at the highest elevations, was a species of *Hedychium* with bright red bracts and flowers. I eventually determined that this species was new to science and named it after Mike as *Hedychium bordelonianum*.[5]

The first morning was indeed a good beginning to our trip. The evergreen forests where we collected the specimens were just east of the border, so we were technically still in Magway Division, but these botanical discoveries encouraged us as to what we would find in Rakhine State. One of the gingers that I was particularly interested in finding was *Globba arracanensis*. This species was named after the state where it was first discovered by Wilhelm Sulpiz Kurz,

ABOVE: Mike Bordelon collecting *Hedychium bordelonianum*, a plant named after him, in the trees on a cloud forest ridge above the Bay of Bengal.

LEFT: The red inflorescence and yellow flowers of *Hedychium bordelonianum*.

CHAPTER II

one of the earliest British botanists and foresters to explore Burma in the mid-nineteenth century.[6] I knew very little about this plant except what I could determine from Kurz's description and a single specimen I had seen in the herbarium at Kew Gardens. It was reported to have pale purple and white flowers with a bright yellow lip and a rather strange anther. The locality written on the specimen indicated simply that it had been collected in the Akyab District, now called Sittwe, of Arakan in October 1869. This information was not much to go on, but we would search for *Globba arracanensis* nonetheless.

As our vehicle headed down the slope toward the town of Ann, my euphoria from the plant collections we made on the ridge above us suddenly began to dissipate. As soon as we crossed the border into Rakhine State, which was marked by a large concrete signpost, immense stands of bamboo appeared. About ninety-five species of bamboo have been recorded from Myanmar. Stretching out before me on both sides of the road as far as I could see was a dense colony of one of these species of bamboo, which the Burmese call *kayin-wa* and is known botanically by the Latin name *Melocanna baccifera*. This particular species had stalks fifteen feet (about 4 m) tall and thickly covered the gently sloping hills in every direction. I was stunned. I knew that some grasses—and bamboos are considered to be members of the grass family—can grow

Dense thickets of bamboo carpet the hillsides that descend to the western coast of Myanmar in Rakhine State.

very fast and spread over large areas of disturbed habitats. I had seen bamboos cover relatively large areas in breaks in the forests at other places in Myanmar. But I was not prepared for the dense covering of *kayin-wa* that seemed to choke out every other plant in its path. A few medium-size trees were scattered across the bamboo-laden hillsides, but I doubted if anything else would grow under this thick mat of green. As I gazed out the window of our vehicle, the distant landscape gave me the impression of a well-manicured golf course, except that the lawn of grass was fifteen feet tall.

The professors told me that they did not know how long these bamboo forests had been here, nor whether they were natural or the result of a massive clearing of the hardwood forests, which were now present only on the tops of the ridges, out of the range of the bamboo.[7] If these lower hills had once been covered by forest, it must have been a long time ago, perhaps centuries. Were the British responsible for this immense clearing of the forest as part of their insatiable thirst for teak during the colonial occupation? Or did this destruction pre-date even the British, from the time when the Arakan dynasty ruled the land? I do not yet know the answer to this mystery. I do know that biodiversity, especially of plant life, is drastically reduced in these areas that are covered by an

The wild bamboo *Melocanna baccifera* rapidly spreads and takes over when forests are cut down.

unending monoculture of bamboo. Perhaps this is why my colleagues in the Forest Department had never wanted me to go to Rakhine State. But I was here.

Late in the afternoon we finally reached the lowlands at Ann, where we uneventfully passed through an immigration checkpoint. The guesthouse in Ann was once again nonexistent, so we pressed onward through the relentless bamboo that lined both sides of the road. Occasionally the bamboo was broken by small villages of wooden huts surrounded by parched cultivated fields. Finally, long after dark, we reached a large village called Dalet, situated along a river choked by the forests of mangroves that line the contours of the coast in Rakhine. Our guide was able to convince the caretaker of the local government guesthouse, which was officially reserved for visiting generals of the military, to open up a few rooms where we could spend the night. We more or less repeated

CHAPTER II

The flat agricultural lands of the floodplains on the western coast of Rakhine State.

the sequence of events of the night before, but this time instead of the cool breezes of the mountain ridge, I fell asleep in the sticky, humid atmosphere of the lowlands. I was not in the mood for even forced smiles. I had seen enough bamboo to last me the rest of my life.

The next day we were up at dawn and on our way. We were in land flat enough for rice cultivation. Bamboo, interspersed with scattered patches of ratty forest, still covered the hillsides. The most interesting plants were located in the roadside ditches, where aquatic species abounded. We made a few, but not many, specimen collections during the day and rolled into Mrauk U late in the afternoon.

Mrauk U (also called Mrohaung or Myohaung or Mynhaung) was the last capital of Arakan for over three hundred and fifty years before the land was conquered by the Burmese in the eighteenth century.[8] The kings of Arakan had constantly moved the location of the seat of government for various reasons before it was situated at Mrauk U on the banks of a tributary of the Kaladan River. The port city was crisscrossed with numerous canals and small lakes that

served as byways for transportation and communication, and for protection. Eventually the entire city was surrounded by a moat filled by the tidal waters of the bay. King Narameikhla, who founded Mrauk U in 1433, started a tradition of building impressive pagodas that was continued by later kings, and the ancient city rivals Bagan in the number and diversity of Buddhist temples and stupas. Eventually both internal and external wars by and among the feuding dynasties in Arakan, together with a series of devastating earthquakes in the mid-1770s, resulted in the decline of the Arakan empire and the successful invasion of the Burmese in 1785. Today the city is at the heart of the agricultural center of Rakhine State.

Mrauk U is an interesting city with a long history, and I spent some time exploring the ancient buildings and pagodas. Although most of the people of the region are Muslim, there is a small Buddhist monastery on the edge of town. At dusk one evening I happened upon a trio of young monks maybe ten or twelve years old. They had slipped out of the confines of the monastery and were sitting and laughing behind one of the three-hundred-year-old pagodas. One was smoking a cigarette and another had on earphones and was listening to a portable cassette player. They were surprised to see a foreigner, but were friendly

Young boys from the local monastery at Mrauk U.

and wanted me to take their photograph. These boys were spending their two-year obligatory term in the monastery, but obviously needed some "down time" to unwind after a day of prayer and giving merit. I knew just how they felt.

The heat of the coastal plain must have gotten to me, as I was feeling rather under the weather the morning we left Mrauk U for Sittwe. My body ached from head to foot with a deep fatigue, and the nausea was at times intense. Mike tried to encourage me over a cup of morning tea, but I was not looking forward to the long trip to Sittwe through never-ending rice paddies. We had to head northwest, across many small waterways, to reach the new bridge across the Saingdan River, then head due south to Sittwe. It was a dismal ride through boring agricultural fields, intensely degraded habitats, and inundated mangrove swamps, but we were able to find a few partially undisturbed areas in which to collect some gingers. Just above Sittwe we stopped at a dry creek bed that drained a rocky hillside covered with leafless trees and bamboos. It didn't look like much, but Mike and I decided to give it a try. Mike went ahead, and I pulled my aching body out of the vehicle. The professors from the university smoked a cigarette while we climbed.

Misty dawn among the ancient pagodas of Mrauk U.

A statue of the Buddha at Mrauk U.

The understory of the deciduous forest was very dry, but we did find a few plants, which had recently entered dormancy. As we headed back down the slope, I spotted a few shriveled rhizomes of what appeared to be a ginger clinging to a large moss-covered boulder that probably dripped water during the rainy season. I pulled the ginger from the rock and shoved it into my pocket. We hadn't found much, but at least we'd tried.

A pagoda overlooking the flat agricultural lands surrounding Mrauk U.

That evening I spent a nearly sleepless night at the Sittwe Hotel overlooking the Bay of Bengal. Our professors decided to celebrate our arrival in the capital city at a local restaurant, a place they had never visited. I just wanted to sleep. The next day I awoke feeling better. Mike cleaned our plants, I finished writing my field notes, and we took a very short flight back to Yangon. All in all we had collected fewer than one hundred plants in Rakhine State, which was not very much for the time we had spent getting there. Now I understood why Kingdon-Ward had never gone to the western coast of Burma. I am convinced that even during his era the habitats in this region were already heavily degraded and disturbed. I am sure that the bamboo was as aggressive then as it is now. But I had to see it firsthand.

Before leaving Myanmar, I decided to pay a visit to U Thet Htun and the Kandawgyi National Botanical Garden in Pyin-Oo-Lwin to see what progress had been made. Once again I was astounded at the level of activity in the gardens and the extent of development of both the garden and the town. U Thet Htun met me at the new airport in Mandalay. He brought his wife Daw Hnin

Hnin and their six-month-old son Pei Pyo Kyaw to welcome me. U Thet Htun
was looking a little domestic. We took a new shortcut to Pyin-Oo-Lwin and
were at the garden in less than two hours.

Yes, Pyin-Oo-Lwin was changing. The government was obviously putting
a lot of money into the development not only of the botanical garden but of the
town as well. It was not clear to me whether this development was associated with
the expanding military college and garrison just north of the town or whether the
government was developing Pyin-Oo-Lwin as a tourist destination. Whatever
the reason, the number of new guesthouses, hotels, restaurants, and commercial
garden nurseries and plant shops was impressive. U Thet Htun checked us into
the renovated Kandawgyi Lodge before we proceeded to the garden.

I barely recognized the National Botanical Garden. The new visitor entrance
was lined with towering wooden arches and trellises dripping with giant aroids
and vines. The newly-built visitor center included an entrance kiosk and gift
shop. Many of the features of the garden that were under construction when I

ABOVE AND RIGHT:
Bamboo poles tied
into rafts are floated
down the rivers to
construction markets.

CHAPTER II

had last visited Pyin-Oo-Lwin a year earlier were completed and fully functional. As we entered the garden, we were greeted by a stone elephant sculpture surrounded by a waterfall and bubbling fountain. The rock garden was now fully landscaped, with an entranceway constructed of huge trunks of petrified wood, probably from the area around Mount Popa. The path through the rock garden led to a "jungle walk," with a raised wooden platform that wound through what was previously considered an off-limits swampy zone of tangled vegetation. The bamboo garden, which had been revitalized by U Thet Htun, was now supplemented by a new planting of native species of bamboo from Myanmar that he had personally designed and labeled. An enclosed nursery of rose cultivars was nearly complete. The innovations were endless, and I was immensely impressed with the overall design, construction, and beauty of the garden.

Yet all of these new plantings, walkways, and designs were dwarfed by the most striking construction project at Kandawgyi. To the east on a small rise overlooking the lakes and ponds, a horde of workers swarmed over the scaffolding that enclosed a giant wooden tower that soared to 330 feet (100 m) in height. This "observation tower" built in a neo-Burmese style was evidently the brain-

child of Secretary One, who wanted a lasting monument to mark the power of his regime. Evidently a similar tower was being built at Bagan to rival the numerous temples and pagodas constructed by past kings and royalty of Burma. My earliest vision of developing a plant research center at Myanmar's only significant botanical garden was now clouded and overshadowed by this gigantic memorial to the current rulers of Myanmar.

Later that evening I sat in my room at the Kandawgyi Lodge, listening to the peaceful outdoor sounds as the night began to fall. I realized how much I loved this little town and this country, despite the eccentricities of Secretary One and the obsessive actions of the military. They could build as many colossal towers as they wished, but the serenity of Pyin-Oo-Lwin and its botanical garden would continue on as it had for centuries, from kings to conquering invaders to dictators. The cool highland breezes blew gently through my open window.

Myanmar in the dry season is very difficult for botanists. Although the roads are passable, and it is easy to get around, the plants of interest are dormant and generally inaccessible. Still, during this trip we had been able to find some important species to add to our plant inventory. A year after our journey to Mrauk U, Mike was able to propagate in our research greenhouses many of the plants that we had collected in their dormant phase in Rakhine State. The most exciting was the shriveled rhizome I had torn off the big moss-covered boulder right before we reached Sittwe. At that point in my fever the plant didn't look like much, but when Mike coaxed it into flower back in Washington, it had purple and white flowers with a bright yellow lip. It was *Globba arracanensis*, one of the prime objectives of our trip. We had succeeded in finding one of the least-known species of the region, but we didn't know it at the time. I also learned after I returned home that the fever and other symptoms I had been suffering at Mrauk U were due to a latent case of Lyme disease, probably contracted from ticks in the woodlands along the Potomac River in Maryland, where I frequently walked with my dog. So much for the perils of exotic places.

"A king, forced by the hazards of war or maybe only to gratify a whim, will change his capital and, founding a very new city, build a palace and temples and richly ornament them; and in a few generations the seat of government, owing to another hazard or another whim, moving elsewhere, the city is abandoned and desolation usurps the place of so much transitory pleasure."

W. Somerset Maugham,
The Gentleman in the Parlour, 1930

Globba arracanensis,
a ginger fortuitously
found after 130
years near Sittwe in
Rakhine State.

Buddhist Reverence and Respect Help Protect the Forests

"Most of the focus at the Earth Summit at Rio was on the definition of sustainable development. Buddha had already defined its principles twenty-five centuries ago. But Buddhism has a practical element. Its philosophy is not about life, but of how to live it."

Ven. Dharmaviriyo Mahathero. *Natural Environment and Buddhalogical Perspective*

It was late in the afternoon of the first day of the festival of Kathina, the celebration during the full moon of November when new robes are respectfully presented to all Buddhist monks. I was sitting on top of an ancient pagoda in the city of Bagan as the day was coming to an end. The deep saffron-colored sun was setting in the west over the Irrawaddy River. Simultaneously the full moon was rising on the opposite horizon, above the hundreds of pagodas and shrines that mark this site as one of the most sacred in Myanmar. The air was still, and from my vantage point the country seemed to be at peace. I was to learn that this serenity could be easily broken at any time in Myanmar.

The calm I had witnessed in Bagan on that November day was shattered a few years later by a rare and massive public protest against the ruling military government. The protest had started in reaction to a fivefold increase imposed by the government in the price of fuel, including gasoline and cooking fuel. Previously gas and oil prices had been heavily subsidized by the military and were therefore affordable for most of the population. The escalating conflict in the Middle East, especially after the invasion of Iraq by the United States in 2003, and the subsequent increase to nearly one hundred dollars per barrel of crude oil on the global market had affected the struggling economy of Myanmar, already suffering from years of international trade sanctions. The military junta, which had maintained artificially low fuel prices for years, could no longer

A guardian spirit of the pagoda on Mandalay Hill.

provide significant subsidies. Overnight, costs for running the buses, the trucks, and the few cars in Myanmar, as well as for cooking on gas stoves and powering the many privately owned generators, which provided reliable electricity to small shop owners, skyrocketed. For the local Burmese, who were dependent on various types of petroleum and petroleum products for their livelihoods and everyday activities, this situation rapidly became a crisis.

The first marches on the streets of Yangon to protest the increase in fuel prices started during the week of August 15, 2007. A few hundred civilians, mostly students and pro-democracy advocates, paraded through the city carrying hand-painted signs and chanting well-worn anti-government slogans. Onlookers were sympathetic, but did not join the protesters in any large numbers. Within a few days it was reported that many of the protesters had been arrested or had gone into hiding after intimidation by plainclothes police. Unexpectedly, several days later, a long line of four hundred monks walking in two solemn rows quietly marched to Shwedagon Pagoda in a silent protest at the government's action. This time the public did take notice.[1] Thousands of local citizens cheered and encouraged the mostly young, maroon-robed monks,

Sunset over the city of Bagan.

The Shwezigon Pagoda, one of the more recent temples built at Bagan.

especially when they were locked out of their destination at the world-famous pagoda by government forces.

Within days the number of monks marching in protest in Yangon and other major cities around the country swelled to thousands, with an even larger number of civilians rallying alongside, symbolically protecting them. The reason that the normally reserved residents of the many Buddhist monasteries suddenly became involved in these protests was never completely clear to observers outside of the country. However, it was known to everyone inside Myanmar that several weeks earlier, in the city of Pakkoku, soldiers had manhandled a small group of monks who were protesting the increase in fuel costs. Pakkoku, a small city in central Myanmar on the banks of the Irrawaddy River just northwest of Bagan, is the site of several large, old, and revered monasteries. Expecting an apology that never came for the government's harsh treatment of the protesting monks in Pakkoku, monks throughout the country took to the streets in peaceful demonstrations.[2] In some cases, the monks marched with their alms bowls held upside down, in a figurative gesture of refusal to accept alms from members of the military and police forces.[3]

At first the military simply monitored the marches and refrained from any direct confrontation with the monks. After five days of continuing protests, the number of marchers in Yangon surpassed a hundred thousand, led by ten thousand monks. At that point the ruling government issued the first warning of a crackdown if the protestors did not cease their marches.[4] The demonstrations continued, with the monks denouncing the "violent, mean, cruel, ruthless, pitiless kings, the great thieves who live by stealing from the national treasury."[5] Nine days after the monks began their protests in Yangon, the crackdown began, first with a ban on all rallies, then the use of tear gas to disperse the marchers, then finally a violent confrontation between soldiers and protesters.[6] Within two days the monks had been effectively confined to their monasteries, the streets were completely cleared of civilians, a curfew was imposed, and most communications with the outside world were cut off. A week after the crackdown began, little news was coming out of Myanmar. The headlines describing the protests and demonstrations by the monks, which had filled the front pages of major Western newspapers such as *The New York Times* and *The Washington Post*, were quickly replaced by short, single-paragraph reports buried in the back pages of the international section.[7] The ruling junta, which had been in control since 1988, had efficiently suppressed another uprising by the Burmese people, this time initiated and led by the much-respected Buddhist monks of the country.

"And there was silence too in the monasteries. There are perhaps a dozen of them in Keng Tung and their high roofs stand out when you look at the town from the little hill on which is the circuit-house. Each one stands in its compound and in the compound are a number of crumbling pagodas. The great hall in which the Buddha, enormous, sits in his hieratic attitude, surrounded by others, eight or ten, hardly smaller, is like a barn, but its roof is supported by huge columns of teak, gilt or lacquer, and the wooden walls and the rafters are gilt or lacquered too. Rude paintings of scenes in the Master's life hang from the eaves. It is dark and solemn, but the Buddhas sit on their lotus leaves in the gloaming like gods who have had their day, and now neglected, but indifferent to neglect, in their decaying grandeur of gilt and mosaic continue to reflect on suffering and the end of suffering, transitoriness and the eightfold path. Their aloofness is almost terrifying."

W. Somerset Maugham,
The Gentleman in the Parlour, 1930

It was a mistake, as some media reports suggested at the time, to interpret the social and political crisis that struck Myanmar in August and September of 2007, as solely based on the desire of the Myanmar people for democracy.[8] The confrontation was about more than the right to self-determination, although many joined the marches in protest against the repressive government. The standoff between the Buddhist community and the military junta during those months revealed two important aspects of life in Myanmar, one social and the other environmental. The first was that Buddhism as practiced by most Burmese provides the foundation for much of the community and social structure in Myanmar, and hence the political stability of the country. When the monks joined and then led the protests, the entire populace followed their example. The second aspect was that Myanmar's natural and environmental resources, which had been degraded and unwisely managed by the government for decades, were the only hope for economic development. The rising fuel costs, despite the rich natural gas and petroleum deposits known to exist in Myanmar, were a symbol of corrupt resource management by the ruling junta. The economic hardship caused by the jump in prices and immediately felt by the people was the spark that set off the demonstrations, which were subsequently taken over and directed by the monks.

King Anawratha, who oversaw the construction of thousands of religious shrines and temples, which still exist in the magnificent city of Bagan, introduced Theravada Buddhism into Myanmar from India in the eleventh century. From that early time Buddhism then spread throughout the broader region of Southeast Asia to eventually include the countries now called Thailand, Laos, and Cambodia.[9] Today Buddhism is practiced by over 90 percent of Myanmar's population. Theravada Buddhism, in its essence, is not only a religion but a way of life that permeates interactions among people as well as between people and their environments. The interconnectedness of Buddhism and social organization in Myanmar is long-standing and strong. After Cyclone Nargis devastated the Irrawaddy Delta region of Lower Myanmar in May 2008, the government was slow to deliver help and obstructed the distribution of foreign aid. However, monks from the local Buddhist monastery, or *kyaung*, quickly came to the aid of villagers and provided critical assistance for recovery.[10]

Three central notions are at the core of Theravada Buddhism: the Buddha, who is the teacher of self-discipline; the Dharma, which is the body of wisdom that the Buddha teaches; and the Sangha, where the teaching is done. It has been said that the Burmese people's dedication to the Buddha, the Dharma, and the Sangha provides stability, continuity, and unity for individuals, communities, and the country. For example, nearly all male Burmese (as well as some female) spend a part of their early lives as novices in a local *kyaung*. A young boy will enter the *kyaung* for one to two years, usually before he is married. It is common for an elaborate ceremony to precede the shaving of the boy's head and his entrance into the Sangha. Although a male may commit to spending a fixed period in the monastery, he may also leave at any time, even before the year is up. No stigma is attached to an early departure because it is recognized that one's status as a layperson has been enhanced by any time spent in the monastery learning the Dharma. An older male at a later time in his life may also shave his head and return to the Sangha for a "refresher" period. This early direct exposure

OPPOSITE, TOP: The wooden Shwe Nandaw Kyaung Monastery in Mandalay.

OPPOSITE, BOTTOM: Detail on the facade of the Shwe Nandaw Kyaung Monastery.

RIGHT: Young monks on the streets of Pyinmina.

of all males to monastic life is emblematic of the social stability and tradition that Buddhism provides for the population at large. The top monk of a monastery, called the *pongyi*, serves as teacher, councillor, and healer in the village or town where the *kyaung* is located. The *pongyi* rarely participates in any political activities that take place in the town.

Monks do not beg, even though it is quite common in the morning to see long lines of monks of all sizes and ages in their red robes and bare feet going from house to house and from shop to shop to receive food for the day. Through this activity monks allow laypersons to earn merit by giving food and money. This merit is important in determining how a person will be reincarnated in later lives. The great number of Buddhist pagodas in Myanmar is a result of the merit earned by the people who have financed these shrines. The fifty-eight tons of gold leaf that have been applied to the Shwedagon Pagoda in Yangon, the most sacred of all Buddhist sites in Myanmar, are also a result of such merit earning. Monks, through their monastic activities, and the laity, through their donations to the Sangha, are constantly awarding merit to each other, and thereby establishing a universal pattern of socialization that serves to bind the community together.

The tradition of training all boys for a period of time in the monasteries of Myanmar accounted in part for the large number of young monks who participated in the antigovernment demonstrations of 2007. It was no coincidence that once the Buddhist monks rose up against the injustice and economic hardship imposed by the military regime on the people, the general populace followed their actions.[11] The normally apolitical Sangha gave an obvious signal that everyone in the community should participate in the marches. It was also not surprising that the military rulers were for a long time reluctant to suppress the monks; they and their soldiers had been educated in the very same monasteries where the discontent had surfaced. When the protesting monks, as they marched through the streets of Yangon, turned their alms bowls upside down, the generals and soldiers, almost all of whom practice Buddhism, clearly understood that they would be prevented from earning merit by giving to the monks, and ultimately condemned to a lower form of life in the next incarnation. This same confrontation of the regime by the Buddhist Sangha had occurred seventeen years earlier, after the military junta discounted the results of the 1990 elections in which Aung San Suu Kyi and her National League for Democracy had won an overwhelming majority of the votes.[12] Then as now, many observers viewed the military's eventual crackdown on monks and monasteries as a moral insult and an attack on the basic social order of Myanmar, and thereby not only a demonstration of the junta's weakness but the first sign of its eventual downfall. Only time will tell if this interpretation was correct.

"In the full tide of the noon the sun burned all the color from the landscape so that the trees and dwarf scrub that grew wildly where in time past were the busy haunts of men, were pale and grey; but with the declining day the colour crept back, like an emotion that tempers the character and has been submerged for a while by the affairs of the world, and trees and scrub were again a sumptuous and living green. The sun set on the other side of the river and a red cloud in the west was reflected on the tranquil bosom of the Irrawaddy."

W. Somerset Maugham,
The Gentleman in the Parlour, 1930

In addition to providing an essential part of the social fabric of Myanmar, Buddhism has had a significant influence on the relationship of the Burmese people to their environment. In learning the Dharma, monks are taught that decisive events in the Buddha's life occurred in natural settings and usually under important trees.[13] All Buddhists know that Siddhartha Gautama was born on a full-moon day in the month of May in the shade of a grove of *sala* trees (*Shorea robusta*), that he attained enlightenment thirty-five years later under a *bodhi* tree (*Ficus religiosa*), and that he eventually passed into *parinirvana* (the final deathless state) under twin *sala* trees at the age of eighty years.[14] For this reason, both the *bodhi* tree and the *sala* tree are treated with great respect. The Buddhist philosophy of nonviolence, benevolence, and compassion toward living beings, which is also taught in the monasteries, is responsible for instilling a universal respect for nature. Yet this respect, whereby all animals (and sometimes plants) are viewed as sentient, living individuals deserving of compassion as taught by the Buddha, has not been immediately transferred to species,

CHAPTER 12

landscapes, and ecosystems. Hence, the followers of Buddhism have not been expected to engage in the "active" promotion of conservation except as a corollary of the protection of individuals. The concept of environmental conservation is compatible with, but not actively promoted by, Buddhism in Myanmar.[15]

In some parts of the world, the modern environmental movement has adopted certain Buddhist practices. These conservation practitioners are often referred to as "eco-Buddhists" or "Green Buddhists." Many books and papers on Buddhism and nature have been written, and the basis for a Buddhist environmental ethic discussed and debated. Organizations and groups such as the Alliance of Religions and Conservation and the Forum on Religion and Ecology are attempting to integrate religious traditions with environmental ethics.[16] Environmentalists who practice Buddhism in developed countries appear to be the most energetic in promoting conservation. As stated by one eco-Buddhist, "Buddhism places more emphasis on our 'internal ecology.' A person enlightened with Buddhist ideals and practicing the same can contribute valuably in saving the physical, biological, and social environment. The Buddhist Way of Life is ultimately compatible with the conservation of Nature. Therefore if the destruction of Nature follows from the human folly, following the Buddhist attitudes will reverse that folly and preserve Nature."[17]

In some countries, such as Thailand, monks have begun to take a more vigorous stance in protecting habitats and in conserving species. In Myanmar the practice of Theravada Buddhism by the majority of the population has not resulted in the development of an active conservation movement among either the monks or the laity. When appropriate, local people take some actions to protect the environment in order to gain merit, but no concerted effort has been made by the Sangha to conserve species or endangered habitats.[18] In general nongovernmental organizations, especially international conservation organizations, have been less active in Myanmar than in other countries of Southeast Asia, especially with regard to conservation of plants. Although some of these organizations, such as the Wildlife Conservation Society, have been instrumental in working with the military government of Myanmar to establish large tracts of land as nature reserves and protected areas (such as the Hukawng Valley Tiger Reserve), these areas are still vulnerable to exploitation by the government itself.[19] With a large part of their country still covered by pristine and forested habitats, and many species of plants and animals still undiscovered and undocumented by scientists, the Burmese people's active role in the protection of their unique environments and natural resources will be an essential ingredient for successful conservation in Myanmar.

Despite the absence of a unified conservation movement in the Sangha and general population of Myanmar, Buddhism has been responsible for the

protection of habitats and species for centuries, albeit in a more passive way. Its role in long-term conservation is evident in the protection and preservation of forests and natural landscapes around Buddhist monasteries and shrines through-out the country. In practice, the passive activities of monks led by the *pongyis* in following the principle of nonviolence toward all life, including the local flora and fauna, have indirectly protected habitats and the species diversity they contain. Many sacred shrines are located in natural forested areas. During certain Buddhist festivals held at various times of the year, pilgrims, often in large numbers, visit these shrines to honor the Buddha. In some cases the pilgrims, who walk for many miles carrying their food and clothing, camp near the sacred sites during the festival. At these times, pristine areas are transformed into small cities, with thou-sands of pilgrims making the trek to pay homage to the Buddha's footprint or a strand of his hair kept in a local shrine. The monks, who tend to these shrines throughout the year, play an important role in urging the pilgrims to respect the natural environments during these brief visits. In nonfestival times, the forests are maintained as sacred areas off-limits to agriculture and the timber industry.

A tin pagoda along the banks of the Irrawaddy River, below Bhamo.

CHAPTER 12

The Nature and Wildlife Conservation Division of the Forest Department has taken advantage of the natural sites associated with sacred shrines in their development of a system of protected areas in Myanmar. My friend and mentor U Uga, who was director of the division when I first visited Myanmar, was particularly instrumental in establishing national parks and wildlife sanctuaries in Buddhist sacred areas. As of 2005 Myanmar had designated thirty-four parks and sanctuaries across the country in many different localities that represented a broad range of habitat types, from mangroves and marine environments in the south to dry zone sanctuaries in the center of the country to high montane alpine forests in the far north. Of course, not all of these protected areas are sacred Buddhist retreats. However, in many of the wildlife sanctuaries that I visited it was possible to find an important Buddhist shrine. More than once I was able to see these nature sanctuaries transformed over the course of a few days from isolated pristine forests to makeshift villages teeming with pilgrims during a three-day festival.

Popa Mountain National Park, Alaungdaw Kathapa National Park,

Shwesettaw Wildlife Sanctuary, Shwe-U-Daung Wildlife Sanctuary, Chatthin Wildlife Sanctuary, Tamanthi Wildlife Sanctuary, and many others include forested habitats that have been maintained for many decades and even centuries as sacred Buddhist sites. The larger, more important nature sanctuaries have been assigned support staff by the Forest Department to maintain and patrol their borders. Many of the smaller, more isolated protected areas have been designated as sanctuaries on paper only. These latter areas are especially dependent on local monks and monasteries for protection and care. In a fundamental way Myanmar must rely on its own unique form of biodiversity conservation through a combination of the Buddhist principles of nonviolence and respect for all living things and the efforts of a core of foresters dedicated to the sustainable management of their natural forests and resources. New opportunities for forging

BELOW LEFT: The misty tree-covered cliffs in the second defile of the Irrawaddy River, below Bhamo.

BELOW RIGHT: A small forest shrine on "Elephant Rock."

CHAPTER 12

Early morning along a small stream at Alaungdaw Kathapa National Park.

alliances between Burmese conservationists, academic institutions, and international NGOs may be the only way forward in future conservation efforts.[20]

From my vantage point atop the pagoda in Bagan, I could better understand how the Buddhist way of life had shaped the daily activities and social interactions of the Burmese people. I could only hope that this same way of life would also protect the forests and natural areas of the country for centuries to come.

CHAPTER 13 *Mount Victoria: Walking in the Steps of a Giant*

The botanist need never burden himself with much apparatus in the field. A bag for plants is better than the metal vasculum sold to budding botanists in England; one or two tobacco tins are carried in the pocket for very small specimens, and a biscuit tin may be taken as well for fragile flowers. Field-glasses, a pocket lens for resolving doubtful points quickly with fresh material, a note-book and pencil, a compass, a strong knife, a pair of Rolcut secateurs for cutting prickly shrubs and the tough stems of Rhododendrons, and some string—the sort of miscellania a schoolboy might cram into his pocket—completes the list. A lunch ration consisting of several biscuits, a few raisins or figs, and a slab of chocolate is also taken, more in case of accident than to be eaten at a fixed hour.[1]

—Frank Kingdon-Ward, *Plant Hunting on the Edge of the World*

In this passage Kingdon-Ward was most likely understating the botanical equipment he carried on his plant-collecting expeditions in Upper Burma in the early 1900s. After all, on each trek into the mountains he traveled with a large cadre of local porters and pack animals who carried all of the equipment he needed. Omissions from his botanist's list were the plant presses, straps, and drying ovens he undoubtedly used to prepare his scientific specimens. In addition to his many popular books, we know most about what Kingdon-Ward saw and discovered during his explorations from his field notebooks and his botanical specimens, which are housed in museums and herbaria in Europe, North America, and Asia.

Today's plant explorers carry all the same apparatus as Kingdon-Ward (without the vasculum), plus more. The preparation of dried and pressed plant specimens remains the standard method for field documentation of plant diversity around the world. The labor-intensive process of making specimens has not

Curcuma roscoeana, a wild ginger of Myanmar.

My field assistants from Yangon University preparing botanical specimens.

changed for over one hundred years. What has changed is the introduction of electronic data-gathering and field-recording paraphernalia that are now carried by nearly all botanists as they travel for fieldwork into remote places. Electronic global positioning systems (GPS), which used to weigh several pounds, now fit on one's wrist and can pinpoint to a few feet the exact locality where a plant specimen has been found. Field data, instead of being scribbled into small note-books or recorded on paper tags, as was the preferred habit of Kingdon-Ward, are now directly entered into electronic databases on lightweight laptop or handheld computers. Digital cameras are routinely used to snap high-resolution photos of the flowers and fruits of a specimen as it is collected to provide a more accurate portrait of the plant than can be described in field notes. And don't forget the mobile or satellite phone that may be used to connect the field botanist to the outside world. I have even seen a new-generation botanist intimately connected to his iPod as he tramped through the rain forests of South America.

The other aspect of plant collecting that has been developed since Kingdon-Ward's time is the application of DNA sequencing to the botanical sciences. Much of what we know today about the evolutionary relationships and classification of plants is the result of DNA studies carried out in laboratories by botanists after they return home with their specimens. Whether it is used in determining the relationship of one species to another or devising an entirely new classification of flowering plants, DNA sequence information has become critical for most botanists as they explore the natural world.[2]

It is generally difficult to obtain high-quality DNA from traditionally dried and pressed plant specimens. In order to conduct DNA-based studies, one of the new responsibilities of taxonomists is to preserve tissue samples in tanks of liquid nitrogen or packets of silica gel along with the field-collected specimens. When the preserved tissue samples are brought back to the lab, DNA can be more readily extracted and sequenced. Giant tissue banks of tens of thousands of such samples are now being assembled at major research institutes, including the Royal Botanic Gardens at Kew, the Missouri Botanical Garden, and the Smithsonian Institution. As the world's natural habitats are shrinking at an ever-accelerating rate, our knowledge of biodiversity is inversely burgeoning at an equal speed. However, this rate may not be fast enough for us to be able to record and analyze the many species that are going extinct.

Kingdon-Ward, along with many other plant explorers of his day, greatly enlarged our knowledge of the plant life in Asia through his many expeditions to Burma and surrounding countries. Yet it is clear from his books that his field trips during the latter part of his career were increasingly hampered by the political situation in the countries where he was working. Reading through some of his archived correspondence at the Natural History Museum in London, I found a number of letters to and from local magistrates and British officials in which he was denied permission to travel to parts of Assam, Tibet, and China. In a few instances he was scolded by an officer for crossing a border or entering a town for which he had not been given permission. I found letters in which directors of botanical institutes in the West refused to help Kingdon-Ward import plant specimens into the United States and England, even after he had painstakingly collected them in the most obscure regions of Burma. I am not sure if it is comforting or disturbing to know that we still encounter today the same resistance from local government officials to our botanical efforts to explore and document the flora of new places; it seems ironic, when one considers that these habitats are being continually degraded by over-exploitation.

One of Kingdon-Ward's last plant-collecting trips to Burma was in the 1950s. His career had stretched over four decades since his first visit to Burma in 1914. This last trip was centered on an expedition to Mount Victoria in the southern Chin

A letter of reprimand from Lord Zetland, noting that Kingdon-Ward had illegally entered Tibet on several occasions.

COPY.

India Office,

Whitehall,

6th May 1937.

My dear Lloyd,

I have looked into the case of Kingdon Ward about whom you wrote to me on 27th April. In 1935 he penetrated into Tibet from Assam without the permission of the Lhasa Government, which is of course required, and the Tibetans protested to us about the incident. They said that it would be no use Kingdon Ward applying for permission to visit Tibet in future.

More recently another case in which two British explorers entered Tibet from Burma without the necessary passport caused the Tibetans to protest to us again. We do not want a third such incident, because of its likely effect on our general relations with Tibet, which are rather at a turning point.

It was for this reason that the Government of India obtained from Kingdon Ward, before he left Burma for Yunnan in March, an undertaking not to cross the Tibetan boundary, which it was explained to him meant that he must keep out of the area north of the latitude 28° North and West of longitude 102° East. The Government of India are being asked whether some relaxation of this interpretation of Kingdon Ward's undertaking may be possible and if so to inform Kingdon Ward direct. I am, however, afraid that they will not in any case be able to allow him to go as far west as longitude 98° East, which would open to him an area under the effective control of the Tibetan Government.

Yours sincerely,

(Signed) ZETLAND.

The Rt. Hon. Lord Lloyd, GCSI, GCIE, DSO.

Hills in the western part of the country. At over 10,000 feet (3,000 m) in elevation, Mount Victoria (now called Natma Taung) is one of the tallest peaks in that region of Burma. Kingdon-Ward was particularly interested in the alpine species that occurred at the summit of the mountain, and he collected plants on Mount Victoria over a period of eight months, from the middle of the dry season through the time of the monsoons. When he first reached Mount Victoria, as he described in *Pilgrimage for Plants*, "the grass slopes, smarting under the fierce sun, were completely dried up, with many bare patches, and it was difficult to tell what plants had grown there."[3] But when he returned several months later "the rains had been going full-blast for five weeks, and the grass slopes facing south were emerald-green, and brilliant with flowers."[4] A species he discovered after the monsoons had started was of particular interest to me. "Very prominent was Roscoea, only a few inches high, each plant was capped by a single (rarely by two) large deep-purple flower, which open in succession. They looked very like orchids."[5] But they were not orchids; they were gingers, and these plants were what I was seeking in my own plant explorations in Myanmar.

After my most recent successful trip to Myanmar, my relationship with the

ABOVE, LEFT: Professors and staff on the campus of Yangon University.

ABOVE, RIGHT: Assistant Professor Aye Pei from Yangon University with *Curcuma roscoeana*.

CHAPTER 13

Botany Department at the University of Yangon had expanded considerably. Now I was back in Yangon. At the invitation of Professor Daw Aye Kyi, I was prepared to deliver several lectures on botany and also conduct a workshop for junior faculty and students in the department. I appreciated her invitation, and hoped to combine the teaching activities with at least one and maybe two plant collecting trips (to Mount Victoria?) during my current visit. I knew that the only way to develop the science of botany and plant taxonomy in Myanmar was to train more young botanists and get them out into the field, collecting plants. During this year I wanted to concentrate on that goal.

The previous year during the monsoon season I had taken a group of university staff, including one assistant professor and two young lecturers, on a trip to collect plants along the west coast of Myanmar. It was an opportunity for them to get out of the classroom and into the field, something they generally do not have the time or the resources to do on their own. On my way to Yangon, as I was flying over the South China Sea, I could sense the monsoons raging below. I knew that any fieldwork during this season would be tough, but it was the right time to find many of the wet-season gingers in flower. When I arrived, I reviewed the preapproved itinerary, spent a few days gathering supplies, and then set off with my colleagues to the west.

Our planned route was to head northwest from Yangon across the lower end of the Rakhine Yoma hills to the coastal town of Gwa; from there we would head north along the coast to the towns of Ngapali and Thandwe, skirting the western slopes of the mountain range that ran parallel to the coast. North of Thandwe is Taunggok, a low-lying delta region and active port town on the Bay of Bengal, where we would spend some time before we headed back east across a mountain pass to the city of Pyay on the Irrawaddy River, then back to Yangon. The plan seemed simple enough.

It was the month of June, and the day we left Yangon it was raining hard. The thick gray sky, typical of the monsoon season, loomed ominously as we loaded up our gear into an old school bus that was to be our transport. Our team included Dr. Aye Pe, who was an assistant professor and a microbiologist by training but who declared himself ready to learn some botany, and Daw Than Than Htay and Daw Win Win Aung, who were both junior lecturers associated with the herbarium. In addition to our driver and his assistant, U Htay Aung and his son had been assigned to accompany us to arrange logistics along the way. Mike and I rounded out the botanical team. The group was large, but I had high hopes for what we might find. Those hopes were soon rewarded as we descended the slopes toward the Bay of Bengal. The evergreen forests were full of gingers, and we collected large specimens of *Etlingera*, *Amomum*, *Alpinia*, and *Elettariopsis*. These plants are characteristic of this type of forest, and it was encouraging to find them so easily. Then, as we reached lower elevations, the habitats quickly changed to more seasonal forests full of very different types of ginger, including *Globba, Curcuma,* and *Zingiber.*[6] Perhaps it was weather patterns or soil types that were responsible for these adjacent, but dissimilar, forest zones. Whatever the ecological reasons for these variations, we were fortunate to find many different species of gingers.

I was encouraged when the sun appeared from behind the thick clouds for a few hours in the afternoon. Even though the heat can be intense when the sun is out, it is much, much easier to collect and prepare plant specimens when it is not pouring rain. The land leeches also seem to be less annoying when the sun is bright. We had already "collected" our share of these blood-sucking creatures, and appreciated the respite from their attacks. But by early evening the rains had returned, and we didn't see the sun again for a week.

On the second day out from Gwa, Mike and I discovered a species of ginger that was exceedingly striking. It was not a large plant, but you couldn't

ABOVE: A lunch break on a rainy mountain road near the border of Rakhine State in the monsoon season.

LEFT: *Globba wengerii,* a ginger with a very bizarre flower that resembles an insect.

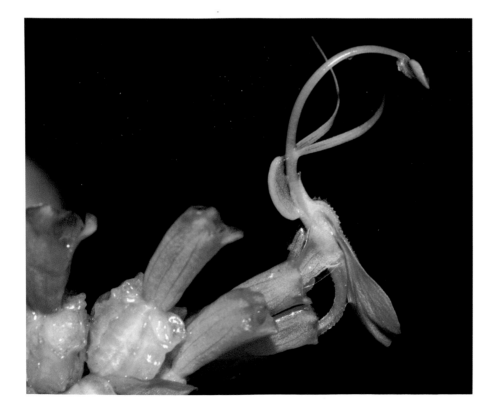

The muddy streets of Thandwe, on the west coast of Myanmar.

miss it because of its bright orange flowers shaped like bizarre insects. It was another species of *Mantisia* (now included in the genus *Globba* by taxonomists).[7] We had collected other species related to this *Mantisia* at Alungdaw Kathapa National Park and along the Chindwin River. But the flowers of those plants, which were locally called the Burmese equivalent of "Dancing Ladies," were pale yellows and lavenders in color and delicately sculpted in form. The flowers of this new species looked more like "Invaders from Mars," with their outstretched tendrils and nodding, hoodlike stamen. The species was an exciting find, but we didn't know until we returned to the Smithsonian that we had rediscovered *Mantisia wengeri*. It was quite abundant in the understory of the forested foothills, and we made many collections for study.

Ngapali Beach is a resort area, to which tourists can easily fly from Yangon or Bagan during the dry season. Now the heavy rains and rough surf were not particularly inviting for tourists, and we quickly passed through the town and headed north to Thandwe and eventually Taunggok. The rains had not let up, but we were collecting quite a few species of gingers and other interesting plants, including many aroids, the white-flowered *Tacca*, various ferns, and some interesting legumes. When we reached Taunggok several days later, one of the hardest sustained torrential downpours I had ever seen hit the town while we were stopped for lunch. Buckets and buckets of rain poured from the sky for about thirty minutes. Everyone on the street was soaked, the main roads were all flooded, and in the side streets people were wading up to their waists in water. This was the monsoon. Taunggok is one of the dingiest towns in this part of Myanmar, and I spent a sleepless night listening to the generator grinding away outside the window of my rather seedy room in a dilapidated guesthouse. As we headed up the slopes toward Pyay, I was not particularly sad to leave Taunggok.

The final leg of the trip was to take us across a pass in the Rakhine Yoma at an elevation of 2,600 feet (800 m) on the way to Pyay. Although this elevation is not particularly high, I had been told that some interesting cloud forest could be found at the top, and I knew that a cloud-forest habitat might hold some potentially new plant species. My expectations were soon dampened as we entered a large expanse of cutover former agricultural land that had eventually been replaced by a massive monoculture of wild bamboo. I had seen this same choking growth of bamboo covering the mountains and hillsides further north in Rakhine State, and it was a great disappointment to think that we would travel through such poor habitats all the way back to Pyay, sixty miles (100 km) away.

At thirty miles (50 km) from Taunggok the bamboo began to thin out, and we finally entered what appeared to be the cloud forest that had been described

A local family in the hills of the Rakhine Yoma. Note the "umbrella" hanging on the wall next to the door.

CHAPTER 13

ABOVE, LEFT: Gingers growing on the branches of trees in the wet cloud forest.

ABOVE, RIGHT: A new species of *Curcuma* growing on steep slopes in the cloud forest above Pyay.

to me. The elevation was around 2,000 feet (600 m), and the area was not large. Here the bamboo had completely disappeared, and the hills were covered in a thick forest of towering trees in the oak family. Epiphytes, including some gingers, hung off the branches in the dense fog. Everything was dripping from the rain and mist. The driver looked at me, and I signaled him to pull the bus to the side of the road. We all jumped out. The hills were very steep, and it was tough navigating the rocky, slippery slopes. I looked across a small valley. In the mist on the other side of the valley, in a small clearing, were a few plants with reddish orange flowers on tall stalks. The more I looked, the more I wanted to see these plants close up. Mike and I plunged off the ridgetop and worked our way laterally along the hillside, hanging onto whatever we could grab. When I finally got to the plant, I knew that the climb had been worth the effort. The plants

An inflorescence of the new species of *Curcuma* with bright orange, wide-open flowers.

were gingers, and belonged to a species that I had never seen before in Myanmar or anywhere else—a new species in the genus *Curcuma*. We collected as many specimens as we could carry, and carefully worked our way back to the road. As we processed the plants, recording localities and elevations with our GPS, taking digital photos, pressing specimens, digging rhizomes to grow in our greenhouses,

The city of Pyay and its golden pagoda on the shores of the Irrawaddy River.

and preserving tissue in silica gel for DNA analyses, I realized that this particular species, with its appendaged leaves, red-bracted inflorescences, and wide-open flowers, had many special characteristics that would undoubtedly make it a major addition to our knowledge of the gingers of Myanmar. When we finished, we headed down the other side of the Rakhine Yoma, leaving this cloud-enshrouded mountain pass behind. After we had traveled for several hours across the flat plains of the central valley, the surreal but beautiful Shwesandaw Pagoda became visible across the river, and we knew we had almost reached Pyay.

In retrospect, that rainy trip along the Ngapali Coast to Gwa, Thandwe, Taunggok, and finally Pyay yielded some very interesting plant collections, including several new species, which significantly added to our inventory and understanding of the flora of Myanmar. Sometimes it is necessary to go a long way for a few very special plants. More importantly, we had to be there during the monsoon season, as some of the plant species that we collected would not be in flower at any other time of the year. And plants weren't the only species we collected on that trip: I had preserved as specimens several leeches that had attached themselves to Mike's leg when we stopped in the cloud forest. Eventually a friend who is a specialist on the classification of leeches at the American Museum of Natural History in New York City would identify the cloud-forest leech as a species potentially new to science.

But that was last year. Now it was November, the monsoons were over, and the cool season with clear blue skies was here in Yangon. This time I arrived in the country ready to give my lectures at the university: first a two-hour talk on gingers and their relatives to introduce the students to these plants, and then a more focused workshop on plant structure and flower biology. I was prepared to teach the courses and excited about interacting with the students, but I was overjoyed when Professor Daw Aye Kyi told me that we had also received permission for a field trip to Mount Victoria once the teaching was over. After many years of waiting and many unfulfilled requests for security clearance, I was finally going to be able to see the locality where Kingdon-Ward had collected some of his most spectacular gingers and alpine plants fifty years earlier. Compared to my last trip to Taunggok in the monsoon season, November was a beautiful time of the year to go to Mount Victoria. I finally had permission, but the logistics of getting there were going to be the next challenge.

The region surrounding Natma Taung, or Mount Victoria, was designated a national park a number of years ago by the Forest Department. Its plants, birds, and mammals have previously been studied by a number of biologists, but I had never been given permission to go there because of the ongoing low-level insurgency that has persisted in the Chin Hills for decades. With the permission that had been granted by the military, our plan was to fly from Yangon to Nyaung-Oo near Bagan, pick up several field vehicles and our logistics guide, and drive through the dry zone south to Chauk, where we would purchase supplies before heading to the village of Kanpetlet on the slopes of Mount Victoria.

The teaching and workshop went well. The students and young professors were very attentive and eager to soak up everything I said. Since the time of the mass student protests in 1988, the universities in Myanmar, especially Yangon University, had been intermittently closed to quell any further discontent. Many of the professors had been transferred out of the city to take up posts at the "University of Distant Learning," which was established to disperse students and faculty into small campuses around the country rather than concentrating them in a central site where large gatherings could erupt into political protests. The Botany Department was struggling to train the few students that remained at the Yangon campus, but the resources for teaching were poor. As I looked around the lecture hall, I was hopeful that at least some of these young Burmese botanists would eventually be able to carry out research on the biodiversity and conservation of their country.

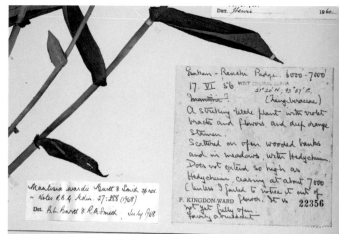

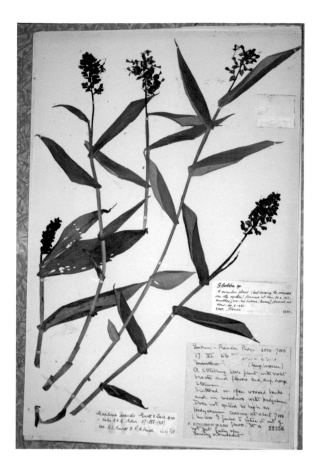

ABOVE LEFT:
The type specimen
of *Globba wardii* kept
in the herbarium of
the Natural History
Museum in London.
This plant was
collected by Kingdon-
Ward on the slopes of
Mount Victoria.

ABOVE RIGHT:
The label of the type
specimen of *Globba
wardii*, with Kingdon-
Ward's handwritten
notes describing the
plant.

The next day Mike and I arrived at the airport
at dawn to catch the earliest flight to Nyaung-Oo.
On the short Air Mandalay flight I reviewed my
notes about Natma Taung, especially the records
that Kingdon-Ward had made during his visit to
the region in 1956. Over the eight months that
Kingdon-Ward spent exploring Mount Victoria, he
collected thousands of plant specimens, including
at least twenty-one species of gingers in eight genera. One of the most interesting gingers, *Globba
wardii*, was eventually named after him. I had found the type specimen of this
new species in the herbarium at the Natural History Museum in London. It
was collected by Kingdon-Ward on June 17, 1956, and his notes read: "A striking
little plant with violet bracts and flowers and deep orange stamen. Scattered on
open wooded banks and in meadows with *Hedychium* [another ginger]. Does
not extend so high [in elevation] as *Hedychium* ceasing at about 7000'. Fairly
abundant."[8] He also found species of *Roscoea*, *Kaempfereia*, *Curcuma*, *Alpinia*,
Curcumorpha, *Rhynchanthus*, and other species of *Globba* and *Hedychium*. I
wanted to see them all.

Upon landing at Nyaung-Oo, we were greeted by our young guide, U Wai
Lwinn, who wanted us to call him "Benjamin." He told me that the distance to
Natma Taung was far, but if we made good time, we could arrive in Kanpetlet
by nightfall. Together with U Tin Maung Ohn and U Ko Tin from the university, we set off in two Russian 1950s-style jeeps. I immediately regretted that my
friend U Thet Htun was not along on this journey. I always trusted him; I was
not yet sure about Benjamin.

The drive from Bagan to Chauk was relatively easy. Impressive pagodas, both ancient and new, lined the roadway. People in the villages seemed to be in good spirits, with the end of the monsoons and the coming of the cool weather in the early dry season. At Chauk we took a break to purchase some supplies, but were soon off again across the Irrawaddy River and the dry plains toward the towns of Yazuma and eventually

"Mount Victoria is inside the tropics, a little north of twenty-one degrees, and there are no surrounding peaks to insulate it and keep it cool."
Frank Kingdon-Ward, *Pilgrimage for Plants*, 1960

Saw, which sits at the base of the Chin Hills on the border of Magway Division and Chin State. The road was in rather poor shape and the going was slow. The only thing working in our favor was that it was the beginning of the dry season, and the ruts in the road, which could be a yard deep in mud in the rainy season, were now at least passable. The dust, unlike the choking substance we encountered during our travels in Kachin State, was annoying but bearable. The semi-deciduous forests along the way, which were interspersed with teak plantations, were not very interesting with regard to plant species. We didn't stop.

Finally, after nearly ten hours of traveling, Natma Taung could be seen in the distance rising above the surrounding hills. Just as we reached the town of Saw, and the sun was beginning to set behind the hills, one of our two jeeps pulled to an abrupt halt with a broken axle. Bad luck. It was not going to be an easy task to repair the vehicle in the current spot, so we piled as many of us as possible into the other jeep and took off up the mountainside in an attempt to get to Kanpetlet before dark.

While we were stopped to assess the disabled vehicle, I had noticed two giant Talipot palms, called *pe-bin* by the Burmese and *Corypha* by botanists, protruding high above the village houses. The Talipot palm is one of the largest in the world and can reach a hundred feet (30 m) in height. The most interesting thing about *pe-bin* is that after growing for many, many years, producing enormously large leaves at its crown, the trunk, when it reaches a particular height, will sprout a huge shoot at its apex that grows above the leaves. This shoot produces a mass of millions and millions of flowers, which in turn are followed by millions and millions of fruits and seeds. Once the seeds are ripe and fall from the plant to the ground, the entire palm simply dies. What was particularly striking about these two individual *pe-bin* was that the local villagers had erected a giant scaffold around the erect flowering shoots and were "tapping" the branches by hanging buckets to collect the sap from the cut stems, much as they tap the toddy palm (*Borassus flabellifer*) for a source of sugar. I had never before seen this done in Myanmar with giant *pe-bin* palms, but I was sure they were going to have enough molasses for the entire village.

As we headed up the hillside toward Kanpetlet in the fading light, I suddenly had a bad feeling that trouble was ahead. With seven of us jammed in the jeep, I couldn't think about much, but I was worried that we were so close to Natma Taung, yet still not there. Just before we entered the town, we stopped for a routine check-in at the military immigration office. I knew that we had the right official papers, with permission to visit the park, so I waited outside while Benjamin and the university lecturers went to talk with the immigration guards.

Two and a half hours later, Mike and I were still standing outside the guardhouse. It was now pitch-black and getting very cold at the high elevation on the side of the mountain. I was worried and angry that something had gone very wrong with our papers. Finally, Benjamin emerged with the bad news that the immigration officers would not accept the permission letter from the military. I could not get the story completely straight, but either we were missing a vital stamp on the letter, or the copies were no good and the originals were needed, or the officers just wanted some type of bribe. Whatever the reason, we were not going to be allowed to proceed to the park that night and would have to go back down the mountain to Saw. I was devastated. After waiting nearly eight years to get the go-ahead to visit Mount Victoria, then traveling to the very gates of the park itself, we could go no farther. I didn't know what to do, and I struggled to control my disappointment and rising fury.

Dejectedly, everyone was about to get back into our jeep when a small vehicle with only one headlight approached the guards' station from the direction of the park. To my immense joy, out jumped U Shein Gay Ngai, the Forest Department Warden at Natma Taung National Park, and one of the participants in the botanical workshop I had taught at Yezin a few years earlier. I had not been in contact with him since the workshop. His sudden appearance was unbelievably good luck. We greeted each other with giant smiles on our faces. He told me that he had heard that I was coming to Natma Taung, but did not know exactly when. I explained the problem we were having, and he headed for the immigration office. Within twenty minutes he had worked out a deal with the officers to let us temporarily pass into the park for the night. We could then work on getting the appropriate papers the next day. Mike and I climbed into U Shein Gay Ngai's vehicle and headed to the park guesthouse before anyone could change their minds. We were here.

The next morning the air was crisp, and the birds were singing on Natma Taung. After breakfast we hiked up the path into the lower levels of the evergreen montane forest; it was comprised of tall Asian oaks interspersed with abundant and dense rhododendrons. The dry season had not yet significantly progressed, and most of the plants were still green. Just as Kingdon-Ward had described in his book, the forest was varied, diverse, and full of gingers. As we trekked up the mountain, we found the purple-flowered Roscoea under the pine trees, the hedychiums, the curcumas, the kaempferias, and finally *Globba wardii,*

which was "fairly abundant" in the "open wooded banks and in meadows," as he had written on the type specimen. Before we left Mount Victoria we collected in just a few days at least twenty species of gingers in eleven different genera. It had taken Kingdon-Ward eight months to record nearly the same number of gingers.

For the Burmese, it is not difficult to visit Natma Taung. When I returned to the university, I was told that many students had hiked to the top of Mount Victoria under the guidance of the Myanmar Hiking and Mountaineering Federation. In fact, 180 university students hiked together to the summit in eight days in 1971![9] In comparison, my trek from Nyaung-Oo to Kanpetlet was not extraordinary at all. For me, however, gaining access to Mount Victoria meant a great deal more than simply completing a hike to the summit. The exploration of Mount Victoria was an ambition that I was obliged to fulfill as a botanist who must follow in the footsteps of other botanists who have come before me. New scientific contributions can only be made by building on the achievements of those who have preceded us. And if not for the smiling and willing help of one of my own students, U Shein Gay Ngai, I never would have succeeded.

ABOVE LEFT: The evergreen forest on the slopes of Mount Victoria in Natma Taung National Park.

ABOVE RIGHT: The pine forests near the summit of Mount Victoria.

OPPOSITE: The flowers of *Globba wardii*.

SMITHSONIAN INSTITUTION
Contributions from the United States National Herbarium
Volume 45: 1-590

A Checklist of the Trees, Shrubs, Herbs, and Climbers of Myanmar

by
W. John Kress
Robert A. DeFilipps
Ellen Farr
and
Daw Yin Yin Kyi

Department of Systematic Biology - Botany
National Museum of Natural History
Washington, DC
2003

CHAPTER 14 *Why the Goldsmith Weeps*

"If foresters and botanists in Myanmar are to sustainably and scientifically manage their natural habitats and resources in the coming decades, it is of utmost importance that they venture to know what these new undiscovered species are and find out their medicinal, food, and other values in order to more fully use and manage our valuable plant resources."

U Shwe Kyaw, Director-General Myanmar Forest Department,
from the Foreword to the *Checklist*, 2003

The cover of the published book entitled *A Checklist of the Trees, Shrubs, Herbs, and Climbers of Myanmar (Revised from the Original Works by J. H. Lace, R. Rodger, H. G. Hundley, and U Chit Ko Ko on the "List of Trees, Shrubs, Herbs, and Principal Climbers, etc. Recorded from Burma").*

Both of my botanical endeavors, the fieldwork in the forests of Myanmar and the compilation of the species checklist at the Smithsonian, were going well. Together with my Burmese colleagues in the Forest Department and at Yangon University, I had by now collected thousands of specimens to document the plants of the country. Daw Yin Yin Kyi and her assistant U Aung Zaw Moe had made another trip to Washington to help put the finishing touches on the species list. In its final form the checklist documented over 11,800 species in 273 families of plants. Information about each species had been noted, including the Latin and common names, habitat, and geographic distribution. We decided to include vegetation maps of the country as well as color photos of some of the important species and vegetation types. For the cover of the book our botanical illustrator at the Smithsonian, Alice Tangerini, drew a magnificent line drawing of the ancient pagodas at Bagan. An illustration of *Hitchenia glauca*, one of my favorite Myanmar gingers, was reserved for the back cover. The final publication, to be called *A Checklist of the Trees, Shrubs, Herbs, and Climbers of Myanmar (Revised from the Original Works by J. H. Lace, R. Rodger, H. G. Hundley, and U Chit Ko Ko on the "List of Trees, Shrubs, Herbs, and Principal Climbers, etc. Recorded from Burma")*, totaled 589 pages![1] We were all very proud of our effort.

235

At the same time that we were completing the book, political trouble was again brewing in Myanmar. Daw Aung San Suu Kyi and members of her National League for Democracy had been savagely attacked in Upper Myanmar, in an area I had visited several years earlier, by unknown assailants who were suspected to be government agents. Several of her supporters died in the attacks, and Daw Aung San Suu Kyi was put back under house arrest by the military junta. The events sparked intense scrutiny and criticism of the military rulers from newspapers and governments around the world.[2] The news was disturbing to those of us trying to make slow headway in the larger task of documentation and conservation of the biodiversity of the country. In developing countries with struggling economies and less-than-democratic governments, politics and conservation efforts are often at odds with each other. Scientists and conservationists at the Smithsonian, who had made extraordinary efforts to advance biodiversity issues in Myanmar, were well aware of the constant tension among the political factions in the country, which had always been a threat to the welfare of the Burmese people as well as to our own activities.

Despite the major clash between Daw Aung San Suu Kyi and the Myanmar government, I continued to think that promoting scientific dialogue between the Ministry of Forests and the Smithsonian would in its own way contribute to a more open country and a greater awareness of the possibility of freedom for our Burmese colleagues. I therefore made plans to travel to Yangon to hand over the final published *Checklist* to the Forest Department in Myanmar.

The chargé d'affaires at the American Embassy in Yangon, Carmen Martinez, who had encouraged me in my work on plants and conservation, offered to host a reception in celebration of the completion of our publication. With several boxes of the book in hand, I boarded my flight in Washington. When I reached Yangon, I was pleased to hear that the American Embassy had invited to the reception my colleagues from both the Forest Department and the University of Yangon. However, at the same time I was cautioned by the embassy staff that the recent attack on Daw Aung San Suu Kyi and the resultant condemnation by Western nations had created considerable anxiety in the capital, and for this reason my Burmese friends from the university and Forest Department might be hesitant to attend the reception. Still, I was hopeful.

Before I left the embassy that day, I learned that one of the major outcomes of the renewed unrest in Myanmar was a revised policy by the U.S. government that would tighten the economic sanctions on Myanmar.[3] To this end the import of all Burmese products into the United States was to be banned. The increased sanctions, like previous economic restrictions on the country, would inevitably have a negative impact on the daily lives and livelihoods of the Burmese. For us this news was particularly devastating because scientific botanical specimens were now to be included in the designation of "products of Burma." We were effectively banned from exporting our specimens out of the country. If we could not bring our botanical collections back to the Smithsonian for study, our work would take ten times longer to accomplish and would very possibly be undermined completely. The new sanctions meant that our biodiversity work in Myanmar was being shut down before my very eyes.

I was beginning to wonder if Daw Aung San Suu Kyi's unwavering support for international economic sanctions and steadfast inflexibility in dealing with the government of Myanmar had enhanced or inhibited the possibility of reforms in the country. Her idealism and charisma had been a unifying force for the Burmese who opposed the military regime, and support for her resistance was widespread. However, politics and social change also require compromise if reform is to move forward.[4] In our case, her relentless support for escalating sanctions had proven counterproductive for our efforts and the attempts by our Burmese partners to understand and conserve the biological resources of the country.

I was understandably discouraged that evening as I headed to the reception being held in honor of our publication. The celebration was to take place at the beautiful home of the chargé d'affaires along Pyay Road on the outskirts of Yangon. It was raining when I arrived, but everyone was upbeat, and I was pleased to see some of my Burmese and embassy friends already there. We had a brief ceremony at which I presented a copy of the book to Carmen Martinez in appreciation of her support. We toasted the future of biodiversity work and our efforts to conserve the biodiversity of Myanmar. No one from the Forest Department showed up at the reception.

When I returned to my guesthouse after the party, I began to ask myself whether my work in Myanmar might be coming to an end. In addition to political events that I couldn't control, I also knew that I was spending more and more time in Asia away from my family. Although I had been determined to finish the *Checklist*, I was beginning to wonder about the next steps. That night before I went to sleep, I wrote in my field journal: "Still I love this country and continue to love it. The land, the people, the plants. Unendingly frustrating but infinitely engaging. I seem to live in two worlds now: one is my nurturing home with the love of my wife and my daughters; and the other is this land I have found halfway around the world that calls me back again and again. How to reconcile the two worlds? I guess I am trying to do just that, but perhaps both are suffering."[5]

The next day I was scheduled to meet with the director general of the Forest Department, U Shwe Kyaw, to make the official presentation of the *Checklist*. Although he had chosen not to attend the reception hosted by the American Embassy the night before, he was exceptionally cordial in his welcome to me that morning. In attendance at the ceremony were many members of the Forest Department, including Daw Yin Yin Kyi and U Thet Htun, as well as Professor Daw Khin Sein and Dr. Daw Aye Kyi from the Department of Botany at the university, and of course Mike. One of my botanical colleagues from Japan, Professor Tetsuo Koyama, who had been working on various local taxonomic projects in Myanmar over the last several years, was also in attendance to showcase his latest work there. The atmosphere was positive, and the director general and I discussed past and future joint projects between the Forest Department and the Smithsonian. We concentrated our talk on the continuation of our documentation of the flora, the development of the Kandawgyi National Botanical Garden and new National Herbarium, and the training of Forest Department staff in plant-collecting and curating techniques. In a slightly staged ceremony I handed over the first official copy of the *Checklist* to the director general and informed him that another thousand copies were in the process of being shipped to Myanmar for distribution by the Forest Department. Everyone seemed extremely pleased that we had finally completed this phase of our collaboration. The ceremony was over.

Later that afternoon, after returning to my guesthouse, I received an awkward note from the director general requesting that I return to the Forest Department to meet with him. This invitation seemed a bit odd to me. As the rains again swept across Yangon, I found myself back in his office. He told me that a number of issues needed to be discussed before I left for a two-week field trip to western Myanmar the next day. To begin with, my offer to provide funds for U Thet Htun to attend a training workshop on medicinal plants in Indonesia was refused. The director general told me that he could not accept the funds until U Thet Htun had been officially approved by the workshop organizers. I explained to U Shwe Kyaw that this situation should not be a problem, and that he could just hold the funds (which I had in my pocket and was ready to hand over) until the approval came through. The director general abruptly stated that it was not possible to accept the funds. I did not look forward to giving U Thet Htun the bad news.

Secondly, U Shwe Kyaw said that we would not be able to proceed with developing the planned National Herbarium in Pyin-Oo-Lwin until I submitted a new proposal to him, which would then have to be approved by the minister of forestry. This new requirement was troubling because I had already submitted two proposals for the initiation of the herbarium over the last three years. I had put much effort into launching this idea of a new herbarium, as well as preparing the previous proposals, so I was a little annoyed that he wanted me to do it again. But of course I would do it again.

Next, the director general told me that my offer to arrange for Daw Kyu Kyu

Thinn, who worked on the orchid collection at Kandawgyi National Botanical Garden and was a participant in our botanical workshop, to receive further training in horticulture and taxonomy at the Smithsonian had been denied because he could not allow a single woman to travel alone to the United States. This reasoning again seemed shortsighted to me, but nonetheless I offered to bring not only Daw Kyu Kyu Thinn but another of his staff to the Smithsonian, so the two of them could travel together. He flatly refused my offer. I was beginning to feel that something had gone very wrong between the time I had seen U Shwe Kyaw at the morning ceremony and now. Then he let the final bomb drop.

To my surprise, and in total contradiction to the praise and congratulations that the director general had expressed to me earlier in the day with regard to the *Checklist*, he now looked at me, shook his head, and said that he regretted that after further consideration the publication was not acceptable to the Forest Department. To my great astonishment he told me that he could not approve the publication in its present form because the cover was wrong. I thought to myself, The cover is wrong? Had I heard correctly? He told me that I had not included the subtitle on the cover of the book (even though it *was* on the title page inside), and that the subtitle was important because it acknowledged the 1912 and subsequent Burmese editions and especially the former Burmese authors of the work.[6] He went on to say that the cover design, which included a stunning illustration of the pagodas at Bagan (and symbolized to me the culture of the country), was also not acceptable. He informed me that the use of such religious illustrations on the cover of a book might even be against government regulations if the books had been printed in Myanmar. It soon became abundantly clear in this private meeting with the director general that the already published and printed volume was being rejected. He told me that the one thousand copies that I had sent from the United States for distribution in Myanmar would all have to be revised with a new cover in a pure white binding that included the full title and subtitle of the book and eliminated the drawing of the pagodas.

I was crushed and disillusioned. The director general's rejection of eight years of work on this book because of the cover design was too much for me to accept. During our conversation U Shwe Kyaw made no mention of the value to his country of the contents of the book, nor of the information we had gathered on the twelve thousand species of plants of Myanmar. He expressed no gratitude for our efforts in training his staff or the training of students from the university. The simple fact was that the facade of the publication was not acceptable. I didn't know how to respond. I smiled, told him that I would do whatever I could to fix the problem, and left his office. I could do no more.

In retrospect, as I think of the golden pagodas I saw, of the openness and kindness of the people I met, of the forests, the rivers, and the mountains that I explored during my time working in the country, I realize that the book cover was not the issue at all. The problem may have in part stemmed from the growing tension between the governments of Myanmar and the United States after the attacks on Daw Aung San Suu Kyi. This tension was in turn transferred to the relationship between the directors of the Forest Department, as representatives of the Myanmar government, and myself, as an American. However, perhaps more relevant in the long term may have been the basic cultural differences between our Western and Eastern societies. My many years of training in botany and taxonomy, along with my own scientific and social perspective, told me that I was doing the right thing by expanding and updating basic knowledge of Myanmar's plants, by training young botanists, and by helping to bring the country into the modern age of science. I realize now that perhaps I failed to understand the priorities of my Burmese friends and colleagues. I had thought that by preparing and presenting this work as a contribution to their knowledge—and hence, their lives—I was performing a good deed. Eventually, I understood that they were fulfilling a more fundamental obligation by allowing me to earn my own merit through giving this work to them. Yet the current state of politics in Myanmar and the world would not allow them to accept my gift. We had reached an insurmountable impasse, one that I had never encountered before and would never encounter again.

In the end I became the Weeping Goldsmith. I had collected the flowers, I had discovered new species, and I had employed all of my skills and training to provide the information necessary for the Burmese to identify and know the plants of their country. After all of this effort, I finally learned that only the Burmese people—in their own fashion, at their own pace, and in their own time—will be able to appreciate their biodiversity in a manner that suits them best. When that time arrives, they will be the best custodians of their land and their natural heritage.

On my first visit to Myanmar I discovered a flower the Burmese call *padeign gno*, the Weeping Goldsmith. Nine years later, after hundreds of miles of travel on land and on rivers, after collecting and documenting thousands of plants and species, after concerted attempts to learn the language and understand the people, and after having my offering to them unexpectedly judged improper, I finally understood why the goldsmith weeps.

Globba radicalis, a ginger collected near the town of Kalewe on the Chindwin River.

ABOVE: The Yin Jiang Valley, in southwestern Yunnan Province, China, near the border with Myanmar.

LEFT: The signpost for the town of Na Bang, spelled in Chinese, Burmese, and English.

Epilogue

"Its most eloquent form is in the reverence the Buddhist has for trees. Trees and forests played an important part in the life of the Sakyamuni. As the story of Gautama's life tells, it was under the shade of the trees at Lumbini grove that his mother Mahamays gave birth to him. Under the branch of the 'Sala' [Shorea robusta] she delivered him. In Lumbini the 'kimsuke' or 'palasa" or flame of the forest [Butea frondosa] was in brilliant bloom. . . . The pipala or bodhadruma [Ficus religiosa], under which Gautama attained Buddhahood on the full-moon day of Vaisakha, became the sacred Botree. . . . Mahaparinirvana was attained by Sakyamuni under the twin sal [Shorea robusta] trees of Kushinagar."

Ven. Dharmaviriyo Mahathero, *Natural Environment and Buddhalogical Perspective.*

I have not returned to Myanmar since my climb of Mount Victoria and final discussion with the director general of the Forest Department. As far as I know, the cartons of books on the plants of Myanmar with their original covers may still sit in a warehouse somewhere in Yangon. A serious illness I suffered a year later, and then a number of new research pursuits at the Smithsonian, were among the reasons that kept me from taking the journey halfway around the planet to Yangon. I continue to work on the plant specimens that I collected while in the country, and I continue to provide updates to the *Checklist* as new discoveries and new materials are sent to me. Many of the living specimens we have grown in the greenhouses have prospered, been propagated, and yielded new data on the plants of Myanmar. My colleagues at the National Zoo and at the National Museum of Natural History carry on with their projects on frogs, birds, and elephants in Myanmar. In the meantime, I have been preparing this book.

Anyone who has read the newspaper or who has watched the latest events on television knows that much has happened in Myanmar in the last few years, despite the attempts by the ruling military junta to further isolate the country

and its people from the outside world. International economic sanctions still persist, although scientists at the Smithsonian were eventually issued an exemption to the "products of Burma" restriction and could once again collect biological specimens in Myanmar. Western governments condemn the military junta at each opportunity for its misbehavior and failings. Reports on the massive protests led by monks in response to rising fuel costs, and crushed by the police, as well as on the devastating cyclone that swept through the Irrawaddy Delta region, killing tens of thousands of people, have been front-page news. All of these events have further eroded the legitimacy of the government of Myanmar. Yet Secretary One and the generals continue to focus inward, on their new capital city of Naypyidaw.

On a recent trip to China to work with my colleagues at the Xishuangbanna Tropical Botanical Garden in Yunnan Province, I had a glimpse of Myanmar from the Chinese side of the border. We had driven from Kunming to the city of Yingjiang, a long trip across new highways connecting distant parts of China. From Yingjiang, which is not far from the Chinese city of Ruili, known

ABOVE: The border crossing between China and Myanmar in the town of Na Bang.

OPPOSITE: Teak and other hardwoods being transported out of Myanmar and bound for the factories of Kunming.

EPILOGUE

for its lawlessness and drug culture, we wound through the mountains to the border crossing at Na Bang. Coming from the other direction, out of Myanmar, was an unending convoy of hundreds, if not thousands, of blue Chinese flatbed trucks, each piled high with teak and other hardwoods. I was watching my beloved forests of Myanmar being carted across the border, bound for the sawmills of Kunming. The grimy border town was half full of Chinese wearing military uniforms and speaking Mandarin and half full of Burmese wearing *longyis* and speaking English and Burmese. Numerous lumberyards stacked with giant logs lined the sides of the roads at Na Bang, waiting for the empty trucks to arrive. Whether this timber market was legal or not, it was discouraging. The exodus to China, India, and Thailand of Myanmar's vanishing biodiversity continues at an ever-accelerating pace.

I will return to Myanmar someday in the near future. After investing so much of my life and myself in the country and its people for nine years, I needed a sabbatical. The quiet study devoted to researching and writing this book has given me an opportunity to think about the time I spent in Myanmar and to contemplate the meaning of the experience to me. But watching the dead bodies of giant trees being carried away on Chinese trucks from their forested homes across the frontier, I knew that my work in Myanmar had only just begun.

Portfolio of Myanmar Plants

Botanical exploration of Myanmar, which lies north of the equator and spans both tropical and subtropical biomes, began in the 1800s, when the country was under colonial rule. The British and their Burmese colleagues produced several partial plant lists for the country as a result of botanical study in India and parts of Asia. However, when Burma gained its independence with the withdrawal of Britain after World War II, botanical investigations sharply decreased. Until recently no modern synoptic inventory of the plants of Myanmar existed, and relatively few scientific plant collections were available for study in or out of the country. Myanmar is exceptionally rich in plant biodiversity, but during the latter part of the last century very few new plant collections were made.

The first list of plants specifically for the region now encompassing Myanmar was compiled in 1912 by J. H. Lace and published as the *List of Trees, Shrubs, Herbs, and Principal Climbers, etc. Recorded from Burma.* The original edition included 2,483 species; a second edition was published by A. Rodger in 1922. In 1961 H. G. Hundley (a silviculturist in Burma) and U Chit Ko Ko (curator of the Herbarium in Rangoon) updated the earlier work with a more complete treatment of grasses, orchids, and herbs. About 7,000 species were included in the edition published in 1987, though this latter edition was not widely distributed outside of Myanmar and is difficult to obtain.

As described in this volume, together with my Burmese colleague I published in 2003 a new list of the plants of Myanmar that built significantly on the versions of earlier botanists. The latest version includes over 11,800 species, a 67 percent increase over previous lists. This modern list is still far from being a complete inventory of the plants of Myanmar, but represents a significant next step in documenting the biodiversity of this land.

The plants displayed and described in this portfolio range from common species used by local villagers to plants that have been discovered for the first time and newly described to science. I have encountered all of these plants in my travels in Myanmar. Although any visitor to the country might readily see some species, others will be difficult to find for even the most experienced botanists. Many of the latter species are endangered, threatened with extinction in their natural habitats. It should be emphasized that the few examples presented here represent a very small fraction of the great diversity of plant species found in the country, and they are meant to provide readers interested in biodiversity with at least a small taste of the plant life of Myanmar.

As part of my scientific research over the last several decades, I have studied the gingers, bananas, and their close relatives in a group of plants called the Zingiberales. During my time in Myanmar I focused in particular on tracking down and collecting members of this group of plants, which are both locally useful and scientifically interesting. Myanmar is a center of diversity for gingers, so it was an especially critical locality to explore for a botanist with my interests.

For each of the fifty species provided in this portfolio, I list the Latin botanical name, common English and Burmese names (if they exist), the plant family, the locality and habitat, the habit and overall size of the plant and its flowers, and a brief comment on the uses, biology, or discovery of the plant.

Non-Gingers

I have selected here twenty-five trees, shrubs, and herbs that can be found in the countryside or villages of Myanmar. These include plants used in the everyday lives of local peoples, as well as a few species that might be encountered in the country's various forest types.

1. *Amherstia nobilis* Wall.
PRIDE OF BURMA, *thawka*
Fabaceae or bean family
Rarely seen in the wild, but cultivated as an ornamental tree in Yangon and other cities
Large tree, to 65 feet (20 m) tall, with flowers 2 inches (5 cm) across

This important ornamental tree is supposedly only native to Myanmar, but little is known about its occurrence in the wild. It is cultivated in botanical gardens and as a street tree in tropical areas of the world because of the spectacular hanging clusters of large deep pink flowers with a yellow center. The specimen shown in the photograph was growing on the campus of Yangon University.

2. *Areca catechu* L.
ARECA PALM, BETEL NUT PALM, *kunthi pin*
Arecaceae or palm family

Cultivated throughout the country and other parts of Southeast Asia for its nuts
Small palm tree to 30 feet (10 m) tall, with nuts about ¾ inch (2 cm) across

Chewing betel nuts is a common custom in many parts of Asia. The plants are native to Malaysia, but have been cultivated throughout the region for millennia. In Myanmar, betel nuts are chopped into small pieces, combined with spices, such as cloves and nutmeg, and an alkaline substance, then wrapped inside a single leaf of the betel pepper vine (Piper betel) to improve the taste. The small "package" is placed inside the cheek, where it is slowly chewed. As the juices from the betel nut trickle down the throat, a slightly euphoric feeling results. The mixture of nut and lime turns the teeth and gums bright red, so it is no secret who is using betel nuts. Chewing betel nuts is an accepted social custom in Myanmar, used by everyone from the most distinguished individuals to common laborers in the field. I have been presented with betel nuts as an after-dinner aperitif in the fanciest restaurants in India.

3. *Arisaema concinnum* Schott
JACK-IN-THE-PULPIT
Araceae or aroid family
Monsoon forests throughout Myanmar
Herb with shoots to 3 feet (1 m) tall, the "jack and pulpit" to 6 inches (15 cm) in height

This striking member of the aroid family has many species in Myanmar. They grow in the seasonal forests and sprout from the parched forest floor after the rains begin. The small greenish flowers are clustered along a spadix, which is surrounded by an enclosing capelike structure called a spathe. The long tail at the tip of the spathe serves to attract tiny insect pollinators that get trapped inside the cape and pollinate the small flowers.

4. *Azadirachta indica* A. Juss.
MARGOSA TREE, NEEM, *tama*
Burseraceae or frankincense family
Common throughout the country, especially the dry zones, usually cultivated

Tree to 20 feet (6 m) tall, with small yellowish flowers

The neem tree is probably native to Myanmar, but is widely grown and naturalized throughout the Asian tropics. It is considered to be a wonder tree because of its many uses: it has edible flowers and leaves, can be used as a medicinal for humans and an insecticide on crops, provides valuable timber products and fuel, and is an ingredient in soaps, toothpaste, and lotions. The neem tree commonly grows along roadsides in the drier regions of Myanmar.

5. *Bambusa tulda* Roxb.
BAMBOO, *chat wa, thaik wa*
Poaceae or grass family
Common throughout the country
Bamboo in clumps to about 10 feet (3 m) in height, with tiny green flowers

Over 125 species of bamboo are native to Myanmar, and many others are cultivated around villages and in household gardens. Bamboos provide habitats for many wild animal species, including deer, elephants, and tigers. Local people use bamboo for many purposes, including house and fence construction, paper making, and chopsticks. Some, but not all, bamboos are edible, and the young shoots are steamed and eaten. Each species has a characteristic clumping or spreading growth habit. The latter types can be significant weeds, spreading over large areas to choke out native vegetation. Cutting and gathering bamboos for sale is a major industry in Myanmar and other Southeast Asian countries.

6. Bombax ceiba (L.) Gaertn.

Kadung, letpan, RED KAPOK, RED SILK
COTTON TREE
Malvaceae (formerly Bombacaceae)
　or mallow family
Cultivated through the country, especially
　the dry zones.
Tree to 65 feet (20 m) tall, with brightly
　colored flowers 4 inches (10 cm) across

*The letpan or red silk cotton tree is most
commonly seen as large isolated specimens
along the roadsides and in villages in the dry
zone. During the season when no rain falls,
the trees have no leaves; not until the rains
begin do the flowers first appear, followed by
a flush of brilliant green leaves. The large,
fleshy, bright red flowers can be seen for miles
when a tree is in full flower. Local people
will gather the flowers when they fall to the
ground and use them in their household
religious shrines as well as in their soups
and curries. If the flowers are pollinated, the
woody podlike fruits will produce fluffy and
cottony seeds that drift for long distances
during the dry season breezes.*

7. Borassus flabellifera L.

Htan, PALMYRA PALM, TODDY PALM
Arecaceae or palm family
Common throughout the country,
　especially in dry zones, where it is
　often cultivated along the margins of
　rice paddies and cultivated fields
Large palm tree to 50 feet (15 m) tall, with
　fruits up to 6 inches (15 cm) across

*The toddy palm is one of the most important
palms in Myanmar. The tips of the large*

*inflorescences that hang under the skirt of
leaves at the top of the plant are sliced off
during the appropriate season, and a bucket
is hung to collect the sap that drips from
the cut end. The exceptionally sweet sap is
boiled down to make a thick brown sugar
that is used in cooking and as a candy. The
raw sap is often allowed to ferment for a few
days, producing a slightly alcoholic beverage
that the locals call "sky beer." On a hot
afternoon in the dry zone, this cooling drink
helps one survive the last few sweltering
hours before sundown.*

8. Butea monosperma (Lam.) Kuntze

Changan, FLAME OF THE FOREST,
pauk, pawpan
Fabaceae or bean family
Common throughout the country,
　often cultivated
Large tree to 30 feet (10 m) tall, with
　flowers about 3 inches (7 cm) in length

*The multitudes of large, pinkish orange
flowers of this well-shaped tree in the
legume family are a welcome relief from
the monotony of the countryside in central
Myanmar. Although it is not as significant
in Buddhist lore as the sala tree under which
the Buddha was born, the flame of the forest
is said to have been in full bloom on his
birthday and is much appreciated by local
peoples for its color and form.*

9. Calotropis gigantea (L.) Dryand.
　ex W. T. Aiton

GIANT SWALLOW-WORT, *mayo gyi,*
VERCUM

Asclepiadaceae or milkweed family
Common in the dry zones
Shrub to 5 feet (1.5 m) tall, with flowers to
　³⁄₄ inch (2 cm) across

*The dry zone is home to many plants
adapted to a harsh environment where rain
is scarce for most of the year. The leaves
are often thick and succulent to retain as
much moisture as possible. The flowers are
similarly fleshy. The pale purplish flowers of
Calotropis are shaped like little stars, with
the sexual parts clustered in the center. The
bee pollinators get their legs stuck between
the points of the star and transfer a small
packet of pollen in the form of a two-lobed
sock from the stamens into a slitlike structure
that accepts the pollen and protects it from
the drying atmosphere. Later the horn-
shaped fruits release floating seeds, which
land on the ground and germinate when the
next rains begin.*

10. Corypha utan Lam.

TALIPOT PALM, GEBANG PALM, *pe bin*
Arecaceae or palm family
Throughout the country, especially around
　villages and among pagodas
Palm tree to 65 feet (20 m) tall, with a giant
　erect cluster of thousands of small
　flowers at the top

*Some of the largest palms in the world are
members of the genus* Corypha. *Unlike
most palms, such as the toddy palm, which
each year produce their flowers and fruits
in structures in the axils of the leaves, these
palms grow larger and larger for decades
without ever flowering. At the right time, the
talipot palm will suddenly produce a single
gigantic branching cluster of flowers at the
very top of the plant above the final whorl of
leaves. I once counted over 17 million flowers
produced by one of these palms, growing in
Florida. The enormous numbers of flowers in
this impressive display attract bees from miles
around, which serve as pollinators. Once
flowering and fruiting is complete, the entire
palm then dies. The next generation of palms
begins to sprout from the thousands of seeds
scattered at the base of the dying mother
plant. In Myanmar, this palm is often
planted around Buddhist monasteries and
pagodas, perhaps because it is so long-lived.*

11. *Cycas siamensis* Miq.
Mondaing, pakut kon
Cycadaceae or cycad family
Monsoon forests in western Myanmar
Small palmlike tree to 6 feet (2 m) tall, with
nutlike fruits 1¼ inches (3 cm) across

Cycads make up an ancient lineage of plants that first originated during the time of the dinosaurs over 200 million years ago. Today about 300 species survive in the tropical zones of the world. Although they look like palms, they are not even remotely related. Only a few species of cycads are native to Myanmar. I found a population of this species, Cycas siamensis, while exploring along the Chindwin River. It was one of the first reports of the plant occurring in the country, and I thought it might be a new species until its correct identity was tracked down a year later. In general these plants grow very, very slowly, and a plant only six feet (2 m) tall may be hundreds of years old.

12. *Dillenia indica* L.
Thabyu
Dilleniaceae or dillenia family
Widely distributed in monsoon forests
Small tree to 6 feet (2 m) tall, with flowers 2
inches (5 cm) across

I collected this plant as I headed back down the Chindwin River on an aborted attempt to reach a remote national park near the border with India. The flooded riverbank was knee-deep in silt, and it was extremely difficult to reach terra firma from our boat. Once we were on secure land, the forest held many exciting gingers, some unexpected relatives of lilies, and this small shrub with

bright yellow flowers. The petals were extremely delicate and started to fall apart as I tried to photograph the flower. Fortunately the plant successfully made it into the plant press and was eventually identified by a colleague at Duke University as a not uncommon plant, characteristic of such monsoon forests.

13. *Duabanga grandiflora* (Roxb. ex DC.) Walp.
Hkalam, shala, thit kazaw
Lythraceae or crape myrtle family
Widely distributed in hill forests in
the central zone of Myanmar
Tree to 16 feet (5 m) tall, with flowers
4 inches (10 cm) across

The lanky, gawky appearance of this tree makes it unmistakable in the forests of Myanmar. The branches hang down in a clumsy fashion from a central trunk that itself can be branched. This drooping habit has a purpose, as each branch holds a cluster of large flowers at its apex. The fruit bats that visit these flowers, which are open and fragrant at night, can easily access these open drooping branches to lap nectar from inside the ring of petals of each flower and thereby ensure that they are pollinated.

14. *Emblica officinalis* Gaertn.
Htakyu, shabyu, tasha, zibyu
Euphorbiaceae or poinsettia family
Common in drier areas
Tree to 13 feet (4 m) tall, with fruits
¾ inch (2 cm) in diameter

Although other plants in the poinsettia family contain some of the most poisonous substances produced by plants—such as

ricin, from the castor bean—small bowls of the grapelike fruits of this plant are commonly served as condiments with traditional Myanmar cooking. The fruits are enjoyed as a bitter and juicy complement to the varied small dishes of vegetables and meats eaten with any meal. The Burmese favor tart and bitter spices and condiments in their everyday cuisine. The tree from which Emblica fruits are harvested has long, soft feathery leaves and grows in the dry zones of the country.

15. *Flagellaria indica* L.
Myauk kyein
Flagellariaceae
Common in wet areas
Climbing vine to the tops of trees,
with small flowers and fruits less
than ½ inch (1 cm) across

Plants have evolved many varied structures for climbing on other plants to reach brighter habitats where they can more easily photosynthesize, grow, and reproduce. Flagellaria possesses leaves with very special tips that develop as tendrils to aid the plant in grasping other vegetation as it pulls itself up into the better-lit zones. This plant, which is related to grasses, bamboos, and rushes, has small white flowers and a reddish orange, grasslike fruit called a caryopsis.

16. *Hesperethusa crenulata* (Roxb.) Roem.
Sansph ka, thanakha
Rutaceae or citrus family
Common in cultivated areas
Small tree to 30 feet (10 m) tall, with
clusters of small flowers ¼ inch
(.5 cm) across.

The Burmese use the bark of this tree, which is related to oranges and grapefruits, extensively as a cosmetic and sunscreen. Chunks of thick branches are sold in markets for this purpose. The bark is grated on a smooth stone into a fine yellowish white paste, diluted with water, and applied to the skin on the face and the arms. Often elaborate patterns of swirls and fine lines are

painted on the cheeks, nose, and forehead as an adornment. When the sun is hot, a thick layer of thanakha is applied to prevent sunburn and cool the exposed skin. The bright yellow flowers are said to bring good luck and are woven into the long braids of girls and young women.

17. *Lagerstroemia speciosa* (L.) Pers.
Hani, pyinma, thwemu, CRAPE MYRTLE
Lythraceae or crape myrtle family
On hillsides in monsoonal, seasonally
    dry forests
Small tree to 30 feet (10 m) tall, with large
    flowers 4–6 inches (10–15 cm) in
    diameter

Pyinma is one of the most colorful trees of the dry forests. At the end of the dry season, the large, bright lavender flowers profusely cover the crown of gangly branches. These small trees, which often grow in dense groves of numerous individuals, are common in the foothills of the western ridges of Myanmar and provide a spectacular sight when in flower. Pyinma is a tropical relative of the crape myrtles commonly cultivated in gardens and around houses in the temperate zone. This specimen was collected just before the "start of rains storm" that crashed down on us as we traveled toward Pyay.

18. *Molineria capitulata* (Lour.)
    Herb.
Kywet malut, tong song kha
Hypoxidaceae
Forested areas
Herb to 2½ feet (80 cm) tall, with flowers
    about ⅜ inch (1 cm) across

This strange-looking plant has leaves that resemble a small palm, but like the screw pines, are not related to palms. They are more closely related to orchids. Found in the herb layer in semi-evergreen forests, this species likes to grow in moist areas bordering small streams and seepage areas. We have found a number of species of Molineria in Myanmar, and collected this one in Shan State near the town of Hsipaw on the road to Lashio and the Chinese border.

19. *Nypa fruticans* Wurmb.
Dani, NIPA PALM
Arecaceae or palm family
Common in mangrove areas along the coast
Palm tree to 13 feet (4 m) tall, with gigantic
    cluster fruits 16 inches (40 cm) in
    diameter

The nipa palm is one of the most abundant palms found in mangrove regions in Myanmar and tropical Asia. The trunks, which are rooted in the mud in inundated areas, run horizontally, with the giant erect leaves forming large forests in coastal swamps. The plants are unisexual, with male and female flowers on separate individuals. The woody fruits are bunched into a huge "head" that is attached to the trunk among the leaves. These fruits are collected, and the young endosperm found within the tough husk, much like coconut meat, is boiled in syrup as a candy.

20. *Oroxylum indicum* (L.) Kurz
Byili pili, CAT'S TONGUE, MOTHER-IN-
LAW'S TONGUE, *kyaung sha*
Bignoniaceae or calabash family
Commonly cultivated
Small tree to 13 feet (4 m) tall, with large
    flowers to 2 inches (5 cm) across and
    fruits up to 3 feet (1 m) long

The long, leathery, strap-shaped fruits of mother-in-law's tongue are sliced, fried, and eaten by the Burmese. The taste is rather bitter, but much enjoyed in combination with other dishes. This slender tree is grown throughout Myanmar and neighboring countries in Southeast Asia for these fruits. The flowers are produced at the ends of long stalks sticking out from the leaves, where the bats that pollinate them after dark can easily reach them.

21. *Pandanus* aff. *wallichianus* Martelli
SCREW PINE
Pandanaceae or screw pine family
Wet areas
Tree to 50 feet (15 m) in height, with heavy,
    globular, pineapple-like fruits to
    12 inches (30 cm) in diameter

The screw pines grow in tropical areas of Africa and Asia, usually in coastal regions bordering the oceans. In Myanmar they are also found in evergreen forests and have tall skinny stems topped with a spiral of long, straplike leaves. Although they superficially resemble palms, these striking plants are not at all related to palms. The screw pines are little used by local peoples except occasionally for thatch to cover their houses. One species has very aromatic leaves and is used as a flavoring for curries.

22. *Prosopis juliflora* DC.
Gandasein, HONEY LOCUST, MESQUITE
Fabaceae or bean family
Dry zones, often cultivated
Small tree to 10 feet (3 m) tall, with small flowers and seedpods to 6 inches (15 cm) long

The mesquite or honey locust trees are a characteristic feature of the dry scrub forests of central Myanmar, and are found in similar habitats in many places around the world. They are native to Mexico and Central America. The dry habitats where mesquite grows receive very little rain and are rather inhospitable. Many of the plants found in these scrub forests are in the bean family and have long thorns on the stems that protect the feathery leaves from grazing animals. The long, narrow fruits with a deep constriction between each seed are easily recognizable, and an important food for stock animals.

23. *Pterocarpus* macrocarpus Kurz
Mai chi tawk, MYANMAR ROSEWOOD, PADAUK
Fabaceae or bean family
Monsoon and semi-deciduous forests
Large trees to 80 feet (25 m) in height, with small, inconspicuous flowers

*Padauk, along with teak (*Tectona grandis*) and pinkado (*Xylia xylocarpa*), is one of the*

major hardwood timber trees of Myanmar. It grows in natural forests and is now also planted in plantations for long-term timber production. The wood is reddish in color and polishes well. It is extensively used in cabinetwork and furniture construction.

24. *Santalum album* L.
Mawk san ku, SANDALWOOD, *santagu*
Santalaceae or sandalwood family
Cultivated
Parasitic small tree to 13 feet (4 m) in height with flowers less than half an inch (1 cm) across

Sandalwood is prized for its hard, fine-grained, fragrant wood. Expert woodcarvers can fashion very detailed figures, such as elephants, nats, angels, and the Buddha, from this wood. The sweet-scented oil can be extracted from the wood and is used as a perfume and in medicine. This species of small tree is native to India and probably Myanmar, but is also cultivated widely as a source of the precious wood. Sandalwood is a parasite on the roots of other plants and cannot live without its host trees growing nearby. The tiny, cross-shaped, deep maroon flowers emerge from the juncture between the leathery green leaves and the stem.

25. *Tectona grandis* L. f.
Kyun, pahi, TEAK
Lamiaceae or mint family (formerly placed in the Verbenaceae or verbena family)
Common in monsoon forest and cultivated throughout the country
Large tree to 100 feet (30 m) in height, with small flowers less than half an inch (1 cm) in diameter

Most of the world's remaining natural teak forests are found in Myanmar, especially in the hills bordering the central dry zone. The giant leaves and clusters of flowers and fruits at the tips of the branches are distinctive. Teak produces its flowers during the rainy season, and the bright yellow flowers adorning the tops of the trees can be seen for miles. For many decades the rich teak forests were carefully managed by the Myanmar Forest Department as an important natural resource for the country. Unfortunately, a recent dramatic increase in illegal logging threatens the long-term existence of these majestic trees.

Gingers and Ginger Relatives

Myanmar is rich in species of gingers and their close relatives. The lower levels of the teak forests, seasonally dry forests, bamboo forests, and evergreen tropical wet forests are full of gingers. Many of these species go dormant during the long, hot dry season, but spring to life with an abundance of flowers from underground stems hidden deep in the soil when the rains begin. Gingers are extensively used by local peoples as foods, medicines, and spices. Much is now known about the diversity of gingers in Myanmar, but many species still remain to be discovered and classified.

26. *Alpinia galanga* (L.) Willd.
GALANGAL, *kunsa gamon*
Zingiberaceae or ginger family
Widely cultivated
Large herb to 8 feet (2.5 m) tall, with flowers 3/4 inch (2 cm) across

This ginger is cultivated in villages throughout Myanmar and other Southeast Asian countries. The underground stems, leaves, flowers, fruits, and seeds, all of which are suffused with a delightfully sweet aromatic oil, are eaten and used as spices or medicinals in many varied dishes. The white flowers are followed by fruits, which are bright red when ripe. Galanga probably originated in India or Indo-China, and it appears to have been used in cooking for many thousands of years.

27. *Boesenbergia pulcherrima* (Wall.)
    Kuntze
Zingiberaceae or ginger family
Common on the floor of monsoon forests
Herb to 3 feet (1 m) tall, with flowers to
    ¼ inch (2 cm) in diameter

Like many gingers, this one grows on the forest floor of monsoonal, seasonally dry forests. The usually green leaves are sometimes deep purple on the back. The flowers, which are nestled down and partly hidden in the crown of leaves, vary in color from locality to locality. They are very ephemeral and last less than a day before they wither.

28. *Curcuma arracanensis*
    W. J. Kress, ined.
No common names
Zingiberaceae or ginger family
Rare on cloud forest ridges
Herbs to 5 feet (1.5 m) tall, with flowers
    1⅛ inches (3 cm) across

This species was unknown to science until we found it on an isolated ridge in cloud forest above the coastal city of Taunggok. The mountainous slopes where this species

grows were very steep, and mosses formed a thick mat on the trees from the daily cover of dense fog and mist. The bright orange flowers of these plants are very different than most species in the genus Curcuma, but DNA evidence told us that it was clearly in this group of gingers. The species name arracanensis means "from the place called Arakan," which is the old Burmese name for Rakhine State, where we discovered it.

29. *Curcuma attenuata* Wall.
Zingiberaceae or ginger family
Common in open growth
Herb to 20 inches (50 cm) tall, with flower
    stalks 8 inches (20 cm) tall and flowers
    about ⅜ inch (1 cm) across

This brilliant species in the turmeric genus was collected on Shwe-U-Daung, an isolated mountain north of Mandalay. It was growing along a small stream on the forest floor in a pristine evergreen forest. We had hiked for hours before we found it. The deep maroon and purple cup-shaped bracts contain the yellow and pink flowers that peer out in search of pollinating bees.

30. *Curcuma cordata* Wall.
Zingiberaceae or ginger family
Forest floor in monsoonal areas
Herb to about 30 inches (75 cm) tall, with
    flower stalks 6 inches (15 cm) tall and
    flowers about ⅜ inch (1 cm) across

When we came upon this plant in the hills around Kandawgyi National Botanical Garden outside Mandalay, it did not have any flowers, so we did not know what it was. We collected the underground stems, and a year later, in our greenhouses at the Smithsonian, the plants broke dormancy and sprouted striking flowering stalks with glowing fluorescent deep purple bracts and yellow flowers. The classification of this group of gingers is very confused at present, but we now know that it is most likely this species that was first named by the British botanist N. Wallich, working on the Indian subcontinent in the early 1800s.

31. *Curcumorpha longiflora* (Wall.)
    Rao & Verma
Zingiberaceae or ginger family
Forest floor in monsoon forests
Herb to 2 feet (60 cm) in height, with
    flowers to 6 inches (15 cm) tall

This species has been classified in a number of genera, including Boesenbergia, and botanists are still debating its correct position in the gingers. We collected this plant while climbing up a small ravine onto the Shan Plateau as we headed toward the city of Lashio. The large flowers, which sprout from underground stems at the base of the plant, are hidden under the leaves and therefore often missed unless one is specifically looking for them. The delicate petals and pouchlike labellum are pale pinkish white and balanced at the tip of a slender tube that is full of nectar. A slightly different form with yellowish flowers is also found in Myanmar.

32. *Ensete superbum* (Roxb.) E. E.
    Cheesm.
Musaceae or banana family
On limestone cliffs east of Mandalay
A large robust herb with shoots to 13 feet
    (4 m) in height; individual flowers are
    1½ to 2 inches (4–5 cm) in length

This plant is one of the most bizarre relatives of the edible bananas. For those who see it for the first time, it is hard to believe that it is not from another planet. The giant bulbous stem, which can grow to thirteen feet (4 m) in height in a few years, sprouts from a hard

brown seed the size of a pea. Once the stem reaches maturity after producing several rings of large banana-like leaves, a massive structure called an inflorescence, or flower stalk, emerges from the center and produces hundreds of separate female and male flowers. After two or three years, the seeds from these flowers mature and are dispersed and scattered, and the entire plant dies. In its natural habitats in the monsoonal forests of the Western Ghats of India and limestone hills of Thailand and Myanmar, the next generation of plants begins to sprout from the seeds produced by the parent plant.

33. Etlingera araneosa (Bak.) R. M. Sm.
Zingiberaceae or ginger family
Rare in wet evergreen forests in
    western Myanmar
Large herb with shoots to 8 feet (2.5 m)
    tall; the flowers are about 4 inches
    (10 cm) long

Unlike many of the gingers of Myanmar, which go dormant during the dry season, species of Etlingera grow in evergreen wet forests and keep their leaves throughout the year. The flowers of E. araneosa, like other gingers, emerge from an underground stem and sit just above the surface of the soil in the leaf litter. Although no animals have been observed visiting these flowers, the bright red and orange color suggests that birds may be the pollinators. This specimen was collected in a small patch of forest in Rakhine State on the way to the Bay of Bengal ten miles from the coast, and marked the first report of this particular species from Myanmar.

34. Globba arracanensis Kurz
Zingiberaceae or ginger family
Restricted to the region around Sittwe
    in Rakhine State
Herb to 18 inches (45 cm) tall with
    flowers about 1½ inches (4 cm) long.

Globba arracanensis *was discovered and named in 1869 by Wilhelm Sulpiz Kurz, who found a single specimen near the city of Akyab, now called Sittwe, on the western coast of Myanmar. Since that single collection, this species had not been found again by botanists. We visited the region around Sittwe at the end of the dry season, when it was extremely hot. At that time very few plants had any flowers, and most were dormant. Fortunately, while exploring a dry creek bed, I spied a shriveled-up ginger that was partly covered with dried-out mosses and clinging to a large boulder. It wasn't until a year later, when this specimen was revived and grown in the greenhouses at the Smithsonian, that I realized we had made only the second collection of* Globba arracanensis *in over 130 years.*

35. Globba magnifica M. Newman, ined.
Padeign ngo, WEEPING GOLDSMITH
Zingiberaceae or ginger family
In semi-deciduous dry forests near the
    Thailand border, commonly cultivated
Herb to 2 feet (60 cm) tall, with flower
    stalks to 6 inches (15 cm) long and
    flowers about ⅜ inch (2 cm) across

The flowers of this species, called padeign gno, *"the weeping goldsmith," by the Burmese, are commonly grown in Myanmar and placed as an offering in Buddhist shrines and monasteries. Even though it is a common*

and conspicuous species of ginger, it was new to science when I first found it in a market. It still does not have an officially recognized botanical name, though we informally call it Globba magnifica. Padeign gno *is an appropriate symbol of how much is still to be learned about the biodiversity of Myanmar.*

36. Globba mogokensis W. W. Sm. & Bane
Zingiberaceae or ginger family
Restricted to monsoon forests north
    of Mandalay
Herb to 30 inches (75 cm) tall, with
    flowers less than ¾ inch (2 cm) long

Globbas are common gingers that grow under teak and other tall trees of the dry and wet forests of Myanmar. This one resembles "the weeping goldsmith," but it is distinctive in the shape of its flower stalks and flowers. Mogok is a small city north of Mandalay, and the center of the country's ruby and gem mining industry. Globba mogokensis *is known only from this area. We collected this plant near the Kyaukgyi Waterfall in Shwe-U-Daung National Park, where it grew on the forest floor along with many other gingers.*

37. Globba radicalis Roxb.
Chauk pan, DANCING LADIES
Zingiberaceae or ginger family
Rare in the western hills of Myanmar

Medium-sized herb to 20 inches (50 cm) in height; flowers are ¾ inch (2 cm) across the width of the "arms"

The petals and anthers of the fragile flowers of Globba radicalis have a very peculiar orientation that makes them appear to be "dancing." This plant was discovered in western Myanmar, growing on steep embankments in the interior of teak forests. During the long dry season, plants of this species, and many other gingers, "hide" underground and wait for the rains to begin with the start of the monsoon-season rains. The flowers are the first parts of the plant to appear aboveground, dancing as they unfold their floral organs to attract insects to pollinate them. The leaves soon appear and expand several weeks later, hiding the flowers beneath. The Burmese name is chauk pan, "rock flower," because the plants often grow on boulders along small streams in the forest.

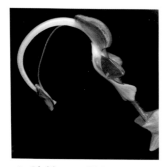

38. *Globba wardii* (B. L. Burtt & R. M. Sm.) K. J. Williams
Zingiberaceae or ginger family
Slopes of Mount Victoria in the Chin Hills
Herb to 2 feet (60 cm) tall, with flowers about ¾ inch (2 cm) long

Frank Kingdon-Ward, after whom this species was named, was one of the great twentieth-century plant collectors in Myanmar, India, Nepal, and Tibet. He discovered many exciting plants of significant horticultural value, which he introduced into the gardens of England and Scotland. One of Kingdon-Ward's last expeditions to Burma took him to Mount Victoria in the Chin Hills in the western part of the country; there he collected some of the first specimens of this ginger, which now holds his name. This species was first classified in the genus Mantisia, but we now know that scientifically it is more appropriate to classify it as Globba wardii.

39. *Globba wengeri* (C. E. C. Fisch.) K. J. Williams
Zingiberaceae or ginger family
Wet areas in western part of the country.
Herb to 30 inches (75 cm) tall, with flowers about 1¼ inch (3 cm) across

This species, similar to Globba radicalis and Globba wardii, was originally classified in the genus Mantisia, but is now also called Globba. The name Mantisia comes from the similarity in appearance of the flowers to a praying mantis with outstretched "arms" and bowed "head" ready to seize its prey. I first collected this species in pouring rain in the middle of the monsoon season near the town of Thandwe, along the western coast of Myanmar. The bright orange flowers were very conspicuous despite the heavily overcast sky and the gloomy shadows of the low forests where the plants were growing.

40. *Halopegia blumei* (Koern.) K. Schum.
Marantaceae or prayer plant family
Common in swampy areas in monsoon forests
Herb to 3 feet (1 m) tall with flowers ⅝ inch (1.5 cm) across

The extremely ephemeral flowers of this species are typical of the prayer plant family, Marantaceae. Opening early in the morning, brilliant white flowers burst from inside the stem to form a structure resembling a ruffled ball of tissue paper at the center of the plant. By midday the delicate petals are already beginning to wilt, and the flowers are no longer available to the insect visitors who pollinate them. This rather unique species usually grows in low-lying swampy areas and is most closely related to another species from far-off tropical West Africa. In contrast to the stark white flowers of the

Burmese species, Halopegia caerulea *from Africa produces bright cerulean blue flowers to attract the native insect pollinators of that distant land.*

41. *Hedychium bordelonianum* W. J. Kress & K. J. Williams
Zingiberaceae or ginger family
Cloud forests in western Myanmar
Herb to 30 inches (75 cm) tall, with flowers 1¼ inches (3 cm) long

Most gingers grow with their roots in the soil of the forest floor. This unique species of ginger, found on the high ridges of the western mountain range in Myanmar, grows with its exposed roots wrapped around branches of tall trees. It is an epiphyte—a plant that grows on other plants—and absorbs the water it needs to grow from the clouds that often enshroud these mountaintops. This species is also special because of its relatively unadorned red and yellow flowers, whose bright colors signals birds that they are ripe for fertilization and pollination.

42. *Hemiorchis rhodorrhachis* K. Schum.
Zingiberaceae or ginger family
Forest floor of seasonally dry monsoon forests in western foothills
Low herb with shoots to over 20 inches (50 cm) tall, with flowers about 1¼ inches (3 cm) across

Botanists have long overlooked this species of ginger, because it comes into flower long before the rains begin, and has rather inconspicuous flowers. In contrast the leaves are very prominent growing along the forest floor, but the flowers are never found in association with the leaves during the rainy season. We found this plant at Alaungdaw Kathapa National Park after a long, nearly fruitless search at the end of the dry season. I had almost given up hope of locating Hemiorchis when we stopped to set up camp on the third day and nearly pitched our tent on top of the plant. The tiny flowering stalks emerge into the light among the dried leaves and are connected to a long, white underground stem, which burrows deep into the soil, and secures the scant, lingering moisture present during the scorching month of April, when we found it.

43. *Hitchenia glauca* Wall.

Zingiberaceae or ginger family
Open seasonally dry areas in central
 Myanmar
Herb to 3 feet (1 m) tall, with flowers up
 to 4 inches (10 cm) in length.

Hitchenia glauca *was one of my most exciting plant discoveries in Myanmar. I first spied the tall, erect leafy shoots with the spiraled flower stalks at the top while riding down a rural road in the center of the country. However, it was the slender, long-tubed white flowers, which glowed in the evening light, and stuck out in every direction from the flower stalks that really caught my attention. The plant was stunning . . . and a mystery. It took me nearly a year to identify it. Although I now know its name, I am still trying to figure out how it should be best classified among the gingers. The process of science is sometimes very slow.*

44. *Kaempferia candida* Wall.

Pa dat sa, panu, taukta
Zingiberaceae or ginger family
Open habitats in monsoon areas of
 western Myanmar
Low herb to 12 inches (30 cm) tall, with
 flowers up to 4 inches (10 cm) in
 length.

Kaempferia candida *is one of the few gingers that produces flowers at the very end of the dry season, just before the rains begin. Most gingers wait to flower until the first rains have arrived. When the flowers of this*

species appear, no leaves have yet sprouted on the trees, and the relentless sun bakes the soil where they grow. The harsh conditions do not deter this species, whose white and yellow flowers joyfully shoot up from the parched and cracked soils. These plants are able to withstand these desiccating conditions by storing moisture and nutrients inside the potato-like structure attached to their roots, which are buried deep in the earth. Weeks later, after the rains have arrived, the leaves sprout. In markets one can find great piles of these flowers, which are collected by local villagers for use as flavoring in soups.

45. *Kaempferia rotunda* L.

Myay padauk, pan gamon,
RESURRECTION LILY
Zingiberaceae or ginger family
Common in monsoon forests
Low herb to 20 inches (50 cm) tall, with
 flowers about 2 inches (5 cm) across

Another one of the early-blooming gingers is Kaempferia rotunda, *one of the commonest species in the seasonally dry forests of Myanmar and the neighboring countries of Thailand and India. Like the ephemeral spring flowers of North America, Europe, and temperate Asia, these delicate blossoms sprout across the forest floor before any new vegetation appears on the trees. The flowers of this species range in color from almost pure white to solid purple and every shade in between. In some areas these flowers will form a carpet of color in contrast to the often charred and burned soils that linger after the rainless dry season.*

46. *Musa laterita* E. E. Cheesm.

Taw nget pyaw, BRONZE BANANA
Musaceae or banana family
Common in open forests, especially
 on slopes
Robust herb to 8 feet (2.5 m) tall, with
 flowers to 1¼ inch (3 cm) long

This wild banana is a common sight in many parts of Myanmar, growing along forest margins and crowding the sides of gullies. The erect, orange and pink flower stalks are filled with yellow flowers. The fruits, which are full of seeds, are not edible for people, although birds and mammals will readily eat them. Because of its swollen underground stem this species, unlike most bananas, has the special ability to go dormant if the dry season is severe. The plants will then grow new shoots once the rains have arrived.

47. *Phrynium pubinerve* Blume

Taungsin phet, taung zin phet
Marantaceae or prayer plant family
Common in monsoon forests
Herb to 5 feet (1.5 m) tall, flower heads
 to 4 inches (10 cm) in diameter

Phrynium pubinerve *is the most common member of the prayer plant family in Myanmar. The small white flowers and bright red triangular fruits congested into a ball in the center of the stem easily identify this species. These plants inhabit evergreen forests and generally do not go dormant during the dry season like many gingers. This specimen was collected, along with many leeches, during the rainy season in the wet lowland forests along the west coast of Myanmar.*

48. *Smithatris myanmarensis*
W. J. Kress

Zingiberaceae or ginger family
Rare in evergreen forests in central
    Myanmar
Herb to 30 inches (75 cm) tall, with flower
    stalks to 4 inches (10 cm) tall

*I had collected this new species several times
in forests north of Mandalay, but did not
know what it was. After finding a similar
species in Thailand, I realized that these two
plants were very different from other gingers
and deserved to be put in a new genus,
which Kai Larsen, a fellow botanist from
Denmark, and I called Smithatris. While
exploring Shwe-U-Daung Mountain I
found a large population of the new species
from Myanmar that had two forms of the
plant: one pink and green, the other pure
white and green, both with yellow flowers.
Smithatris myanmarensis is one of the
loveliest of Burmese gingers.*

49. *Stachyphrynium spicatum*
(Roxb.) K. Schum.

Marantaceae or prayer plant family
Common in monsoon forests of central
    Myanmar
Herb to 3 feet (1 m) tall, with small
    flowering stalks to 2 inches (5 cm) high

*The prayer plants (Marantaceae family)
have a special mechanism at the base of the
leaves that moves the leaf blades into an erect
position at night, making the leaves look like
they are "praying." In Myanmar, there are
fewer species of prayer plants than gingers
in both dry and wet forests, and they are
not as colorful. However, the classification
has proven very difficult, and we are only
recently beginning to understand how these
species evolved. Stachyphrynium spicatum
occurs in seasonally dry forests and has the
ability to go dormant while it is waiting for
the rains to begin.*

50. Zingiber kerrii Craib

Zingiberaceae or ginger family
Common in forests on the Shan Plateau
Herb to 5 feet (1.5 m) tall, with flowers
    about ⅜ inch (1 cm) across

*The most common spice used in Western
cooking is Zingiber officinale. Over one
hundred close relatives of this common spice
are found in Southeast Asia, and many are
native to Myanmar. They come in many
shapes and sizes and are found in all types
of forests. Most have highly aromatic leaves
and underground stems with various odors,
such as wintergreen, licorice, and mustard.
Zingiber kerrii is found at higher elevations
in evergreen forests. The flowers are clustered
in stalks at the base of the leaves and appear
during the wettest months of the year.*

Acknowledgments

I would like to thank all of my colleagues and friends in Myanmar for their support and for taking care of me while I was in their country: U Uga, U Win Kyi, U Shwe Kyaw, U Kyaw Tint, U Khin Maung Zaw, Daw Yin Yin Kyi, U Thet Htun, and all of my other friends in the Forest Department; Prof. Dr. Soe Yin, Dr. Daw Aye Kyi, Dr. Daw Khin Sein, Dr. Aye Pe, Daw Than Than Htay, and Daw Win Win Aung and others at the University of Yangon; the staff at the Highland Lodge, my logistics expert U Hpone Thant; the Charges d'Affaires Priscilla Clapp and Carmen Martinez at the American Embassy in Yangon; and Ambassador U Linn Aung and Daw Ti Ti Ta for their unending support in Washington.

At the Smithsonian Chris Wemmer, Debbie Bell, Ida Lopez, Ellen Farr, Francine Berkowitz, George Zug, and colleagues at the National Zoo all helped to keep my work going through ups and downs. Mike Bordelon was with me for almost every trek in Myanmar and helped me to solve many of the ginger mysteries we encountered. He and Leslie Brothers supplied some of the photographs of Burmese plants growing in the Botany Research Greenhouses. Shirley and James Sherwood, along with the staff on the Road to Mandalay of the Orient Express Company, showed unending kindness during my travels with them. Colleagues at natural history institutions, such as Sandy Knapp from The Natural History Museum in London, provided literary and botanical support. I am especially appreciative of the help with historical photographs of Myanmar and Kingdon-Ward provided by the James Green Centre for World Art and the Royal Geographical Society.

This book was initiated and written while I was a Visiting Scholar in the Garden and Landscape Program at Dumbarton Oaks of Harvard University in Georgetown, DC. I thank Michel Conan, Ned Keenan, Jan Ziolkowski, Xin Wu, Nancy Hinton, Sheila Klos, Gail Griffin, Alison Maffry, and everyone at Dumbarton Oaks for their support and encouragement during my tenure.

It is not possible to express on paper how much my family meant to me while I was away from them for so long. But thanks to LLC, LLK, WLMcK just the same.

My research in Myanmar was supported by the Smithsonian Institution and the National Geographic Society. I could not have done my work nor written this book without that support.

Endnotes

CHAPTER 2. *Waiting in Rangoon*

1. A *longyi* is the traditional tubelike skirt worn by men, women, and children in Myanmar for all occasions. The garment is pulled tight around the waist and secured by twisting the cloth in a specific knot according to the sex and ingenuity of the wearer.

2. For information on the conservation work in Myanmar by the National Zoo, see their Web site at http://nationalzoo.si.edu/ConservationAndScience/CRC.

3. For a discussion of the rise to power of U Ne Win, see David I. Steinberg's *Burma: The State of Myanmar* (Washington, D.C.: Georgetown University Press, 2001), ch. 1.

4. Daw Aung San Suu Kyi provides a detailed account of her father's life in her book *Freedom from Fear* (London: Penguin Books, 1995).

5. See Rafaël Govaerts, "How Many Species of Seed Plants Are There?" *Taxon* 50 (2001): 1085–90.

6. See Jake Brunner, Kirk Talbott, and Chantal Elkin, *Logging Burma's Frontier Forests: Resources and the Regime* (Washington, D.C.: World Resources Institute, 1998).

7. For more discussion of the extinction crisis, see Stuart Pimm, *The World According to Pimm* (New York: McGraw-Hill, 2001).

8. Journal entry, May 10, 1996.

CHAPTER 3. *Ancient Cities and Sacred Mountains*

1. For more information on volcanoes, see http://www.volcano.si.edu/.

2. See U Thant Myint's two books, *The Making of Modern Burma* (Cambridge, U.K.: Cambridge University Press, 2001) and *The River of Lost Footsteps* (New York: Farrar, Straus and Giroux, 2006), for engaging accounts of the three Burmese empires and the history of Myanmar.

3. According to U Thant Myint, *thosaung kala* literally means "sheep-wearing overseas person," a reference to the wool clothing worn by the British invaders.

4. Amitav Ghosh, *The Glass Palace* (London: HarperCollins, 2000), gives a fictionalized account of the last days of the reign of King Thibaw and his exile to India.

5. For a detailed history of Bagan, see G. E. Harvey, *History of Burma* (London: Frank Cass, 1967).

6. The modern military junta currently in control of Myanmar has followed the ancient Burmese tradition of relocating the capital city as a statement of the power of their regime. Outsiders have interpreted the move of the seat of government from Yangon in the south to the newly created city of Naypyidaw in the center of the country as an indication of the military's paranoia, but it is more likely that the relocation was initiated in the tradition of past rulers of the land.

7. Robert Lester, *Theravada Buddhism in Southeast Asia* (Ann Arbor: University of Michigan Press, 1973), provides a good perspective on *nat* worship in Myanmar.

8. For the conservation successes and failures of the protected areas in Myanmar, see Madhu Rao, Alan Rabinowitz, and Saw Tun Khaing, "Status Review of the Protected-Area System in Myanmar, with Recommendations for Conservation Planning," *Conservation Biology* 16 (2002): 360–68.

CHAPTER 4. *The Arrival of the Monsoon*

1. See Paul Richard, *The Tropical Rain Forest* (Cambridge, U.K.: Cambridge University Press, 1996), ch. 16.3, on rain forest, monsoon forest, and savanna in

the eastern tropics.

2. Reports in *The New York Times*, August 4, 5, and 22, 2007, described the widespread flooding caused by the destructive monsoons in India and Bangladesh and suggested that climate change may be increasing the intensity of the storms throughout this part of Asia. The cyclone that hit the Irrawaddy Delta region of Myanmar in May 2008, killing perhaps one hundred thousand people, may also have been a result of this shifting weather pattern.

3. The giant storm of May 2008 affected over one million Burmese and led to further condemnation of the ruling military government, which refused to allow international aid workers into the country to help the survivors. See *Economist*, May 10, 2008.

4. George Orwell, best known for his social commentaries in the novels *Animal Farm* and *1984*, wrote *Burmese Days* (New York: Harper & Brothers, 1934) after spending several years stationed in Burma as a member of the British police force in the 1920's. It has been suggested that the repressive nature of the British control over their Burmese subjects was the inspiration for his description of an authoritarian state in *1984*.

5. Frank Kingdon-Ward, *In Farthest Burma* (London: Seeley, Service, 1921).

6. See William Stern's biographical introduction to Kingdon-Ward, *Pilgrimage for Plants* (London: George G. Harrap, 1960), published posthumously, and Charles Lyte's biography of the explorer, *Frank Kingdon-Ward: The Last of the Great Plant Hunters* (London: John Murray, 1989). Also see the Web site maintained by Kingdon-Ward's grandson at www.geocities.com/tooleywatkins/fkwbiog1.

7. Other gardens in Cornwall where plants introduced by Kingdon-Ward can be seen include Caerhays Castle Garden, Trevarno Estate Garden, and Trewithen Gardens.

8. Although many of Kingdon-Ward's books are now out of print, some are being reprinted and are once more available, such as *In the Land of the Blue Poppies*, Tom Christopher, ed. (New York: Modern Library, 2003).

CHAPTER 5. *Across Two Rivers*

1. See more details on the Second Burmese Empire in G. E. Harvey, *History of Burma* (London: Frank Cass,

1967) and U Thant Myint, *The Making of Modern Burma* (Cambridge, U.K.: Cambridge University Press, 2001).

2. Over 3,290 herbaria are maintained in natural history institutions and universities around the world. A complete list of these herbaria can be found at http://sciweb.nybg.org/science2/IndexHerbariorum.asp.

3. See *Index Herbariorum: A Global Directory of Public Herbaria and Associated Staff*, maintained at the New York Botanical Garden by Patricia and Noel Holmgren, http://sweetgum.nybg.org/ih/.

4. Jake Brunner, Kirk Talbott, and Chantal Elkin, *Logging Burma's Frontier Forests: Resources and the Regime* (Washington, D.C.: World Resources Institute, 1998), documents the overexploitation of the teak forests in Myanmar.

5. The genus *Shorea* in the Dipterocarp family is one of the most important components of these forest formations. Teak, known botanically as *Tectona grandis*, is in the verbena plant family (Verbenaceae). Other important timber species in Myanmar include pyinkado (*Xylia xylocarpa*), in the bean family (Fabaceae), and padauk (*Pterocarpus macrocarpus*), also in the bean family.

6. A mahout is the keeper of an individual elephant used in the practice of forestry in Myanmar. It is not uncommon for a mahout to adopt an elephant when it is an infant and maintain a close relationship with the same animal throughout its entire life. Robert Harvey wrote a children's book about mahouts and their elephants in Burma called *Elephant Boy of Burma* (New York: Random House, 1960).

CHAPTER 6. *Buddha's Garden*

1. The Latin name for teak is *Tectona grandis*. This important timber tree is placed in the verbena family, the Verbenaceae. The genus *Tectona* includes four species, two of which are found in Myanmar. The second species, *Tectona hamiltoniana*, is common in the dry zone at Shwesettaw Wildlife Sanctuary.

2. Journal entry dated April 20, 2000.

3. Botanically known as *Hesperethusa crenulata* in the orange family (Rutaceae).

4. George Orwell, *Burmese Days* (New York: Harper & Brothers, 1934), p. 127.

5. The betel nut palm, *Areca catechu* in the palm family (Arecaceae), is widely cultivated in southern Asia for its intoxicating seeds, which are wrapped in the aromatic leaves of the betel pepper (*Piper betel* in the pepper family, the Piperaceae) and then chewed.

6. The new species of ginger I found in Shwe-U-Daung Wildlife Sanctuary was the second species to be described in the genus *Smithatris*, which was named after Rosemary Smith, a ginger specialist at the Royal Botanic Gardens in Edinburgh, Scotland. In 2001 I described the first species along with the genus from a plant that I originally saw in a flower show in Bangkok in "*Smithatris*, a new genus of Zingiberaceae from Southeast Asia," *Systematic Botany* 26 (2001): 226–30. I later found out that the first species, which I had named *Smithatris supraneeana*, was also used in Buddhist festivals in the region surrounding Saraburi in Thailand.

CHAPTER 7. *The Choir of Cicadas*

1. Journal entry dated April 11, 2000.

2. The Thingyan, or Water Festival, is celebrated over three days every year in the middle of April. The festival marks the Burmese New Year and occurs at the height of the hot, dry season.

3. Poisonous snakes are not uncommon in Myanmar. An accomplished herpetologist from the California Academy of Sciences was killed by a poisonous many-banded krait several years later in Upper Myanmar. See Jamie James, *The Snake Charmer* (New York: Hyperion, 2008).

CHAPTER 8. *Paradise in Maymyo*

1. U Thant Myint gives an extensive and vivid history of the British conquest of the last Burmese empire in his books *The Making of Modern Burma* (Cambridge, U.K.: Cambridge University Press, 2001) and *River of Lost Footsteps: Histories of Burma* (New York: Farrar, Straus and Giroux, 2006). In the latter book he also recognizes the similarity between British behavior in Burma and the American conduct in the invasion of Iraq in 2003.

2. See Thant Myint, *Making of Modern Burma*, and David I. Steinberg, *Burma, the State of Myanmar* (Washington, D.C.: Georgetown University Press, 2001).

3. Anonymous, "Note on the Government Botanic Garden, Maymyo," *Burmese Forester* (1929): 65–82.

4. On August 25, 1999, I sent two reports to the director general of the Forest Department entitled "Recommendations for the Further Development of the Pyin-Oo-Lwin Botanical Gardens and Establishment of the Botanical Research Center" and "Detailed Proposal for the Establishment of the Center for Botanical Research in Myanmar."

5. The notebook was called "Botanical Training Workshop—National Museum of Natural History, Smithsonian Institution and Forest Research Institute, Forest Department, Ministry of Forestry; 5–18 November 1997" and encompassed 363 pages.

CHAPTER 9. *Up the Chindwin River*

1. The Burmese language has its own script. Representing the sounds of Burmese words and sentences with English notation is particularly difficult. The notation used here is that used by one school of Burmese language teachers.

2. See *Practical Burmese*, published by U Kyi Swe at Myan Com Services in Yangon.

3. The first list of plants compiled specifically for the region now encompassing Myanmar was published in 1912 by J. H. Lace as the *List of Trees, Shrubs, Herbs and Principal Climbers, etc. Recorded from Burma* (Rangoon, Burma: Forest Department, CCF, 1912). The original edition included 2,483 species; a second edition was published by A. Rodger in 1922. In 1961 H. G. Hundley (silviculturist in Burma) and U Chit Ko Ko (curator of the herbarium in Rangoon) updated the earlier work with a more complete treatment of the grasses, orchids, and herbs. About 7,000 species are included in the last published edition of 1987.

4. Rudyard Kipling published his poem "Mandalay" in 1892, but was later criticized as a "jingo imperialist" by none other than George Orwell, who had spent several years in Burma in the 1920s.

5. Over 800 species of fig are included in the genus Ficus. The pipal is *Ficus religiosa*, a commonly cultivated fig in tropical regions around the world. Pipal trees can attain massive sizes and may cover large areas, spreading outward with the production of adventitious or prop roots.

6. The Buddha is usually portrayed in a standing, sitting, or reclining posture, and less often walking. Within each of these basic orientations are more stylized postures, each with a specific meaning, suchas *bhumisparsa* ("touching the earth"), *dhyama* ("meditation"), and *dharmachakka* ("turning of the wheel of dharma").

7. For a description of the geologic history of Myanmar, see the account by Gordon Packham in *Tectonic Evolution of Southeast Asia*, ed. Robert Hall and Derek Blundell (London: Geologic Society, 1996).

Chapter 10. *Dust, Jade, and Prostitutes*

1. Kingdon-Ward describes many of his expeditions into the Himalayan region of Myanmar and neighboring countries in his books, many of which were popular in the mid-twentieth century, including *In Farthest Burma* (London: Seeley, Service, 1921), *Plant Hunting on the Edge of the World* (London: Victor Gollancz, 1930), *Plant Hunter's Paradise* (London: Jonathan Cape, 1937), *Burma's Icy Mountains* (London: Jonathan Cape, 1949), and *Return to the Irrawaddy* (London: Andrew Melrose, 1956).

2. Kingdon-Ward, *In Farthest Burma*, p. 157.

3. Ibid., p. 48.

4. Ibid., p. 135.

5. Ibid., p. 143.

6. Ibid., pp. 102–3.

7. Ibid., p. 68.

8. Ibid., p. 157.

9. Lieutenant-General Khin Nyunt, the top military leader of the Myanmar ruling junta in the early years of the twenty-first century, was known as Secretary One.

10. See the book by conservation biologist Alan Rabinowitz, *Beyond the Last Village* (Washington, D.C: Island Press, 2001), for an account of his work in the Putao region of Upper Myanmar.

11. The plant I collected in Pidaung National Park is most likely the second species in a new genus that has not yet been officially described. The other species, which was sent to me by a friend who had found it in Bangladesh, was originally described as a species of *Hitchenia* by a British botanist named George Bentham in 1883. However, further analysis of flower structure and DNA sequence comparisons suggest that neither species belongs in the genus *Hitchenia*, but rather should be placed in a new genus related to *Hedychium*, species of which are also found in Myanmar.

12. Kingdon-Ward's travels in the region of Sumprabum are described in his books *Plant Hunter's Paradise* and *Burma's Icy Mountain*.

13. *Stadiochilus longiflorus*, collected only a few times in the area around Sumprabum in the 1950s and 1960s, was published as a new genus only in 1980, by Rosemary Smith at the Royal Botanic Garden in Edinburgh.

14. See Alan Rabinowitz's account of this controversial incident in *Beyond the Last Village* (Washington, D.C.: Island Press, 2001).

15. See Donovan Webster, *The Burma Road* (reprint, New York: HarperCollins, 2004), on the building and importance of this major route during World War II.

16. Journal entry dated February 27, 2002.

17. The intricate pollination system of *Vallisneria* was described in 1873 by the German botanist Hermann Müller from observations he made in Europe.

18. Kingdon-Ward, *Return to the Irrawaddy*, p. 217.

Chapter 11. *The Arakan Capitol at Mrauk U: Through Bamboo Hell*

1. An intriguing account of the political, economic, and social history of Arakan is provided in G. E. Harvey, *History of Burma* (London: Frank Cass, 1967).

2. Informative botanical treatments of the region included Sulpiz Kurz, *Forest Flora of British Burma* (Calcutta, India: Supdt., Government Printer, 1877), Jatinora Nath Mitra, *Flowering Plants of Eastern India* (Calcutta, India: World Press Private, 1958), and various articles in the *Bulletin of the Botanical Survey of India*.

3. I found this letter in a box of correspondence from and to Kingdon-Ward filed in the Botany Library in the Natural History Museum in London. The correspondence included letters sent to Kingdon-Ward by his wife and two daughters, as well as his children's nanny.

4. Journal entry dated November 10, 1997.

5. Published with my Burmese colleague U That Htun by the Royal Botanic Garden in Edinburgh in 2003.

6. Wilhelm Sulpiz Kurz was an early British forester who wrote the first account of the plants of Burma in his *Forest Flora of British Burma*.

7. For descriptions of bamboo thickets and other vegetation types in Myanmar, see L. D. Stamp, "Notes on the Vegetation of Burma," *Geographical Journal 64* (1924): 231–37.

8. Harvey, *History of Burma*, describes the location and construction of Mrauk U, including the building of the many pagodas.

CHAPTER 12. *Buddhist Reverence and Respect Help Protect the Forests*

1. *The New York Times*, September 19, 2007; *The Washington Post*, September 19, 2007.

2. *The New York Times*, September 21, 2007; "Week in Review," *TheNew York Times*, September 30, 2007.

3. *The Washington Post*, September 26, 2007; "Week in Review," *The New York Times*, September 30, 2007.

4. *The New York Times*, September 24, 2007; The *Washington Post*, September 24, 2007.

5. *The New York Times*, September 21, 2007.

6. *The New York Times*, August 27, 2007; *The Washington Post*, August 27, 2007.

7. *The Washington Post*, October 1, 2007; *The New York Times*, October 3, 2007.

8. *The Economist*, September 29, 2007, and October 13, 2007.

9. See Robert Lester, *Theravada Buddhism in Southeast Asia* (Ann Arbor: University of Michigan Press, 1973), for a detailed account of the introduction, spread, and practice of Buddhism in Myanmar and neighboring regions.

10. *The New York Times*, June 18, 2008; *The Washington Post*, June 23, 2008.

11. "Week in Review," *The New York Times*, September 30, 2007.

12. See Amitav Ghosh, "A Reporter at Large—Burma," *The New Yorker*, August 12, 1996, pp. 39–54; and Justin Wintle's account of the events surrounding the 1990 elections in his book about the life of Daw Aung San Suu Kyi, *Perfect Hostage* (London: Hutchinson, 2007).

13. See Donald Swearer, *Buddhism and Ecology: Challenges and Promise*, Forum on Religion and Ecology, 2004, http://environment.harvard.edu/religion/religion/buddhism/index.html.

14. See S. K. Pathak, ed., *Buddhism and Ecology* (New Delhi: Bauddha Sanskrit Kendra; Patna, India: Om, 2004).

15. See Lambert Schmithausen, *Buddhism and Nature* (Tokyo: International Institute for Buddhist Studies, 1991); the essays in Mary Evelyn Tucker and Duncan RyÐken Williams, eds., *Buddhism and Ecology: the Interconnection of Dharma and Deeds* (Cambridge, Mass.: Harvard University Center for the Study of World Religions, 1997); and Stephanie Kaza and Kenneth Kraft, eds., *Dharma Rain: Sources of Buddhist Environmentalism* (Boston: Shambhala, 2000).

16. For the Alliance of Religions and Conservation, see http://arcworld.org; for the Forum on Religion and Ecology, see http://environment.harvard.edu/religion/information/about/index.html.

17. From Pathak, *Buddhism and Ecology*.

18. See Dominic Nardi, "The Green Buddha: An Analysis of the Role of Buddhist Civil Society in Environmental Conservation in Burma," unpublished ms., Georgetown University Law School, 2005.

19. As described in Alan Rabinowitz, *Life in the Valley of Death* (Washington, D.C.: Island Press, 2007); but see also the book review by Zao Noam, "Taming the Generals to Save the Tigers," *Irrawaddy*, March 1, 2008, http://www.irrawaddy.org/artclefiles/10618-bookreview.gif.

20. See the foreword by U Uga and other materials presented in Andrew Tordoff and colleagues, *Myanmar: Investment Opportunities in Biodiversity Conservation* (Washington, D.C.: BirdLife International, 2005).

CHAPTER 13. *Mount Victoria: Walking in the Steps of a Giant*

1. Kingdon-Ward, *Plant Hunting on the Edge of the World* (London: Victor Gollancz, 1930), 103.

2. See Douglas Soltis, Pamela S. Soltis, Peter K. Endress, and Mark W. Chase, *Phylogeny and Evolution of Angiosperms* (Sunderland, Mass.: Sinauer, 2005), for an introduction to plant molecular systematics.

3. Kingdon-Ward, *Pilgrimage for Plants* (London: George G. Harrap, 1960), 105.

4. Ibid., 106.

5. Ibid.

6. The plant family Zingiberaceae is classified into four major groupings. The evergreen plants, such as

Etlingera, Amomum, Alpinia, and *Elletariopsis,* are in the subfamily Alpinioideae; the plants that go dormant in the dry season, including species in the genera *Globba, Curcuma,* and *Zingiber,* are contained in the subfamily Zingiberoideae.

7. As taxonomists learn more about various plant species through additional field work or using DNA-based techniques, species and even genera are often transferred back and forth between taxonomic categories.

8. I found the type specimen, which Kingdon-Ward had collected on Mount Victoria in 1956, in the herbarium at the Natural History Museum in London. The description was taken from the label on the specimen. In the herbarium I also found specimens of the other gingers he collected at that site.

9. From an unpublished report by U Hla Aung, president of the Myanmar Hiking and Mountaineering Federation, translated by U Hpone Thant.

CHAPTER 14. *Why the Goldsmith Weeps*

1. The final book was published as W. John Kress, Robert A. DeFilipps, Ellen Farr, and Daw Yin Yin Kyi, "A Checklist of the Trees, Shrubs, Herbs, and Climbers of Myanmar (Revised from the Original Works by J. H. Lace and H. G. Hundley)," *Contributions from the United States National Herbarium* 45 (2003): 1–590.

2. *The New York Times,* June 4, 2003.

3. *The New York Times,* June 12, 2003.

4. See Justin Wintle, *Perfect Hostage* (London: Hutchinson, 2007), for a thoughtful and thorough presentation of the influence of Daw Aung San Suu Kyi on the political and economic reform process in Myanmar.

5. Journal entry dated June 10, 2003.

6. H. J. Lace, a British forester, had published the first checklist in 1912, with a subsequent version authored by another British botanist, A. Rodger, in 1922. The first Burmese botanists to work on the checklist were H. G. Hundley, a forester, and U Chit Ko Ko, curator of the herbarium, who published their first version in 1961, followed by a revised edition in 1987.

Bibliography

Over the last decade a number of fictional and nonfictional accounts of Myanmar have been published. *The Glass Palace* by Amitav Ghosh, *The Piano Tuner* by Daniel Mason, and *Saving Fish from Drowning* by Amy Tan are three contemporary novels that convey a sense of the lives and cultures of past and present Myanmar. The first two works are particularly successful in their descriptions of Burma during British colonial rule from both British and the Burmese perspectives. Emma Larkin's *Finding George Orwell in Burma* traces the travels of author George Orwell in Burma during the first decades of the twentieth century, including the publication of his book *Burmese Days*, and provides a modern perspective on the country, especially with respect to the authoritarian rule of the current government. It is interesting that the work of an author contemporary with Orwell, William Somerset Maugham's *Gentleman in the Parlour*, receives so little attention today, when it provides an equally if not more vivid description of Burma during colonial times. Another recently published work by Pascal Khoo Thwe, *From the Land of the Green Ghosts*, is a semiautobiographical account of the struggle that a Burman must endure to escape the repression of the current regime and reach the West. Other books such as Edith Mirante, *Down the Rat Hole* (2005), Andrew Marshal, *The Trouser People* (2002), and Whitney Stewart, *Aung San Suu Kyi: Fearless Voice of Burma* (1997) provide different perspectives on the historical, social and political climates of Myanmar.

Frank Kingdon-Ward was a prolific travel writer and authored many books describing his exploration of the mountainous regions of East Asia in search of new plants. Those books describing his expeditions to Myanmar are listed below. He also wrote a number of shorter papers that were published in scientific journals. Charles Lyte's *Frank Kingdon-Ward: The Last of the Great Plant Hunters* is a vivid biography of the explorer.

Daw Aung San Suu Kyi, the leader of the pro-democracy movement in Myanmar and the recipient of a Nobel Peace Prize, is the subject of a number of books, including her own autobiographies, *Freedom from Fear* and *The Voice of Hope*, and Justin Wintle's *Perfect Hostage*.

Finally, *Beyond the Last Village* and *Life in the Valley of Death* by Alan Rabinowitz are nonfiction accounts of the struggle by a North American biologist to conserve the animal species and forests in northern Myanmar.

Full citations of relevant books and references about the land, biodiversity, politics, history, and culture of Myanmar, which may be of interest to readers and which have been cited throughout the present book, are listed below.

Alliance of Religions and Conservation. http://arcworld.org.

Brunner, Jake, Kirk Talbott, and Chantal Elkin. *Logging Burma's Frontier Forests: Resources and the Regime*. Washington, D.C.: World Resources Institute, 1998.

Christopher, Tom, ed. *In the Land of the Blue Poppies*. New York: Modern Library, 2003.

Ghosh, Amitav. *The Glass Palace*. London: HarperCollins, 2000.

———. "A Reporter at Large—Burma." *New Yorker*, August 12, 1996, pp. 39–54.

Govaerts, Rafaël. "How Many Species of Seed Plants Are There?" *Taxon* 50 (2001): 1085–90.

Hall, Robert, and Derek Blundell, eds. *Tectonic Evolution of Southeast Asia*. London: Geologic Society, 1996.

Harvey, G. E. *History of Burma*. London: Frank Cass, 1967.

Harvey, R. R. *Elephant Boy of Burma*. New York: Random House, 1960.

Hla Aung, U (president of the Myanmar Hiking and Mountaineering Federation). "Expedition to Climb 10200 Feet High Mt. Victoria (Natma Taung) (26th December 1971 to 4th January 1972)." Translated by U Hpone Thant. Unpublished ms. N.d.

Holmgren, Patricia K., and Noel H. Holmgren. "Index Herbariorum: A Global Directory of Public Herbaria and Associated Staff." Virtual Herbarium, New York Botanical Garden (continuously updated). http://sweetgum.nybg.org/ih/.

Hundley, H. G. *List of Trees, Shrubs, Herbs and Principal Climbers, etc. Recorded from Burma with Vernacular Names*. 4th rev. ed. Rangoon, Burma: Forest Department / Swe Daw Oo Press, 1987.

James, Jamie. *The Snake Charmer: A Life and Death in Pursuit of Knowledge*. New York: Hyperion, 2008.

Kaza, Stephanie, and Kenneth Kraft, eds. *Dharma Rain: Sources of Buddhist Environmentalism*. Boston: Shambhala, 2000.

Khoo Thwe, Pascal. *From the Land of the Green Ghosts*. New York: HarperCollins, 2002.

Kingdon-Ward, F. *Burma's Icy Mountains*. London: Jonathan Cape, 1949.

———. *In Farthest Burma*. London: Seeley, Service, 1921.

———. *Pilgrimage for Plants*. London: George G. Harrap, 1960.

———. *Plant Hunter's Paradise*. London: Jonathan Cape, 1937.

———. *Plant Hunting on the Edge of the World*. London: Victor Gollancz, 1930.

———. *Return to the Irrawaddy*. London: Andrew Melrose, 1956.

Kress, W. John, Robert A. DeFilipps, Ellen Farr, and Daw Yin Yin Kyi. "A Checklist of the Trees, Shrubs, Herbs, and Climbers of Myanmar (Revised from the Original Works by J. H. Lace and H. G. Hundley)." *Contributions from the United States National Herbarium* 45 (2003): 1–590.

Kurz, S. *Forest Flora of British Burma*. Calcutta, India: Supdt., Government Printer, 1877.

Larkin, Emma. *Finding George Orwell in Burma*. New York: Penguin, 2004.

Lester, Robert C. *Theravada Buddhism in Southeast Asia*. Ann Arbor: University of Michigan Press, 1973.

Lyte, Charles. *Frank Kingdon-Ward: The Last of the Great Plant Hunters*. London: John Murray, 1989.

Marshall, Andrew. *The Trouser People*. London: Penguin, 2002.

Mason, Daniel. *The Piano Tuner*. New York: Alfred A. Knopf, 2002.

Maugham, W. Somerset. *The Gentleman in the Parlour*. Reprint. Bangkok, Thailand: White Orchid Press, 1995.

Mirante, Edith. *Down the Rat Hole*. Bangkok, Thailand: White Orchid Press, 2005.

Mitra, J. N. *Flowering Plants of Eastern India*. Calcutta, India: World Press Private, 1958.

Nardi, Dominic. "The Green Buddha: An Analysis of the Role of Buddhist Civil Society in Environmental Conservation in Burma." Unpublished ms. Georgetown University Law School, 2005.

Orwell, George. *Burmese Days.* New York: Harper & Brothers, 1934.

Pathak, S. K., ed. *Buddhism and Ecology.* New Delhi: Bauddha Sanskrit Kendra; Patna, India: Om, 2004.

Pimm, Stuart L. *The World According to Pimm.* New York: McGraw-Hill, 2001.

Rabinowitz. Alan. *Beyond the Last Village.* Washington, D.C.: Island Press, 2001.

Rabinowitz. Alan. *Life in the Valley of Death: The Fight to Save Tigers in a Land of Guns, Gold, and Greed.* Washington, D.C.: Island Press, 2007.

Rao, Madhu, Alan Rabinowitz, and Saw Tun Khaing. "Status Review of the Protected-Area System in Myanmar, with Recommendations for Conservation Planning." *Conservation Biology* 16 (2002): 360–68.

Richards, Paul W. *The Tropical Rain Forest: An Ecological Study.* 2nd ed. Cambridge, U.K.: Cambridge University Press, 1996.

San Suu Kyi, Aung. *Freedom from Fear.* London: Penguin, 1995.

San Suu Kyi, Aung, with Alan Clements. *The Voice of Hope.* New York: Seven Stories Press, 2008.

Schmithausen, Lambert. *Buddhism and Nature: The Lecture Delivered on the Occasion of the EXPO 1990; An Enlarged Version with Notes.* Tokyo: International Institute for Buddhist Studies, 1991.

Soltis, Douglas E., Pamela S. Soltis, Meter K. Endress, and Mark W. Chase. *Phylogeny and Evolution of Angiosperms.* Sunderland, Mass.: Sinauer, 2005.

Steinberg, D. I. *Burma, the State of Myanmar.* Washington, D.C.: Georgetown University Press, 2001.

Stern, William T. "Biographical Introduction." In *Pilgrimage for Plants,* by Frank Kingdon-Ward, pp. 1–5. London: George G. Harrap, 1960.

Stewart, Whitney. *Aung San Suu Kyi: Fearless Voice of Burma.* Minneapolis: Lerner, 1997.

Swearer, Donald K. *Buddhism and Ecology: Challenges and Promise.* Forum on Religion and Ecology, 2004. http://environment.harvard.edu/religion/religion/buddhism/index.html.

Tan, Amy. *Saving Fish from Drowning.* New York: G. P Putnam's Sons / Random House, 2006.

Thant Myint, U. *The Making of Modern Burma.* Cambridge, U.K.: Cambridge University Press, 2001.

———. *The River of Lost Footsteps: Histories of Burma.* New York: Farrar, Straus and Giroux, 2006.

Tordoff, Andrew W., Jonathan C. Eames, Karin Eberhardt, Michael C. Baltzer, Peter Davidson, Peter Leimgruber, U Uga, and U Aung Than. *Myanmar: Investment Opportunities in Biodiversity Conservation.* Washington, D.C.: BirdLife International, 2005.

Tucker, Mary Evelyn, and Duncan RyÐken William, eds. *Buddhism and Ecology: The Interconnection of Dharma and Deeds.* Cambridge, Mass.: Harvard University Center for the Study of World Religions, 1997.

Webster, Donovan. *The Burma Road.* Reprint. New York: HarperCollins, 2004.

Wintle, Justin. *Perfect Hostage: A Life of Aung San Suu Kyi, Burma's Prisoner of Conscience.* London: Hutchinson, 2007.

Zao Noam. "Taming the Generals to Save the Tigers." *Irrawaddy,* March 1, 2008. http://www.irrawaddy.org/artclefiles/10618-bookreview.gif.

Index

(Page references in *italic* refer to illustrations. Page references in **boldface** refer to entries in Portfolio of Myanmar Plants.)